DANISH BUT NOT LUTHERAN

Danish but Not Lutheran

The Impact of Mormonism on

Danish Cultural Identity,

1850–1920

Julie K. Allen

THE UNIVERSITY OF UTAH PRESS

Salt Lake City

The Defiance House Man colophon is a registered trademark of
The University of Utah Press. It is based on a four-foot-tall Ancient
Puebloan pictograph (late PIII) near Glen Canyon, Utah.

Library of Congress Cataloging-in-Publication Data

Names: Allen, Julie K., author.
Title: Danish but not Lutheran : the impact of Mormonism on Danish cultural
    identity, 1850-1920 / Julie K. Allen.
Description: Salt Lake City : The University of Utah Press, [2017] | Includes
    bibliographical references and index.
Identifiers: LCCN 2016041710| ISBN 9781607815457 (cloth : alk. paper) | ISBN
    9781607815464 (ebook) | ISBN 9781647691554 (pbk : alk. paper)
Subjects: LCSH: Mormon Church--Denmark--History--19th century. | Mormon
    Church--Denmark--History--20th century. | Mormons--Denmark--History--19th
    century. | Mormons--Denmark--History--20th century. | Group
    identity--Denmark. | Nationalism--Denmark. | Nationalism--Religious
    aspects--Mormon Church.
Classification: LCC BX8617.D4 A45 2017 | DDC 289.3/48909034--dc23 LC
record available at https://lccn.loc.gov/2016041710

Contents

Figures

Acknowledgments

I would like to express my sincere gratitude to the dozens of individuals and institutions without whose assistance this book could not have been written. David Paulsen, emeritus professor of philosophy at Brigham Young University (BYU) in Provo, Utah, deserves credit for starting me on this road by introducing me to Peter Christian Kierkegaard's tract, *About and Against Mormonism*, while I was a visiting lecturer at BYU in winter 2004. Mary Lambert of Salt Lake City, Utah, was also instrumental in the genesis of this project. She enabled my acquaintance with Hans and Mine Jørgensen by allowing me to translate their entire correspondence and use it in my research.

Laying the foundation of this project was made possible by the Memorial Library staff and the interlibrary loan office at the University of Wisconsin–Madison (UW–Madison), who surpassed all expectations in obtaining obscure materials for me. Constructing my argument and supporting it with evidence required archival materials and photographs, which were skillfully and generously made available by the Danish Royal Library and its helpful staff, in particular Bruno Svindborg. I would also like to thank the Danish Film Institute, in particular Lisbeth Richter Larsen and Thomas Christensen, and the LDS Church History Library in Salt Lake City, Utah. The financial costs of this project were significantly underwritten by the UW–Madison graduate school in the form of summer salary and travel funding in 2010, 2012, and 2013. Travel funding from the ScanDesign Foundation in Seattle, Washington, also allowed me to get to Copenhagen on several occasions to conduct the necessary archival research.

In conceptualizing, researching, and writing this book, I benefited from the invaluable intellectual support and stimulation of many wonderful people. A research semester in spring 2011 at UW–Madison's Institute for Research in the Humanities gave me not only freedom from instructional duties as I mapped out the scope of this project, but also valuable feedback from many insightful colleagues, including Nevine El-Nossery, Steve Hutchinson, Susan Stanford Friedman, and Steve Nadler. I am indebted to Ian Macfarlane for his organization of a fall 2011 conference commemorating Ditlev Gothard Monrad's bicentenary in Wellington, New Zealand, which allowed me to explore Monrad's life and political activities in depth. I'm grateful to Ryan Gesme—who worked with me in the summer of 2012 under the auspices of the UW–Madison Welton Honors Summer Sophomore Research Apprenticeship Grant— for helping me to see this project from the outside and in a comparative perspective. Nate Kramer and Leonardo Lisi were excellent collaborators on a Kierkegaard panel at the Modern Language Association conference in Boston in January 2013, in commemoration of Søren Kierkegaard's two hundredth birthday, and Deidre Green and Nate Kramer (once more) deserve thanks for organizing an excellent bicentennial conference on Kierkegaard at BYU in November 2013, where I was given the opportunity to present part of this project. For careful reading of my draft chapters and making valuable suggestions, I want to thank my "writing buddy" Sonja Klocke, my father Phillip C. Smith, Jes Fabricius Møller, Sarah Reed, Richard Jensen, Jennifer Lund, and Bruce Kirmmse. I also owe a debt to Jørn Brøndal, Sophie Wennerscheid, and Stephan Michael Schroeder for bringing some fascinating Mormon references in rather obscure Danish texts to my notice very late in the game. John Alley, Kelly Neumann, and the staff of the University of Utah Press have been wonderful to work with throughout the production process, and Mel Thorne and the BYU Humanities Publication Service deserve credit for the index.

Most of all, I want to thank my husband Brent and my children Clark, Emily, Soren, and Alice for their patience with me throughout this long process. I am also grateful to all of my friends, siblings, colleagues, neighbors, and casual acquaintances who feigned enthusiasm (or at least concealed boredom) and allowed me to ramble on at length about whatever aspect of the project I happened to be working on when they ran into me.

None of the chapters in this book have been published previously, but a portion of chapter 2 is closely related to the introduction of my translation of Peter Christian Kierkegaard's *About and Against Mormonism*, which appeared in *BYU Studies* 46:3 (2007), and a portion of chapter 3 appeared in the online Danish film journal *Kosmorama* in May 2013.

Preface

Very few of the Danes I have spoken with over the past twenty years are familiar with the fact that tens of thousands of their countrymen joined the Church of Jesus Christ of Latter-day Saints in the late nineteenth and early twentieth centuries and immigrated to Utah. Most of them aren't even aware of the stately Mormon temple on Priorvej in the Frederiksberg district of greater Copenhagen, or of the congregations of Latter-day Saints that still exist throughout the country. On the American side of the Atlantic, I know hundreds of people who are proud of their Danish Mormon ancestors—convert-immigrants who made up the second largest ethnic group in Utah for many years. Yet, although they value this heritage, most of these descendants of early Danish Mormons know little about the country and culture from which their ancestors came, nor about the social conditions attendant upon their ancestors' conversion and emigration. This book attempts to help both of these groups learn more about their own histories by shining a light on Danish society's responses to Mormonism during the period when the greatest number of Danes were joining the LDS Church and immigrating to Utah.

This isn't just a book for or about Mormons, however. It also aspires to contribute to broader discussions about cultural identity in Denmark, the United States, and around the world. It was inspired, to a certain degree, by the international crisis that erupted over the September 2005 publication in the Danish newspaper *Jyllands-Posten* of twelve cartoons depicting the Muslim prophet Mohammad. At the time, I had just finished translating Danish Lutheran pastor Peter Christian Kierkegaard's 1854 treatise *Om og mod Mormonismen* (*About and Against Mormonism*), which played an important part in generating anti-Mormon sentiment among Danes when it was published in a Danish newspaper in 1855. The aggrieved response to the Mohammad cartoons by the Danish Muslim community in 2005 reminded me of the social turmoil that accompanied the early years of Mormon missionary work in Denmark in the 1850s, although the protesters in that case were Danish Lutherans. Just as the cartoons in *Jyllands-Posten* made light of Muslim beliefs about the sanctity of the prophet Mohammad (as much by the fact of their publication as by their precise content), Kierkegaard's text—and many others like it that appeared in the same time period—denigrated the character of Joseph Smith, founder of the LDS Church, and derided Mormon beliefs. Both incidents pitted the rights of a minority religious group against the fears and concerns of the majority of Danes, most of whom were at least nominally Lutheran. While many aspects of the two situations are very different, particularly their respective global political contexts, both engage with questions about the power and responsibility of a free press, the conditions for acceptance within a national and cultural community, the ways in which majority and minority groups within a given society relate to each other, the role of religion and religious difference in shaping cultural and national identity, and the interplay of modernity, globalization, migration, and secularization in setting the parameters of the discussion.

Cultural identity negotiations are not only relevant to discussions of national communities. Institutions also create their own cultures that have to be constantly renegotiated with respect to the conditions of the world in which they operate. As scholars of Mormonism—such as Kathleen Flake and Jan Shipps—have shown, the Church of Jesus Christ of Latter-day Saints has redefined its institutional identity many times over its nearly two-hundred-year history, transforming itself from yet another revivalist utopian experiment to an embattled frontier theocracy to a socially integrated, economically powerful, global corporation. Less visible to the casual observer, however, is how Mormon cultural identity has also undergone tremendous change during this period, as the ethnic composition and self-conception of the church membership has reacted to: (1) shifting demographic patterns, from the influx of tens of thousands of primarily European immigrants in the nineteenth century to the predominance of Hispanic and Latino Mormons in the twenty-first; (2) major doctrinal shifts, such as the renunciation of the practice of polygamy in 1890 and 1904, as well as the decision to extend the LDS priesthood to men of African descent in 1978; and (3) changing social norms regarding gender equality and marriage, among others.

As the LDS Church approaches its bicentenary in 2030, it continues to grapple with new challenges to its cultural identity—as do Denmark, the United States, and, in fact, all nations. It is my hope that this book will be a useful tool in this process, allowing people to look back in time to see how early Danish Mormons constructed a new cultural identity for themselves and how their efforts intersected with Danish society's contemporaneous attempts to come to terms with the effects of modernity, migration, democracy, and secularization. It is a fascinating story of reaction, adaptation, and transformation on the part of both the Danish Lutheran majority and the Danish Mormon minority, a process that not only changed individual lives but set in motion much farther-reaching social changes within Danish society and the LDS Church that affect millions of lives today.

Introduction

The title of this book may prompt two questions. First, what does Mormonism have to do with Danish cultural identity? Second, since many Danes today are not Lutheran, why do nineteenth-century debates over Danish religious norms matter? With regard to the first question, although Mormonism is widely perceived as an American religion, the prevalence of surnames ending in *-sen* among Utah's residents hints at the prominent role of Danish Mormon converts in the early history of the Church of Jesus Christ of Latter-day Saints, often referred to as the Mormon or LDS Church.[1] In fact, around twenty-three thousand Danes joined the LDS Church between 1850 and 1920, and nearly fourteen thousand of them immigrated to Utah, making them one of the largest non-English ethnic groups in both the early church and Utah. Quite a few early Danish Mormons became prominent in Utah society, including the painter Carl Christian Anton (C. C. A.) Christensen, the historian Andrew Jenson, and Apostle Anthon H. Lund. The vast majority of nineteenth-century Danish Mormon immigrants, however, made their mark on the development of the LDS Church simply through their hard work settling Utah, their numerous descendants, and the perpetuation of certain uniquely Danish customs, names, and traditions—including a fondness for gelatin-based dishes that may well have contributed to Utah's prodigious consumption of Jell-O, the official state snack.[2]

Rather than providing a comprehensive history of the LDS Church in Denmark or of Danish Mormon settlers in Utah, however, this book considers how Danish cultural identity was affected by the introduction of Mormonism into Danish society. It focuses on several critical moments in the reception of Mormonism in Denmark, specifically in popular culture and mass media between 1850 and 1920, a period of intense social and political change for both the LDS Church and Danish society and the era during which the largest numbers of Danes joined the Mormon Church.

In answer to the second question posed above, analyzing how Danes reacted to the spread of Mormonism among their countrymen offers insights into how societies can come to terms with foreign elements that may initially seem threatening. The evolving public reception of Mormonism in late nineteenth- and early twentieth-century Denmark, in conjunction with other social movements and trends, reveals how Danish attitudes toward religious difference, cultural identity, and the validity of divergent conceptions of Danishness have evolved and expanded over time, far beyond the Danish Lutheranism that defined Danish society in the mid-nineteenth century. It also illuminates what was at stake for Danish Mormon converts, whose decision to embrace a new religion entailed, at minimum, negotiating a new cultural identity as a non-Lutheran Dane. In most cases, conversion to Mormonism led to emigration, which required Danish Mormons, after an often arduous and hazardous transatlantic and transcontinental journey, to adapt to an ethnically heterogeneous, theologically unique American Mormon frontier culture in the territory, and later state, of Utah.

Mormonism's reception in Denmark between 1850 and 1920 offers a valuable historical template for the way new elements may be incorporated into a largely homogenous culture: initial rejection—marked by both agitated resistance and isolated but sincere attempts at understanding—gives way to self-reflective mockery and, finally, acceptance as the otherness of the new identity construction is gradually eroded by time, increased familiarity, and efforts at mutual rapprochement. While the present study confines itself to the relationship between Danish identity and Mormonism in the late nineteenth and early twentieth centuries—a time when Denmark was struggling to transform itself from a rural, agricultural, Lutheran absolute monarchy into a modern, urbanized, industrial, secular parliamentary democracy—similar patterns recur with regard to other minority religions and groups into otherwise largely homogenous cultures. The synthesis of Lutheran religion and national identity that characterized Danish culture—officially until 1849 and unofficially for decades beyond that—may have been unique to Denmark at that time, but other cultures have institutions and practices that occupy a similarly monolithic position with respect to collective identity construction, whether it be religion, political ideology, race, gender norms, or something else entirely, to which this history may be relevant.

Religion has been a central constitutive feature of Danish national identity for centuries, but its social significance has changed dramatically in the past two hundred years, concurrent with major demographic shifts in Denmark. Although neighboring Sweden and Norway have severed their ties between state and church, evangelical Lutheranism is still the official religion in Denmark. Relatively few Danes attend church with any regularity, but nearly 80 percent of the population is legally affiliated with the Danish national church, known as *Folkekirken* (the People's Church),[3] which receives significant financial support from tax revenues. Despite the constitutional protection of religious difference in Denmark since the mid-nineteenth century, public acceptance of the exercise of religious freedom in Denmark came about very gradually and only after considerable social unrest, much of it directed at the LDS Church and Danish Mormons.

Danes' shifting attitudes toward Mormonism in nineteenth-century Denmark share some common features with contemporary Danish society's struggles to come to terms with its increasingly heterogeneous population, in particular its growing population of Muslims, who made up nearly 5 percent of Denmark's residents in 2016.[4] The history of Mormonism's gradual, contested incorporation into Danish culture illuminates how religious belief and cultural identity in Denmark inform each other in an era of global migration and ethnic diversity, as well as what role popular media can and should play in such discussions. More than 165 years ago, the establishment of religious freedom in Denmark's first democratic constitution in June 1849 precipitated a paradigm shift in Danish cultural identity by facilitating the emergence of modern Denmark's religiously pluralistic society. While adherents of other minority religions were already present in Denmark during the same time period—notably Jews, Catholics, and Baptists—the scale of the public and private response to Mormonism in the wake of the June Constitution is unparalleled in Danish history. The mass conversion of thousands of Danes to Mormonism and their large-scale emigration in the late nineteenth and early twentieth centuries delivered a shock that prompted a groundswell of private and public reflections on the

relationship between religious difference and cultural identity. The following chapters will consider how these reactions to Mormonism in
Denmark reveal the evolution of the answer to the question of what it
means to be Danish but not Lutheran.

The Revolutionary Nature of Religious Freedom in Denmark

Giving Danes the right to choose a religious affiliation other than evangelical Lutheranism disrupted the previously symbiotic relationship
between Danish national identity and Lutheran Christianity, which
had been a defining feature of Danish political and social life since the
official adoption of evangelical Lutheranism as the national religion by
King Frederick II in 1536. Prior to 1849, the only non-Lutherans officially
permitted to live and work in Denmark were foreigners working in the
embassies of foreign nations, as well as small groups of Jews and Huguenots who had been permitted to reside in certain designated parts of
Denmark since the seventeenth century, albeit with limited rights and
without full fellowship in the ethno-religious national community. For
more than three centuries following the Protestant Reformation, the
option of being a Dane but not a Lutheran simply did not exist. Until the
mid-nineteenth century, residents of Denmark who were not Lutheran
were not Danish.

As a result of this fusion of religion and national identity, the introduction of religious freedom into Danish society functioned essentially as a large-scale social experiment in redefining Danishness. The
official establishment of religious freedom in 1849 and the subsequent
proliferation of new religious (and nonreligious) communities and
ideologies in Denmark undermined the power of the state church
as an institution and Danish clergymen as a class, while simultaneously destabilizing the social homogeneity and class hierarchy upon
which Danish society had traditionally rested. In the mid-nineteenth
century, the Danish church was a homogenous evangelical-Lutheran
church with an emphasis on the oral confession of faith and the congregation. Today it is an undogmatic civil religion with an emphasis on individual belief.[5] In terms of religion's influence on Danish
cultural identity, however, it is not the character of particular religious institutions that is decisive, but rather the conceptualization

of religious homogeneity as a fundamental part of being Danish. In a society where religious uniformity had long provided the foundation for both official and private conceptions of Danishness, the explosion of religious difference post-1849 became symbolic of the fragmentation of Danish society and national identity in the same period.

Many prominent Danish intellectuals and writers—including the philosopher Søren Kierkegaard, his older brother the Lutheran minister Peter Christian Kierkegaard, and the religious reformer, folklorist, and poet N. F. S. Grundtvig—were influential commentators on Danish cultural identity, but their views were shaped, adapted, and enacted by the Danish public in their attempts to come to terms with the redefinition of what it meant to be Danish and who belonged in Danish society. While few individuals recorded or preserved their explicit personal views on this matter, it is possible to explore how Danes reacted to this dramatic and momentous shift by examining the way religious difference is treated in Danish literary, artistic, and popular culture productions of the period (such as street ballads and silent films), which both reflected and directed changing discourses about Danish cultural identity.

Mormonism in a Nineteenth-Century Danish Context

The contentious public reception of Mormonism in the second half of the nineteenth century illuminates the perceived challenge to Danish cultural identity that the (nearly) unfettered expression of religious difference seemed to pose at the time. Although founded in upstate New York in April 1830, Mormonism was not introduced in Denmark until 1850, where it attracted tens of thousands of converts over the course of just a few decades. Although other non-Lutheran religious groups, notably Baptists, also established a presence in Denmark in the mid-nineteenth century, the Mormon phenomenon represented the largest and most controversial movement away from the Lutheran Church. This exercise of religious freedom by those Danes who embraced Mormonism in this period initially aroused vocal and sometimes violent public opposition, before gradually subsiding into a subtler but still persistent probing of the extent to which Mormonism was compatible (or not) with Danishness.

This book investigates the social effects of decoupling Danish identity from membership in the Lutheran Church by analyzing depictions of and reactions to Mormonism in various Danish cultural products of the late nineteenth and early twentieth centuries. The authors and audiences of these texts, which took a wide range of forms and cover more than half a century, represent not only different ideological camps within nineteenth-century Danish society (high vs. low culture) but also the perspectives of ordinary Danes whose neighbors, friends, and relatives had adopted these new ideas (insiders vs. outsiders). In order to get a sense of how this debate affected individual and collective Danish cultural identity among both Lutherans and Mormons, this book examines the kinds of stories Danes told about who belonged in Danish society and who didn't. Some of these stories were told publicly, in newspapers, books, films, and other forms of public entertainment, while others took the form of private letters, diaries, and memoirs.

While public narratives indicate that the majority of Danes felt threatened and destabilized by the sudden emergence of a relatively large group of people whose interpretation of Danishness challenged prevailing norms, private narratives confirm that individuals were often more open to adapting their own sense of identity and definition of what constitutes Danishness. Over the course of the late nineteenth and early twentieth centuries, as the notion of religious difference as a negotiable attribute of Danish culture became familiar, public and private anxieties about Mormonism subsided. During this period, Danish social norms gradually shifted enough to encompass a much broader view of Danish identity that contributed to the establishment of Denmark's social liberalism today. However, despite the much greater tolerance of contemporary Danish society, the growing electoral success of anti-immigrant, right-wing parties in Denmark during the early twenty-first century suggests that concerns about the influence of foreign religions and minority groups on Danish cultural identity continue to percolate beneath the surface.

The transformation of Danish cultural identity—which has undergone major shifts over the last two hundred years—is of course intertwined with larger trends affecting Danish society. These developments, including industrialization and democratization, inform the ways in which religious freedom and religious difference were perceived by Danes at any given time. The mid-nineteenth century was a politically turbulent era for Denmark, bracketed by two wars between Denmark and Germany. When the German-speaking duchies of Schleswig and Holstein sought to break away from Denmark in 1848 they were supported militarily by Prussia and Austria, but the intervention of Britain and Russia led to a withdrawal of German support and a Danish victory. When Denmark violated the terms of the treaty ending the First Schleswig War, however, hostilities resumed in 1864 and Denmark suffered a crushing military defeat in the Second Schleswig War, losing both duchies.

Danish nationalism had a major influence on Danish identity throughout the nineteenth century, but its character and orientation changed in response to geopolitical events. Nationalistic fervor was boosted into euphoric self-confidence by the success of the Danish army in the First Schleswig War. Denmark's first progressive constitution was written and adopted in 1848–1849, while Denmark's army was still fighting and winning on the battlefields of Kolding and Sundeved. The violent opposition that characterized the initial reception of Mormonism in Denmark thus coincides with the peak period of Danish nationalism. Less than two decades later, however, Denmark was severely chastened by its devastating defeat by the Prussians and Austrians in 1864 and the economically—and psychologically—crippling loss of territory, population, and status. Perhaps as a result of the radically different social climate after 1864, the dramatic increase in Mormon converts during the late 1860s and 1870s did not arouse even a fraction of the antagonism Danish Mormons faced in the 1850s, even when conversion led to mass emigration.

Prior to the arrival of Mormon missionaries in Denmark and their well-organized efforts to "gather Saints to Zion" by facilitating the group emigration of converts beginning in 1851, there had been no significant waves of emigration from Denmark, in contrast to the surge of emigration from its neighbors, Norway and Sweden, that had begun in the 1820s. Yet, although emigration from Denmark began relatively late, it did eventually become a major force for social change, with more than three hundred thousand Danes—out of a total population of roughly two million—emigrating between 1850 and 1920. The two Schleswig wars had a significant effect on Danish emigration patterns, with German speakers from Schleswig-Holstein emigrating in large numbers after 1848, followed by waves of Danish speakers who emigrated after 1864 in respone to the incorporation of the duchies into what would shortly become the German Empire.

While the majority of Danish immigrants to the United States left for economic reasons and settled in the Midwest, particularly Iowa, Nebraska, Illinois, and Wisconsin, as well as in California, nearly fourteen thousand Danes followed the call to gather with the Mormons to Zion, in Utah. Those Danes who were most receptive to the lure of America, namely those who had the least to lose by leaving home to start afresh, were often attracted to alternative political and religious philosophies such as socialism and Mormonism. As Jørgen Würtz Sørensen argues, emigration for political, ideological, and/or religious reasons, particularly in the 1850s and 1860s (before large-scale emigration from Denmark had begun), functioned as a "protest against the entire Danish societal system."[6] With regard to members of religious communities that diverged from *Folkekirken*, Sørensen explains:

> Their emigration was due in part to the desire to get away from Denmark, where religious minorities were still persecuted by the authorities and the people, and in part to reach the "land of freedom" USA, where precisely religious freedom and tolerance were a defining feature relative to Europe. . . . Members of these sects [Baptist, Methodist, and Mormon] often belonged to the poorest groups in society, with the result that their religious motives often fused completely with economic and social motives.[7]

The converance of Danish Mormon emigrants' economic, social, and religious motivations did not mean they had an easier time leaving home than Lutheran Danes—on the contrary, their decision to emigrate entailed a much greater existential burden than that of economically-driven emigrants. All Danish emigrants had to say goodbye to their homeland, relatives, neighbors, and friends, face the dangers of the journey, and adapt to a new land. On top of these challenges, however, Danish Mormon convert-emigrants abandoned both "their previous beliefs about life, death, and fate"[8] and their sense of cultural belonging in Denmark by aligning themselves with this new, foreign religion and settling among fellow Mormons in Utah rather than among Danish Lutherans in the Midwest or on the west coast.

Mormon integration in late nineteenth-century Denmark was closely connected to migration, both outward and inward. Given the American origins and distinctively American institutional character of the LDS Church, Mormon missionaries were often perceived as emissaries of

American culture as much as LDS theology. Thus, in adopting the Mormon faith Danish converts acquired not only a new religious identity but also a perceived association with American culture. Converts who chose to "gather to Zion" in Utah further distanced themselves, both geographically and psychologically, from the Danish Lutheran mainstream. As William Mulder points out in *Homeward to Zion*, the Danish Mormon migration was unique in its multidirectionality. Not only did most converts leave Denmark for the United States, many of them returned to Denmark after ten, twenty, or thirty years as missionaries for the LDS Church, hoping to win over their erstwhile countrymen.[9]

Although statistically significant and highly controversial at the time, the Mormon dimension of Danish migration history has largely vanished from Danish cultural memory, which celebrates the connections between Denmark and Danish Americans through, for example, the annual Fourth of July celebration at Rebild National Park in Denmark, established by a group of Danish Americans in 1912. In contrast to this mutually appreciative relationship, the influence of Mormonism on Danish cultural identity and Danish contributions to Mormonism in Utah have received relatively little attention. Danish historian Margit Egdal explains:

> Mormonism was a movement that came and swept over the country. It aroused strong emotions and was an issue that everyone had an opinion about, either because the local pastor had warned them against the Mormons or perhaps they had themselves encountered the Mormon missionaries who proselytized actively everywhere in Denmark. It may seem incredible that the events that caused such uproar in the 1850s have been completely forgotten by Danes. This is due primarily to the fact that those who converted to Mormonism emigrated, as a rule. They took their history with them.[10]

The fact that the majority of nineteenth-century Danish Mormons emigrated, with the result that the LDS Church in Denmark did not establish a permanent institutional presence in Denmark until the early 1900s, has effectively erased the Danish Mormon phenomenon from collective Danish memory. Since, as Spanish philosopher George Santayana asserted, "Those who cannot remember the past are condemned to repeat it,"[11] understanding the history of how Danish Mormons negotiated their cultural identity, and how Lutheran Danish society responded to those negotiations, can be useful in navigating current tensions between religious difference and cultural identity in Denmark and the rest of the world.

Theoretical Toolbox

In order to discuss the role of religious difference in Danish society and identity, whether individual or collective, national or cultural, we first need to identify the theoretical tools that make it possible to analyze public and private attitudes toward events that happened so long ago. As Stephen Greenblatt asserts, every culture is constantly in transition; the ideas and traditions that define and demarcate the cultures with which we identify—whether religious, national, ethnic, linguistic, or otherwise—are always in flux.[12] One example is the adoption of the potato, which was introduced from South America in the eighteenth century but rapidly became a staple of the Danish diet. It is so closely identified with Danish cuisine today that the Danish Potato Council was established in 1996 to combat the growing popularity of "foreign" carbohydrates such as pasta and rice. Underscoring the significance of this imported food tradition for Danish cultural identity, June 15, a date that already commemorates the miraculous appearance of the Danish flag in 1219 and the reunification of northern Schleswig with Denmark in 1920, was designated in 2008 as Denmark's "National Potato Day."[13] Similarly, the Lutheran religious culture—which was so integral to the early modern Danish state that the *Kongelov* (King's Law), ratified in 1665, essentially defined the state's function as preserving the Lutheran faith—was itself a sixteenth-century import from Germany, as Catholicism had been nearly six hundred years earlier, when pressure from Catholic rulers of the Carolingian Empire induced Danish kings to adopt Christianity.

In light of the inherently transitory nature of culture, it may seem pointless to speak of cultural identity at all. However, the relationship between culture and identity is central to the human experience. People define themselves according to the discursive practices of the groups with which they associate, even if only in opposition to them. Our sense of ourselves as subjects is predicated on the process of identification with certain values and norms rather than others. As Stuart Hall explains,

In common sense language, identification is constructed on the
back of recognition of some common origin or shared characteristics with another person or group, or with an ideal, and
with the natural closure of solidarity and allegiance established
on this foundation. In contrast with the "naturalism" of this
definition, the discursive approach sees identification as a construction, a process never completed—always in process. It is
not determined in the sense that it can always be "won" or "lost,"
sustained or abandoned.[14]

Although cultural identity is never fixed and is therefore indeterminate
to a degree, it nonetheless exists and shapes individuals' perception of
themselves and the world around them. Like culture itself, an individual's
or a group's cultural identity is continuously subject to redefinition and
renegotiation of the categories of sameness and difference. Hall stresses
that cultural identity cannot "stabilize, fix or guarantee an unchanging
'oneness' or cultural belongingness underlying all the other superficial
differences" between members of a group. He explains that identities are
"never singular but multiply constructed across different, often intersect-
ing and antagonistic, discourses, practices and positions."[15] The gradual
transition from a Danish identity that was once dependent upon Lutheranism to a new, more secular and more religiously tolerant conception of
Danishness—which underlies the evolving reception of Mormonism in
Denmark—reflects precisely this kind of constantly shifting construction
of cultural identity.

Processes of identity construction require the presence of difference as a means of demarcating the shape and limits of one's identity
by contrasting it with what it is not. Difference is integral to meaning.
As the Swiss linguist Ferdinand de Saussure argued regarding language,
meaning is relational and relies upon contrast with its opposite, often in
binary oppositions that oversimplify the nuances of reality and promote
the exclusion of those in the weaker pole rather than the recognition of
the many similarities that bind members of both groups together. Hall
notes that since identification "operates across difference, it entails
discursive work, the binding and marking of symbolic boundaries."[16]
At a time when Denmark's physical boundaries were unstable and the
definition of Danish identity was in flux, the role of the "Other" was

assigned to Danish Mormons in the late nineteenth century by means of predominantly negative depictions of Mormonism in Danish culture and media. Such strategic representations have the symbolic power to "mark, assign, and classify,"[17] solidifying stereotypes and shaping public opinion. Although the number of Danish Mormons residing in Denmark has stayed relatively steady (around five thousand) since the early twentieth century, the Mormon phenomenon retains significance in late nineteenth-century Denmark as an Other against which the emerging mainstream cultural identity could define itself.

Chapter Overview

While the general starting point for any study of the reception of Mormonism in Denmark is fairly simple to determine—namely, the establishment of religious freedom in 1849 and the arrival of the first Mormon missionaries in 1850—the ending date is more negotiable, falling somewhere around the outbreak of World War I, with some spillover into the 1920s. This study extends from the events leading up to the passage of the June Constitution in 1849 through the initial wave of Mormon conversions in the 1850s, considering various responses to this phenomenon in the Danish media by Lutherans and Mormons alike, up through the early 1920s, when both Denmark and the LDS Church completed fairly radical processes of reorientation. This book cannot provide exhaustive chronological coverage of this complex three-quarters of a century, but focuses instead on several distinct periods during which popular reactions to Mormonism took particularly visible form—either in public demonstrations or in a profusion of media treatments—in order to offer a representative sample of how these depictions relate to the development of political, religious, and cultural identity in Denmark.

The first period under consideration centers on the decade immediately following the arrival of the first LDS missionaries in Denmark. Their proselytizing success resulted in the rapid growth of LDS congregations around the country, particularly in greater Copenhagen and northern Jutland, as well as the beginning of large-scale Danish Mormon immigration to Utah. The second period falls later in the century, spanning the 1870s and 1880s, after Danish emigration had become widespread enough to be a matter of public concern and the Mormon practice of polygamy well-known enough to be fodder for ridicule. The final period, which encompasses the

1910s and early 1920s, showcases various new media and forms of popular entertainment that used Mormonism as a symbol for the dangers of modernity, globalization, and women's emancipation.

In addition to the June Constitution's expansion of Danish civil rights in 1849, many other factors influenced the development of Danish culture and society during the late nineteenth century. Perhaps the most significant of these was Denmark's catastrophic defeat in the Second Schleswig War in 1864, which brought about a fundamental reorientation of Danish political and intellectual life. As a result of the war, Denmark lost 40 percent of its territory to Germany and more than a third of its population, marking a new low point in Denmark's long decline from its status as a major power in northern Europe in the late Middle Ages. Marginalized in global political affairs, Danish society focused deeply inward, which led to both extensive socioeconomic reforms and a national preoccupation with Danish cultural identity. Industrialization and urbanization offered expanded opportunities for the Danish peasantry, while the rise of the cooperative movement allowed even tenant farmers to earn a decent living. Widespread anti-German sentiment created an opportunity for French realistic literary aesthetics, mediated by the Danish literary critic Georg Brandes (1842–1927), to inspire a new generation of writers and artists who came to be grouped under the moniker *det Moderne Gennembrud* (the Modern Breakthrough).

Both conversions to Mormonism and Mormon emigration from Denmark dropped off beginning in the 1880s, in part because innovations such as the dairy cooperative led to a more flexible economic market and more options for Danish laborers. Intensifying federal prosecution of polygamy among Mormons in the United States in the 1880s also played a role in diminishing Danish interest in the LDS Church, in part because of resulting difficulties for LDS missionaries in Denmark. In the wake of the U.S. Edmunds Act of 1882, which declared polygamy to be a felony, U.S. consuls and ambassadors were instructed not to extend protection or aid to American citizens engaged in missionary work abroad on behalf of the LDS Church.[18] In response to this development, many Danish civil authorities began banning Mormon missionaries and deporting them to England, which had an inhibiting effect on conversions.

The turn of the twentieth century witnessed additional dramatic shifts in Denmark's political and economic situation that also affected the reception of Mormonism in Denmark. One such watershed was the *Systemskifte* (system change) of 1901 that brought Denmark's first majority prime minister to power and confirmed the extent to which Denmark had finally become the parliamentary democracy the June Constitution prescribed. Another important development was the emergence of film as a powerful medium of communication and entertainment for broad swaths of the population. Thanks to cinema pioneers such as Ole Olsen, Valdemar Psilander, Asta Nielsen, Benjamin Christensen, and Carl Theodor Dreyer, Denmark became an early leader in the global film industry, though films also enjoyed strong domestic popularity. A third factor that profoundly influenced Danish society was World War I, which ravaged Denmark's economy (despite the country's official neutrality in the conflict) and paved the way for the kind of far-reaching governmental intervention in public life that led to the establishment of the Danish welfare state in the 1930s.

Moreover, by the early 1920s, the tide of Danish Mormon emigration had largely subsided due to a change in LDS Church policy regarding immigration, nativist legislation in the United States prompted by World War I, and fundamental shifts in the nature of Danish Mormon identity in both Denmark and the United States. The LDS Church had officially discontinued the practice of polygamy in 1890, but did not begin to rigorously enforce this change until the first decade of the twentieth century, when the U.S. Senate held investigative hearings into Mormon practices in connection with the dispute over seating Utah senator Reed Smoot. Under the leadership of its sixth president, founder Joseph Smith's nephew Joseph F. Smith, the LDS Church finally subordinated itself to the U.S. government in order to bring its persecuted isolation in the Rocky Mountains to an end.[19]

In the wake of the Smoot hearings, a final outburst of anti-Mormon sentiment erupted in Denmark around 1910–11, exemplified by a series of anti-Mormon rallies, informative lectures, restrictive legislation, and popular media representations, including several silent films. Historian Andrew Jenson, while serving as president of the LDS Scandinavian Mission from 1909 to 1912, worked to counter negative stereotypes about Mormonism, in particular through a series of illustrated lectures that he delivered a total of seventy-eight times in venues across Denmark, Norway, and Iceland.[20] While the socially and politically turbulent years surrounding World Wars I and II in both Denmark and the United States had a repressive effect on Mormon missionary work, conversions, and emigration, the Danish state and Mormonism achieved a calm, mutually accepting relationship by the mid-1920s.

Chapter 1 establishes the sociopolitical context of Danish engagement with Mormonism by describing the state of religion in Denmark in the early nineteenth century and outlining the social and political changes that led up to the ratification of the 1849 constitution. Looking at this history allows us to situate the reception of Mormonism in relation to the larger changes taking place in Danish society. In the early nineteenth century, Denmark experienced a Pietist revival led by lay clergymen across the country, whose meetings the government unsuccessfully attempted to outlaw. During and after the revival movement, the emergence of divergent Christian groups—particularly the Baptists—and the so-called Baptist crisis in 1842 and its repercussions brought the issue of religious difference to the forefront of Danish political debate. This emerging pattern of religious division prompted the establishment of freedom of religion in the 1849 constitution, which was drafted almost entirely by the Danish bishop and later prime minister D. G. Monrad, although the religious reformer and scholar N. F. S. Grundtvig also played an influential role in the process.

When Mormonism emerged soon thereafter as the primary threat to the monopoly of the Danish Lutheran Church, positive and negative reactions to the missionaries reflected current social and political conditions. Arriving in 1850, the first four Mormon missionaries in Denmark baptized more than three hundred people in their first year. Over the next decades, more than twenty thousand Danes converted to Mormonism, with converts drawn primarily (but by no means exclusively) from the most impoverished classes of rent farmers and day laborers. The unfamiliar doctrines of Mormon theology and the movement's viral spread throughout Denmark, as well as the resulting loss through emigration of the cheap labor upon which prosperous Danish farmers relied, led to public outrage toward the Mormons. Tacitly encouraged by the priests of the Danish Lutheran Church, this opposition took the form of libel, harassment, and mob violence. This crisis put Denmark's constitutional guarantee of religious freedom to the test and sparked a range of literary, artistic, and popular cultural articulations of the relationship between religious difference and Danish identity, discussed in subsequent chapters.

Chapter 2 considers the relationship between Danish religious and cultural identity as it was expressed in several "high culture" texts produced in the 1850s. This chapter places philosopher Søren Kierkegaard's final work, a series of essays known as the *Kirkekamp* or, in English, the *Attack on Christendom* (1854-55), in dialogue with his brother the Reverend Dr. Peter Christian Kierkegaard's 1855 book *Om og mod Mormonismen (About and Against Mormonism)*, as well as Danish realist painter Christen Dalsgaard's 1856 painting "Tvende Mormoner på Besøg has en Tømrer på Landet" ("Two Mormons Visit a Country Carpenter") and Baroness Elise Stampe's unpublished manuscript "Mormonismen" ("Mormonism"), (1858) in order to illustrate how the Danish educated elite dealt with the relationship between religion and cultural identity during this tumultuous era. Although the brothers became estranged in 1850, their contemporaneous texts on different aspects of the same subject offer a unique opportunity to compare and contrast their positions.

The arrival of the Mormon missionaries and the unrest caused by their followers' attempts to take Denmark's religious freedom at face value coincided with Søren Kierkegaard's *Attack on Christendom*. Although perhaps best known today as the "father of existentialism," Kierkegaard was a devout Christian and many of his works deal with questions of faith, particularly the individual's responsibility for his or her own relationship with God. Søren ultimately concluded that the social systems of Christendom, in particular *Folkekirken* and its professional clergy, were the primary obstacles to the individual's development of a personal Christian faith. For this reason, in 1854 he embarked on a public campaign of newspaper articles attacking the Danish church and clergy.

Around this same time, pastor Peter Christian Kierkegaard accepted an invitation to speak at one of the cottage meetings held by the Mormon missionaries preaching in his parish. In his remarks, which were published in 1855 under the title *About and Against Mormonism*, Peter outlines his objections to Mormonism in a serious manner that distinguishes itself from the scandalmongering tone of many other early Danish anti-Mormon publications. His opposition to Mormonism has primarily theological grounds, but his defense of Danish Lutheranism intersects at several points with his brother's attack on the same, particularly regarding the capacity and responsibility of the individual to determine his or her own religious views.

Baroness Elise Stampe, who drafted an unpublished manuscript about Mormonism in 1858, was, like Peter Christian Kierkegaard, a devoted disciple of the poet-theologian N. F. S. Grundtvig. Her parents, Baron Henrik and Baroness Christine Stampe, were the primary Danish patrons of the neoclassical sculptor Bertel Thorvaldsen, who created the statue of the Christus that graces Vor Frue Kirke in Copenhagen. Elise Stampe, who had been confirmed by Grundtvig and corresponded with him throughout her life, authored several books about religious and nationalistic issues. When one of her dear friends converted to Mormonism, she decided to write a treatise about the religion, looking at its theological basis as well as its implications for the individual convert, perhaps with Grundtvig himself as her audience. Although Stampe was opposed to Mormonism and remained a staunch Lutheran throughout her life, her book is in many ways quite sympathetic to the Mormon cause. Stampe's book—analyzed in light of Grundtvig's public pronouncements and private counsel and compared with her many other religious and nationalistic publications—offers an intimate look at the effects of the exercise of religious freedom in Denmark in the second half of the nineteenth century.

Widening the focus from individual authors representing Copenhagen's educated bourgeoisie to Danish society more generally, chapter 3 analyzes depictions of Mormons and Mormonism in late nineteenth- and early twentieth-century Danish popular culture, including newspaper articles, art, music, and film. These often caricatured portrayals of Mormons exemplify the way in which Mormonism was perceived by the Danish public in this period, through such varied media as *Skillingsviser* (street ballads) published between the 1850s and 1880s; a 1911 Tivoli cabaret song titled "Mormons, Mormons!"; and several silent films from the 1910s and early 1920s, the most successful of which was *Mormonens Offer* (*A Victim of the Mormons*) (August Blom, 1911), starring Valdemar Psilander and Clara Wieth. These prominent treatments of Mormonism in Denmark confirm that the question of religious difference continued to resonate with Danish audiences more than half a century after the establishment of the LDS Church in Denmark. Each of these cultural "texts" provides insight into the ways in which Mormonism in particular and religious difference more generally intersected with public discourses about Danish identity, modernity, and secularization.

Finally, in order to balance out the representation of Danish Mormons by outsiders, chapter 4 gives voice to individual Danes who chose to convert to Mormonism. Given the high propensity for Danish Mormons to immigrate to America, this chapter also considers the phenomenon of Mormon emigration in terms of its economic impact as well as its implications for the cultural identity of the emigrants. Drawing on both public self-representations in the print media and personal narratives contained in journals, memoirs, and letters, this chapter attempts to tease out converts' individual experiences of diverging from the Danish mainstream—first by embracing a controversial doctrine condemned by *Folkekirken*'s ministers and second by emigrating across the ocean to the Utah Territory, which would later, due in no small part to the efforts of these Danish immigrants, become a state.

The overwhelming majority of the Mormon missionaries in Denmark in the late nineteenth century were themselves Danish converts to the church (often very recent), who shared their new faith with their friends, neighbors, and countrymen prior to emigrating and later returned on two- to three-year missions to Denmark. With little formal education or training, these lay representatives covered the Danish countryside and cities on foot, making the case for their new religion, often with remarkable success. The Scandinavian Mission, as it was known, made extraordinarily effective use of print media to spread the Mormon message, publishing the periodical *Skandinaviens Stjerne* (*Scandinavia's Star*) as well as numerous pamphlets and brochures. Danish-language publications, such as *Morgenstjernen* (*The Morning Star*) and *Bikuben* (*The Beehive*), were also produced and circulated among Danish immigrants in Utah. By analyzing both the public documentation of the Danish LDS community in the late nineteenth century and the personal narratives of several Danish Mormons—the pioneer couple Hans and Wilhelmine Jørgensen, the prosperous farmer Mads Nielsen and his family, and F. F. Samuelsen, the first Mormon member of a national parliament outside the United States—this chapter documents the estrangement of Danish Mormon emigrants from their homeland and native culture and outlines the ways in which they gradually redefined their cultural identity.

The conclusion takes a step back from these detailed analyses of individual lives in order to more broadly consider the influence of the Danish Mormon phenomenon on the evolution of Danish society and cultural identity over the course of the late nineteenth and early twentieth centuries. It demonstrates that this period of social upheaval and cultural transformation is still relevant to contemporary discourses about religious difference, migration, and cultural identity in Denmark and elsewhere in the world, as well as within the LDS Church.

1

Uncoupling Danish National Identity from Lutheranism

The Advent of Religious Difference in Denmark

During the "Arab Spring" uprisings in 2011, political commentators often invoked the European revolutions of 1848 as a cautionary tale, as a means of lowering expectations that the unrest in the Middle East and North Africa would lead to lasting, positive governmental and social changes. However, these commentators generally failed to mention that the 1848 revolutions did contribute to the democratization of one country ruled by an absolute monarch, a society in which common people had no say and few civil rights, where religious leaders were also powerful politicians, and where religious affiliation was inextricable from national identity.

That country was Denmark, which has since become one of the most democratic, egalitarian countries in the world. Accomplishing this transformation required the country to undergo a slow, conflicted, and often painful process of social, economic, and political modernization that called into question long-held and dearly-cherished national institutions, traditions, and values. Foremost among these was the national religion—evangelical Lutheranism—and the state church that defined and administered it. The Danish Lutheran Church served the crucial social and political functions of underpinning governmental control of society and grounding ideological constructions of Danish identity.

The Danish constitution of June 1849, known as the "June Constitution," brought about an unprecedented, though not universal, enfranchisement of Danish commoners. Although the right to vote was initially limited to male heads of households, the constitutional guarantee of civil rights applied to all citizens, but was of particular significance for cottagers and day laborers, who had been trapped in unrelieved poverty and exploitative working conditions since the emergence of the self-owner farmer class in the late eighteenth century. Moreover, the inclusion of religious freedom as one of these civil rights challenged the primacy of the Danish church and opened the door for all manner of alternative religious views, ranging from Catholicism to atheism to Mormonism.

Although it came about later than in the United States, Great Britain, or Germany, Denmark's introduction of limited religious freedom was nevertheless revolutionary in terms of its effect on the structure and self-conception of Danish society. The civil rights codified in the June Constitution grew out of more than half a century of ideological and social liberalization in Denmark. They in turn set the stage for a fundamental redefinition of Danish national and cultural identity over subsequent decades, particularly with regard to the role of religion as a constitutive factor of that identity. Prior to 1849, the Danish state and the Danish Lutheran Church were essentially indivisible, as were Danish citizenship and Lutheran confirmation. Denmark's Jewish community, whose members were given citizenship in 1814,[1] represented the sole exception to the legal unity of religion and citizenship, alongside small groups of Huguenots and Catholics, but the extent to which Danish Jews were regarded as Danish varied over time. Very few Danes converted to Judaism, which was generally regarded as a hereditary affiliation rather than the result of individual choice. Giving Danes the legal right to choose and publicly practice alternate religions disrupted the previously symbiotic relationship between Danish national identity and evangelical Lutheranism, which had been a defining feature of Danish political and social life since the Reformation.

Prior to 1849, even the theoretical possibility of religious freedom was unsettling for many Danes, including Jacob Peter Mynster (1775–1854), bishop of Zealand and primate of the Danish church. Mynster argued vehemently against the inclusion of religious freedom in the June Constitution, warning that the measure "purports to grant a freedom that no human law can either grant or revoke. Faith resides in the innermost part of a person, and people retain their complete freedom to believe or not, even under the strictest inquisition. Nor does Denmark at the present time lack the freedom to express one's belief or disbelief."[2] In Mynster's opinion, freedom of conscience was sufficient for individuals, whereas the legalization of religious freedom would effectively dissolve the state church and open the door to the eventual abolishment of religion:

> Although people who have reached their majority ought not be subjected to any kind of force compelling them to significant participation in any religious organization, a state that does not wish to abolish all involvement with religion must, for its part, be able to categorize each of its citizens within the existing religious community, [for] . . . being without religion means precisely that nothing is acknowledged as sacred.[3]

Mynster's objections to the constitution reveal that while he did not aspire to control individuals' private religious views, he regarded state religion as an essential element in maintaining social order and public morality.

The fact that the exercise of religious freedom on a large scale did in fact prove quite disruptive to Danish society seemed to confirm Mynster's fears of disorder and apostasy. Less than a year after the adoption of the June Constitution, successful proselytizing efforts by missionaries of the Church of Jesus Christ of Latter-day Saints (widely known as the LDS or Mormon Church) brought to a head the question of how to deal with the sudden emergence of religious difference in culturally homogenous Denmark. Arriving in the spring of 1850, the first four Mormon missionaries in Denmark baptized more than three hundred people in their first twelve months in the country. By 1855, more than two thousand Danes had joined the LDS Church. Many of the earliest converts were Baptists who had suffered legal persecution during the 1840s because of their illegal religious affiliation. Over the next half-century, tens of thousands of Danes converted to Mormonism, with the bulk of converts drawn from the impoverished classes of rent farmers and day laborers, most of whom subsequently immigrated to Utah. Although many other Scandinavians—from Norway, Sweden, Iceland, and Finland—also joined the LDS Church during this period, the scale of the Mormon phenomenon in Denmark was much greater than in any of the neighboring Nordic countries and had a correspondingly larger impact on public discourse in Denmark.

The provocative and outspoken Mormon view of mainstream Christianity as being in need of restoration, the American origins of the religion, and its viral spread throughout Denmark led to public hostility toward Mormonism, particularly in the early 1850s. Tacitly supported by pastors of the Danish Lutheran Church (which was renamed *den danske Folkekirke*, or the "Danish People's Church," in 1849), this opposition initially took the form of libel, harassment, and mob violence. These public expressions of hostility put the viability of Denmark's constitutional guarantee of religious freedom to the test. The tension between Danish Lutheranism and Mormonism also inspired a range of literary, artistic, and popular culture explorations of the relationship between religious difference and Danish identity that will be discussed in later chapters. In order to understand the significance of these texts, however, we must first establish the sociopolitical conditions that led to the advent of religious freedom in Denmark and its immediate repercussions for the introduction of Mormonism. This historical backdrop explains the anxiety religious freedom generated among the Danish people about their national and cultural identity.

The Road to Religious Freedom

Political conditions in Denmark in the early nineteenth century were far from democratic, although not egregiously oppressive either. Since 1660, the king of Denmark had ruled as an absolute monarch, a system that was instituted in reaction to widespread abuse of power by the Danish nobility in the early seventeenth century. The absolutist system in Denmark was conceived of as paternalistic, with a benevolent father-king ensuring the well-being of his children-subjects. This arrangement functioned relatively well throughout the eighteenth century, but an adscription law passed in 1733 illustrates its disadvantages. Known as *stavnsbåndet* (estate binding), adscription made it illegal for male Danish peasants between the ages of fourteen and thirty-six to leave the estate where they were born, ostensibly to ensure that they would be readily available for military conscription in the event of a war, but also allowing them to be easily exploited as cheap labor by feudal landlords in peacetime. This law was repealed in 1788 as part of a broader land reform designed to improve the efficiency of Danish agricultural production. Although the main focus of this reform was economic (and the law did not repeal military conscription but merely centralized it), the reform still improved living and working conditions for much of the Danish peasantry.

The absolutist system of government in Denmark concentrated political power in the hands of a very small group of men, who managed the country's affairs according to their personal preferences, whims, prejudices, and mental health. The dangers of such a closed system became apparent in 1770, when Johann Friedrich Struensee (1737–1772), a German doctor attending to the mentally ill King Christian VII (1749–1808), seized power and ruled for sixteen months in the king's stead. He issued more than a thousand cabinet orders to enact Enlightenment-style reforms, including freedom of the press, but he also had an affair with Queen Caroline Matilda (1751–1775), the youngest sister of Britain's King George III. Struensee fathered the queen's second child, Princess Louise Augusta, who was born in July 1771. A coup orchestrated by Dowager Queen Juliane Marie and politician Ove Høegh-Guldberg in January 1772 sent Struensee to the executioner's block. Caroline Matilda was divorced by decree from her husband in April 1772 and exiled to Celle, in the Kingdom of Hannover, where she died of scarlet fever in 1775 without ever having seen her children again.

Under normal circumstances, however, the concentration of power facilitated by absolutism allowed the Danish king to maintain tight control of the country's affairs. When Christian VII and Caroline Matilda's son Frederik (later Frederik VI; 1768–1839) took power back from his step-grandmother's council and became prince regent in 1784, he set the national tone, first through the extensive economic reforms he pioneered in his liberal youth and later—in his reactionary older years—when his alliance with French emperor Napoleon ultimately led to national bankruptcy and the loss of Norway in 1814. The Danish Lutheran Church was the most influential of the institutions that promoted and policed national unity and homogeneity in absolutist Denmark, not least because its clergy were among the monarchy's most loyal supporters and the state's most talented bureaucrats.

As a result of the state's stranglehold on both the press and the political sphere in the late eighteenth and early nineteenth centuries, the Danish public—including most of the privileged, educated bourgeoisie in Copenhagen as well as rural farmers—paid little attention to politics, though there was considerable political agitation in other parts of the kingdom, such as Norway and Holstein.[4] The Danes directed their energies instead toward economic affairs, technological advances, and artistic accomplishments that ushered in a golden age of Danish culture. This same period witnessed a dramatic increase in religious fervor that manifested itself as a grassroots Pietistic revival, primarily among the Danish peasantry (who made up 85 percent of the population), that became known as the *de gudelige Vækkelser*, or "the godly awakenings."

One reason for the popularity of this revival was the loss of social cohesion stemming from the erosion of village life in the wake of Frederik VI's land reforms. These late-eighteenth-century reforms had enabled farmers to consolidate their land holdings into single parcels instead of strips of land distributed across the district (as had previously been customary), and to purchase their farms outright instead of leasing them from large landowners. This development laid the foundation for the transformation of peasants into farmers, a shift that resulted in increased individualization and a decline in traditional communities. As more and more farmers moved out to their newly consolidated farms and abandoned communal cultivation, the rural village ceased to function as the center of social and cultural life. A new middle class of *selvejer* (self-owning) farmers emerged, while the number of tenant farmers and landless farm laborers who could not afford to buy their land grew exponentially and was exploited by self-owning farmers and large landowners alike. The growing geographic and socioeconomic divisions within the Danish peasantry led many people to embrace religious revivalism as a new source of community identity.

Although the religious revivalism of the 1820s was not directly associated with a political movement, it contributed indirectly to an increase in political consciousness, if only as a result of increased self-confidence arising from religious autonomy. This is perhaps not surprising given the inherently anti-authoritarian character of the revivals themselves. P. G. Lindhardt explains their significance as Denmark's first general public meetings: "Revivals represent a break with the old life, not just in a *religious* sense, but precisely also to a high degree in a *social, economic,* and thereby *political* sense. . . . *The godly awakening is the cradle of religious developments and popular self-governance*"[5] (emphasis in original). The same peasants who defied authority to attend revival meetings soon embraced ideals of democracy and parliamentary government. Wary of the danger that religious meetings could lead to political agitation, the government tried unsuccessfully to suppress the revival movement. A 1741 ordinance (*Konventikelplakaten*) forbidding public gatherings without the approval of a minister was used to justify fining or imprisoning lay preachers suspected of fomenting political unrest along with their message of literal Biblical interpretation and intense empathy with Christ's suffering.

Such stringent measures, which were in effect until the passage of Christian VIII's edict of toleration in 1840, had the opposite effect than intended. Indeed, they contributed to the rise of pro-democracy political parties—such as *Bondevennernes Selskab* (the Society of the Friends of the Peasants)—by mobilizing the peasantry to support a "long-term project of economic self-improvement, the acquisition of literacy, and the quest for adulthood in religious and political affairs."[6] Thus, although the June Constitution was a direct outcome of the revolution of 1848, it was also the gradual outgrowth of half a century of gradual liberalization in Danish politics and society.

The modernization of Denmark's political culture in the nineteenth century was accelerated by the catastrophic consequences of Frederik VI's alliance with Napoleon after the British bombarded Copenhagen and confiscated the entire Danish fleet in 1807. These consequences included the Danish state's declaration of bankruptcy in 1813 and loss of Norway to Sweden in 1814. Dissatisfaction with absolutism increased, particularly among students, as the aging, authoritarian king tightened censorship laws in an attempt to quell dissent and ignored, until 1830, the requirement of the 1815 Congress of Vienna that he establish advisory legislative bodies. Since Frederik VI's successor, Prince Christian Frederik (1786–1848), had been instrumental in the drafting of the Norwegian constitution in 1814 (as part of Norway's unsuccessful bid to avoid being forced into union with Sweden), hopes were high among national-liberals when he became King Christian VIII in December 1839 that he would support a shift toward republican government and greater civil rights. They were, however, disappointed in these expectations; Christian VIII made token efforts at administrative reform, but would not support any steps toward a Danish constitution or an elected, representative legislature.

As soon as Christian VIII's son, Frederik VII (1808–1863), ascended the throne in January 1848, the national-liberals began pressuring him to abandon absolutism in favor of a constitutional monarchy that would incorporate the largely Danish-speaking duchy of Schleswig into the kingdom of Denmark. That same month, a revolution in support of democratic self-government erupted in Italy and spread quickly throughout Europe, from Paris to Vienna, Frankfurt to Berlin, and finally to Copenhagen. Unlike the 1848 revolutions elsewhere in Europe, the Danish revolution was bloodless but nonetheless momentous in terms of its abiding impact on Danish society. Although many Danish national-liberals were skeptical of democracy, they took advantage of the situation to advance their own agenda of political reform. Nationalistic unrest among German speakers in Schleswig-Holstein lent urgency to their demands.

On March 21, 1848, a delegation of leading Copenhagen citizens presented the new king with a resolution demanding that he "immediately surround the throne with men whose insight, energy, and patriotism can give the government power and the nation trust." The king reputedly answered, "I am pleased that our views are so completely in harmony, for that which you desire, gentlemen, was already accomplished this morning. The old ministry has been dissolved. If you, dear gentlemen, will put the same trust in your king as I have in my people, then I will lead you faithfully in honor and freedom."[7] He appointed Adam Wilhelm Moltke as *Statsminister* (prime minister) and commissioned him to form a government. The *Martsministeriet* (March Ministry), as it came to be known, was tasked with drafting a constitution and organizing elections for a Danish legislature. Without a shot being fired, absolutism in Denmark came to an end and parliamentary democracy was introduced. However, the struggle to redefine Danish national and cultural identity outside of the state's control had just begun.

D. G. Monrad and the June Constitution

Although many individuals contributed to the crafting of the June Constitution, the pastor and national-liberal politician Ditlev Gothard (D. G.) Monrad (1811–1887) was arguably its single most influential architect. As *Kultusminister* (minister for religion and education) in the March Ministry, Monrad played a central role in writing the constitution, with particular influence on the paragraphs dealing with religious matters.

Monrad's reputation in Denmark today is negatively colored by the fact that he—while serving as prime minister and suffering from manic-depressive disorder[8]—presided over Denmark's defeat by Prussia and Austria in the Second Schleswig War of 1864. He has been almost universally blamed for Denmark's loss of the economically and psychologically significant duchies of Schleswig and Holstein. While Monrad was technically responsible for the course of the war and its consequences, the root causes of Denmark's humiliation and diminution— self-aggrandizing nationalism and political discord in Copenhagen, rapid German militarization and imperial ambitions under Chancellor Bismarck, and the indifference of the great powers, among other factors— were largely out of his control. Monrad's more positive legacy lies in his contributions to the Danish constitution. His central role in the establishment of religious freedom in particular justifies closer examination of his biography and his motivation for promoting the cause of religious liberalization in Denmark.

Monrad's long and influential career in Danish politics offers evidence of his own intelligence and ambition as well as the opportunities for social mobility available through the church during the absolutist era. Although he came from a long line of priests and lawyers, Monrad's immediate family was impoverished—his father suffered from mental illness and had difficulty providing for his family.[9] At the age of ten, Monrad went to live with his uncle, Rasmus Kornerup, who operated a general store in the small town of Præstø. As his uncle's apprentice, Monrad learned the shopkeeper's trade, but his interests lay in a more scholarly direction. Inspired by Thomas Paine's treatise *The Age of Reason*, which laid the foundation for Monrad's later fascination with democratic ideals, and sponsored by his parish priest, the poet Nicolai Bierfreund Søtoft, Monrad was able continue his education at a boarding school in Vordingborg in 1826.[10] There he lived and studied with Lauritz Christian Ditlev Westengaard, an ardent proponent of both political and religious freedom. Enthusiastically recommended by Westengaard, Monrad was accepted into the University of Copenhagen to study theology.

Monrad arrived in Copenhagen in 1830, the year of the July revolution that shook Paris and brought down the French king Charles X, but there was no hint of revolution in Denmark at that time. Nearly all of Copenhagen's considerable intellectual energies of the era were directed into the arts and sciences, as exemplified by the poetry and dramas written by Adam Oehlenschläger, the scientific discoveries of Hans Christian

FIGURE 1.1 *D. G. Monrad* (1846), painting by Constantin Hansen. Lutheran bishop and statesman D. G. Monrad was the primary architect of the Danish constitution, adopted in June 1849, which established the right of religious freedom for all Danes. Reproduced courtesy of the Danish Parliament, Copenhagen.

Ørsted, and the norm-setting aesthetic critiques that Johan Ludvig Heiberg published in his influential literary journal. Short on funds but rich in ambition, Monrad carved out a niche for himself in Copenhagen's elite society, forming lifelong friendships with many of the men who would play a central role in nineteenth-century Danish politics, such as the pastors Vilhelm Birkedal and Victor Bloch, the historian Frederik Barfod, the doctor C. E. Fenger, and the statesman C. C. Hall, among others. Monrad's student years were marked by feverish productivity—of poems, plays, and scholarly endeavors—but also by recurring crises of faith and a nervous breakdown in the summer of 1832. Over the course of the 1830s, Monrad gained confidence in his own ideas and a reputation as a skilled debater, daring enough to take on even the most venerable professors. Monrad's engagement to Emilie Lütthans in 1838 motivated him to abandon his plans for pursuing a professorship in Semitic languages in favor of the security provided by a career in the Danish national church.

The ascension of Christian VIII to the Danish throne in 1839 gave Monrad the opportunity to demonstrate his political acumen, setting the stage for the fusion of political and religious interests that would shape Monrad's professional life and allow him to make a lasting contribution to Danish democracy. On the evening of December 3, 1839, the day King Frederik VI died, Monrad accepted an invitation from his friend Frederik Barfod to attend a gathering of students at the Hotel d'Angleterre. These students intended to present the new king with a resolution in support of a democratic constitution and freedom of the press. Barfod, who was a loyal monarchist at the time (although he later became an ardent democrat), initially wanted to oppose this venture, but Monrad surprised his friend by speaking out in favor of the resolution, which was subsequently adopted. It was at this meeting that Monrad first met the journalist and politician Orla Lehmann (1810–1870), who would be Monrad's most effective partner over the next decade in the struggle to inculcate the Danish public with democratic ideals. Both Lehmann and Monrad were members of the delegation that presented the resolution to Christian VIII on December 4, 1839. Although the new king rejected the resolution out of hand, Monrad had started down a path that would lead to a long, energetic career as a proponent of democratic ideals in Danish politics and an architect of the modern Danish state.[11]

One of the most important ways in which Monrad helped shape public opinion in favor of democratic principles—and, not incidentally, work out his own view of democracy—was through print media. Despite the generally apolitical bent of Copenhagen society and Denmark's strict press censorship laws at the time, Monrad, Lehmann, and others devoted themselves to spreading liberal political ideas through newspapers and circulars. On December 7, just three days after the failed appeal to the king, Lehmann published the first issue of the liberal newspaper *Fædrelandet* (*The Fatherland*), the editorial board of which Monrad joined in April 1840. In 1843, he became the editor of *Dansk Folkeblad* (*Danish People's Paper*), and between 1839 and 1842 he published a series of five circulars that he called *Flyvende Politiske Blade* (*Flying Political Papers*), which explained and illustrated his political ideology. In the first circular, published on December 23, 1839, Monrad rejected the rhetorical norm of referring to the king as "the father of the country" because of the way it implicitly infantilized the Danish people.[12] In a later article in the *Fatherland*, he takes pains to differentiate between the king's official role and his private life, noting that "the king can go without sleep just as little as any other person, but when he sleeps, he does it as a person and not as the king."[13]

Although he challenges the king's position as absolute monarch in his articles, Monrad does not blame the king for Denmark's political problems. Instead, he chastises Danes for their passivity in political matters and lays the burden of democracy upon their shoulders. He warns that Denmark's future depends on individuals "taking upon themselves the responsibility for regarding themselves as members of the society of the state and exercising that right."[14] Despite having passed his theological exams with honors, Monrad did not seek an appointment as a pastor until 1846, when he was assigned a parish on the island of Lolland. Even at the height of his activism, Monrad infused his political discussions with religious imagery and Biblical allusions. For example, in April 1840 he published an article in which he compares Christian VIII to Moses, who has been called to lead the people out of the land of Egypt but will not act without a sign from God. "People of Denmark," Monrad exhorts, "it is you who must give your king a sign, for Jehovah no longer performs miracles. Dead and torpid and drowsy is a mute people that does not lift up its voice and speak. . . . Verily I say that a people that does not even have the power to ask for freedom is unworthy of it."[15] Monrad's outspokenness in the media gave him a reputation as an agitator, which cost him a position as superintendent of schools in 1844, when the queen opposed his candidacy on the grounds that he was too critical of the king and his government.[16]

In his political philosophy, Monrad regarded freedom as synonymous with democracy, which he believed could only be instituted by means of a constitution. Monrad's newspaper articles present a democratic constitution as the answer to many of Denmark's domestic and foreign challenges, including the pro-German separatist movements in the duchy of Holstein that flared into war in both 1848 and 1864. In the second *Flying Political Paper*, he argues that only a democratic constitution could "transform the divided province to a single kingdom, the scattered crowds to one people. . . . Regional differences are mighty, cultural traditions are mighty, but mightiest of all is freedom."[17]

These arguments reveal that Monrad, in contrast to many of his contemporaries, viewed national identity primarily in civic rather than ethnic or linguistic terms. He regarded freedom of thought and expression as universal truths, on par with the Christian gospel and available to all, as the following excerpt from a speech he delivered on May 31, 1840, illustrates:

Gentlemen! There are some truths, which are of an entirely unique nature, which are not restricted to any particular stage in life nor to a particular educational level, but which accompany all people from the cradle to the grave. . . . Such truths are knowledge of God, of free will, and immortality, which, although they are the subject of the most serious analysis by the keenest thinkers, are taught to children by their mothers, who point toward Heaven and say that we have a Father there, to whom we all will be gathered.

Yet it is not only the church, it is also the state, not only religion, also politics, which are in possession of such deep and yet universally accessible truths: that there is something called laws, holy, unbendable, strict, to which we owe unconditional loyalty, and whose righteous punishments we should accept without murmur, if we have transgressed them; that there is something called freedom, which requires that thoughts shall be free of all constraints, that words should not be muzzled, and that the press should not be subject to the despotism of power; that there is something called guarantees of freedom, which ensure that the welfare of thousands upon thousands is not sacrificed for anyone's whims and irrational impulses.

These truths are not the exclusive property of the highly educated or the nobility or the ancients; they can be recognized by young and old, weak and mighty; they can be understood by everyone, without exception.[18]

Despite his belief in the universal validity of these truths, Monrad recognized that it would take a great deal of work to ensure their acceptance among people of all social classes. He admonishes his audience not to rely on the efforts of journalists and activists, but to help defend truth and right with "a power and enthusiasm that never dulls, never tires, never fails, for which every obstacle is encouraging, every resistance a prod. Not until political life bubbles forth from thousands and more thousands of small, unknown springs will the efforts for freedom grounded in laws and limited by laws swell to a mighty river that nothing can withstand."[19]

After years of efforts first as a journalist and later as a pastor, Monrad saw the streams of political activism in Denmark swell to a mighty river. In the spring of 1848, the revolutions across Europe and the coronation of a new king in Denmark reignited hopes for a democratic constitution. Reprising the meeting in December 1839 where Monrad and Orla Lehmann first met, the two men were among the main speakers at a meeting of leading Copenhagen activists at the Casino Hotel on March 21, 1848, where the demand for a free constitution was adopted, with both Lehmann and Monrad as signatories. Rumor had it that Monrad visited the king on March 20 in order to prepare him for the delegation's petition.[20] Whether or not Monrad deserves credit for easing the transition, Frederik VII's ready acceptance of the delegation's demands—in contrast to his father's unwillingness to do so eight years earlier—reflects the traction that democratic ideas had gained in the intervening years. Nevertheless, they still had plenty of vocal opponents among the Copenhagen elites, whose fears were bolstered by reports of an armed insurrection in the provinces of Schleswig and Holstein. The so-called "March Revolution" gave the king a popular platform from which to quell the rebellion and preserve the monarchy, at least for the time being.

In recognition of his representative role within the liberal movement, Monrad was appointed minister of religion and education in the new government, headed by A. W. Moltke. Acting on provisional authority, the March Ministry formed a committee consisting of Minister of Justice C.E. Bardenfleth, Minister without portfolio L. N. Hvidt, and Monrad, on June 9, 1848, to draft a proposal for a constitution to be discussed at a constitutional convention. In only two days, Monrad produced eleven folio-sized pages containing his draft of the constitution,[21] drawing on various foreign models for inspiration but striving to make it "as comprehensible and popular as possible."[22]

Although Monrad was relieved of his office after only eight months due to the formation of a new, more conservative government[23] and was not elected or appointed to the constitutional convention, the fundamentals of his proposal were retained to such a degree that he is widely regarded by Danish historians as the father of the Danish constitution. Monrad's constitution was flexible and farseeing enough that nearly three-quarters of it is still included in the present constitution, though the concepts underlying the actual text of the constitution have, of course, shifted significantly over time in favor of increased social equality and participation in government.

Strictly speaking, Monrad was not so much a democratic ideologue as a Hegelian pragmatist, who strove to achieve a balance between freedom and order. He regarded the constitution less as an ideological manifesto and more as a mechanism designed to achieve harmonious cooperation between the branches of government, between different social classes, between the individual and society, and between the church and the state. As much as he believed in participatory government, he worried about replacing the tyranny of the few with the tyranny of the many and strove to ensure that no single group or institution would have disproportionate influence.

Monrad was initially skeptical of the common man's ability to rule himself. In the early 1840s, Monrad opposed universal suffrage for peasants, trusting instead in the enlightened ability of the educated middle class to represent the peasants, selflessly "safeguard the welfare of the country, and resolve conflicts between opposing interests."[24] By 1849, however, his fundamental belief in the inherent potential of all people persuaded him to support the radical position of universal suffrage. In an article in the *Fatherland,* Monrad explains his change of heart regarding the empowerment of the working classes:

> We do not believe that poverty or wealth makes any material difference with regard to the deepest content of the human soul; we assume that a working man can master the highest truths with the same warmth and fervor as a wealthy man, that he possesses the same strength of will to fulfill his duty in all respects, the same faithfulness and love. We admit, that there was a time when we were less persuaded of this belief and that we have later come to this realization by means of careful observation of and communion with the common people. The worth of the individual in a Christian state, the independence of its being, with regard to purity or evilness, from earthly conditions are of great importance for us in deciding the question now before us. In our opinion, this view of the common man is tied to our conviction of the Christian religion's accessibility for all.[25]

The decisive change in Monrad's life that lay between his opposition to universal suffrage and his support of it was his appointment as a pastor in Vester Ulslev in 1846. Despite the financial difficulties he had experienced as a child and young man, Monrad was still a member of the educated bourgeoisie and had not had any close contact with the Danish peasantry before taking responsibility for his parish. He was pleasantly surprised by the sincerity and goodness of his parishioners, but was also taken aback by the political apathy evident among people of all classes in his rural area.

It was at this point that Monrad realized democracy could not take root in Denmark, either among peasants or merchants, if the people were not willing to speak out. They must ask for their own freedom, as he had proclaimed in the above-mentioned article in which he compared King Christian VIII to Moses waiting for a sign to lead his people out of bondage. In short, Monrad believed the Danish people must first be enfranchised in order to be effective participants in a democratic society.

In addition to freedom of the press and freedom of assembly, both of which had been sorely lacking during his time as a newspaper editor in the 1840s, Monrad initially proposed merely ensuring freedom of conscience, in keeping with Bishop J. P. Mynster's approach. However, Monrad soon became an advocate of freedom of religion, specifically citizens' rights to join together in communities to worship God according to their own beliefs, as long as such worship did not offend public order or morality. This proposal broke with one of the central tenets of Danish absolutism, namely that it was the king's responsibility to ensure his subjects' fidelity to the pure and unadulterated (Lutheran) Christian faith. Monrad believed the state should be responsible for the spiritual needs of its people, for which reason he proposed defining the evangelical Lutheran religion as the church of the Danish king and his people, which should therefore be supported and administered by the state. At the same time, however, he wanted to ensure the church's independence of state interference and therefore proposed that a future law should codify *Folkekirken*'s precise relationship to the state. In preparing his draft of the first Danish constitution, Monrad tried to find a solution that would be acceptable to the majority of Danes, preserve public order, and protect the preeminent position of the state church.

Once he completed the draft that would form the basis for the constitutional assembly's discussions, Monrad circulated it among the Danish clergy and recommended—in his capacity as minister of religion—that they gather to discuss the provisions relevant to the exercise of religion. Although a church-wide convention never came about, both the Roskilde and Copenhagen pastoral councils debated Monrad's proposals in the summer of 1848. The members of both councils, who had been discussing the issue of religious freedom since at least the early 1840s, represented the full range of positions on the matter, but they ultimately endorsed Monrad's proposals, albeit with a few amendments. The constitutional assembly then discussed the draft over several months, finally adopting a slightly modified version in June 1849.

The State of Religion in Denmark

The Danish people officially became Christian after the formation of a unified Danish kingdom around the mid-tenth century, when King Harald Bluetooth mandated his people's mass conversion to Christianity. The Catholic Church was, however, legally and financially independent of the king and free to act against his wishes in support of its own priorities. Although the church in Denmark was a "highly centralized religious organization that could be of immense political use"[26] on occasion, it was not synonymous with the state and had a complex relationship with the king and Danish nobility.

After the country's royally mandated conversion to Lutheranism in 1536 the de facto symbiosis of church and state was regularized, such that "the Danish government has continuously enjoyed sovereign authority in the affairs of the State Church"[27] since that time and continues to do so today. (Sweden severed its ties between church and state in 2000, and Norway did the same in May 2012.) The Danish monarch became the leader and protector of the Danish church, a relationship that was formalized and heightened by the 1665 *Lex Regia* or *Kongeloven* (king's law), which established absolute monarchy in Denmark and specified not only that the religion of the state was the king's religion, but also that it was the king's responsibility to ensure his subjects' conformity to the same, which meant that being Danish became synonymous with being Lutheran.

Until 1849, therefore, there was not just complete unity between church and state—there was no distinction between the two. The Danish monarch functioned as the head of the church and its pastors were often an extension of government bureaucracy. Clergymen in the Copenhagen area played prominent roles in Danish government, bureaucracy, and society, especially after the emasculation of the Danish nobility by the implementation of absolute monarchy in the 1660s. Rural pastors functioned simultaneously as spiritual shepherds and government administrators in matters such as conducting the census and enforcing military conscription. These university-educated men were the king's loyal servants and were often the only academically trained person in the parish, which made them influential defenders of official policies and practices.

This conflation of church and state permeated many aspects of everyday life for Danes. With very few exceptions, baptism into the Danish Lutheran Church was required for all children born in Denmark and was carried out by force, if necessary. Regular church attendance in geographically determined parishes was mandatory for all citizens, while confirmation, which was reinstituted in 1736, was a prerequisite for receiving communion, being a godparent, getting married, receiving an inheritance, and getting a job. Beginning in 1814, graduation from school was also predicated upon being confirmed, which indicated a person's eligibility to join the ranks of adult Danes. The introduction of religious freedom thus required both a fundamental redefinition of the conditions of membership in the Danish nation and the creation of secular institutions to perform the many functions previously carried out by the church.

For practical reasons, the religious affiliation of Danish citizens living outside the Danish kingdom was less strictly regulated, but this flexibility was accompanied by ambiguity about their Danishness. Certain non-Lutheran Protestant groups and Jews were allowed to live and practice their religion in the German-speaking duchies of Schleswig and Holstein, for example, but the rise of linguistic nationalism in the late eighteenth and early nineteenth centuries further divided these subjects of the Danish king from their Danish-speaking compatriots and led to the two Schleswig wars in 1848 and 1864 that ultimately resulted in the separation of these territories from the Danish state. No particular religious affiliation was mandated in the Danish colonies or trading outposts in West Africa, India, and the West Indies, where Danish citizens mingled freely with Frenchmen, Portuguese, Brits, Americans, and native peoples, among others. Danish forts along the Gold Coast in Africa maintained Lutheran chaplains and schools, but many Danish men posted at these forts married local women in traditional ceremonies.[28] Some of the Afro-Danish children of these unions became Lutherans, but racial politics meant they were not fully accepted as Danish citizens, either when they visited Denmark or in terms of their employment options at the Danish forts in Africa.

Conditions within the Danish kingdom were more highly regulated, with one notable exception. In 1682, King Frederik III granted religious freedom to all inhabitants of the newly established fortress town of Fredericia in central-eastern Jutland in order to entice settlers to the area. The tactic worked and the town soon became home to both a garrison of Catholic mercenaries and Denmark's largest Jewish community, primarily made up of Ashkenazi Jews from Germany who worked in tobacco manufacturing and retail trading. A smaller group of Jews in Copenhagen, led by the court jeweler Meyer Goldschmidt, were granted the right to hold private religious services in Goldschmidt's home in 1684, which they did for the next fifty years.

As a rule, non-Lutheran religious communities in Denmark prior to 1800 were made up of foreigners, who were subject to a plethora of legal restrictions on where they could worship, whom they could marry, and the religious education of their children, all of which underscored their cultural difference from the Danes among whom they lived. Similar to the above-mentioned Jewish community holding services in a private home, Catholic and Reformed services could at first only be conducted in chapels attached to foreign embassies (notably the Austro-Hungarian embassy) and later in a few specially designated churches, such as the St. Thomas Reformed Church on Store Kongensgade in Copenhagen. Members of foreign, non-Lutheran groups who married Danes had to get special permission from the king and commit to raising their children as Lutherans.

The state exhibited a degree of tolerance for certain immigrant religious communities that had received royal permission for limited freedom of worship, but this tolerance was predicated upon political calculation. Royal concessions were typically granted only when the group in question was in a position to provide economic benefit to the Danish state, such as German Catholic craftsmen or wealthy Jewish merchants, or if the royal family had a particular partiality for the group—for example, Queen Sophie Magdalena's fondness for her cousin Nikolaus Ludwig von Zinzendorf, a Pietist nobleman in Saxony who became the protector of the Moravian Herrnhuters in 1722, prompted her to extend protection to Pietists in Denmark. Poor Jews or Catholics, on the other hand, were often treated harshly or deported. Permission to reside in Denmark could also be revoked if an immigrant was unable to support himself, broke the law, or attempted to win converts to his faith.

Such religious liberty for average Danes as existed in Denmark prior to 1849 took the form of freedom of conscience—you could believe whatever you wanted as long as you observed the outward forms of Lutheranism. However, Danish citizens were still forbidden by law from converting to a different religion. If they did so anyway, they forfeited any property or inheritance they held in Denmark and were required to leave the country.[29] The most public cases of conversions that invoked such penalties involved Danish students at various European Catholic universities, as well as one instance of five theology students at the University of Copenhagen in 1706 who converted to Catholicism. Two of the five eventually returned to the fold and served as Danish Lutheran priests, while the other three found employment, respectively, as a librarian in the Vatican, a Jesuit and professor of theology in Cologne, and a librarian at the Royal Library in Madrid, then Mexico, and finally London.[30]

Fear of the possibility that Danes might be lured away from Lutheranism into the service of a foreign political entity resulted in laws forbidding Catholic monks, Jesuits, and papal representatives—with the exception of priests employed by foreign embassies—from setting foot on Danish soil (although such draconian measures were rarely, if ever, enforced). The potency of this perceived cultural and political threat was demonstrated as late as 1839, when a scandal erupted over Pope Gregory XVI's selection of a conservative Belgian Jesuit, Johannes Laurent, as a Nordic apostolic bishop based in Hamburg. This move was widely regarded, in Denmark as well as in other Protestant states in northern Germany, as the beginning of an attempt to reconquer northern Europe for Catholicism, and the pope was forced to replace Laurent with a moderate German bishop based in Osnabrück. Even then, Bishop Mynster persuaded the king to specifically prohibit the new bishop, Carl Anton Lüpke, from physically entering Denmark, a law that was invoked in 1846 when Bishop Lüpke attempted to come to Denmark to dedicate a new Catholic church.[31]

The complete unity of church and state in Denmark was largely undisputed until the spread of Enlightenment rationality from Germany in the late eighteenth century called it into question. The lay revival movement among Danish Pietists in the 1820s, discussed above, treated religion as a realm of individual self-expression rather than state control and gave the pursuit of religious individualism political significance. The king's edict of toleration in 1840 brought the persecution of *de vakte* (the awakened) to an end and allowed them to meet freely anywhere in the country without fear of government opposition.

Such freedoms did not, however, apply to other dissident religious groups, as illustrated by the furor sparked by the (illegal) establishment of the first Danish Baptist congregation in Copenhagen in 1839, under the leadership of an engraver named Peter Christian Mønster (1779–1870).

Unlike the revivalists, who still belonged to the state church, or Catholics and Jews, who belonged to officially recognized foreign religious groups and were not allowed to convert Danes, Baptists represented a new religion without precedent in Denmark. Not only were "new and unknown sects" specifically forbidden by a 1745 law, but the Baptists declared themselves independent of the state church and openly proselytized.[32] The so-called "Baptist crisis" of 1842 brought the issue of religious difference and its political repercussions to the forefront of Danish political debate during the years leading up to the adoption of the June Constitution.

Originally one of the "awakened" who doubted the practice of infant baptism, Mønster embraced the Baptist faith in October 1839, after learning of it from J. G. Oncken, a German Baptist minister who was visiting Copenhagen. Before returning to Germany, Oncken baptized the first eleven Danish Baptists and organized the Copenhagen congregation with Mønster as its leader. Mønster and his fellow converts baptized 267 people between 1839 and 1844, primarily members of the most disadvantaged socioeconomic classes—craftsmen, journeymen, soldiers, and servants. By the 1850 census, there were 360 Baptists in Copenhagen, while other Baptist groups sprang up in western Zealand, on the island of Langeland, and in northern Jutland. The Baptist congregation in the city of Aalborg boasted a membership of 689 between 1840 and 1856 under the leadership of O. N. Føltved.[33] While Føltved enjoyed the respect of the local Lutheran bishop and his congregants continued to attend their local Lutheran churches, Mønster was imprisoned on at least three occasions for proselytizing.

Undaunted, in 1840 Mønster submitted a petition to the Danish government in which he outlined the tenets of the Baptist faith and demanded religious freedom for all Danes. Both the liberal newspapers *Fædrelandet* and *Dansk Folkeblad* (the latter edited by Monrad) and Pastor Nikolaj Frederik Severin (N. F. S.) Grundtvig spoke out in support of Mønster's cause, while two British Baptist ministers and the British Quaker Elizabeth Fry presented his case to the king. However, Mønster's efforts were not successful, although they did result in a special ordinance concerning Baptists. The *Baptistplakat* (Baptist Ordinance) of 1842 granted Baptists the status of a "tolerated" foreign religion, but also stipulated that their adherents must register with the local police magistrate, refrain from proselytizing, and present their infant children for baptism into the Lutheran Church. This final, highly controversial provision had been the subject of heated debate within the government prior to passage of the law, but it was retained in the final version, on Bishop Mynster's insistence, in order to protect the absolutist principle of the Lutheran identity of all Danish citizens. Mynster regarded the Baptists' refusal to accept Lutheran baptism as a valid Christian ordinance as a threat to the state church and the unity of Danish Lutheran society.

The failure of Danish Baptists to obey the provision requiring the infant baptism of their children into the state church precipitated the Baptist crisis. The measure aroused opposition among both Baptists and Lutherans; many pastors, particularly those of a Grundtvigian or Pietist persuasion, disliked the idea of forcing the church's sacraments upon unwilling recipients, while some Baptist congregations threatened to excommunicate members who obeyed the law. Bishop Mynster, however, insisted that Danish Lutheran pastors forcibly baptize the children of Danish Baptists, which escalated the conflict. Having counseled with his mentor, Pastor Grundtvig, on the matter, Peter Christian Kierkegaard, pastor of Pedersborg parish, refused to perform the forcible baptisms, despite the threat of dismissal. Queen Caroline Amalie also opposed the policy, which caused the king to waver in his support of Mynster's hardline view.

Other critics were even more outspoken. In 1843, Pastor Hans Lassen Martensen published *Den kristelige Daab (Christian Baptism)*, in which he argues against both forcible infant baptism and the adult baptism practiced by Baptists.[34] Liberal professor H. N. Clausen contributed to the discussion with an 1845 pamphlet urging the state to rescind this demand, which he believed contradicted the personal religious freedom of conscience endorsed by Martin Luther. Clausen recommended that the government adopt an earlier proposal requiring the children of Baptists to be baptized no later than the age of nineteen—the maximum age for confirmation in the Lutheran Church.[35] Despite ongoing discussions within the government, the Baptist law was not repealed before the adoption of the June Constitution in 1849. However, the crisis made it clear, as Martin Schwarz Lausten argues, "that time had run out on attempts to use force in matters of faith and conscience."[36] Yet old habits die hard—the requirement that all Danish citizens present their children for baptism was not officially rescinded until 1857. Even today all births in Denmark must be reported to the local parish for recording, regardless of the child's or parents' religious affiliation.[37]

The Baptist crisis was a public relations disaster for Bishop Mynster and the Danish Lutheran Church, as well as an immediate justification for the inclusion of religious freedom in the new constitution. Although not even the opponents of the forcible baptism policy initially supported full religious freedom for all Danes, debates about the Baptist problem prompted calls for some degree of religious freedom beyond the freedom of conscience that Mynster felt was sufficient. The ensuing discussion, which informed deliberations about the constitution in 1848–49, weighed the benefits of the British model of retaining an official state church but tolerating dissidents versus the American model of exclusively independent congregations with no connection to the state. Revivalist preacher and schoolteacher Rasmus Sørensen (1799–1865) ardently advocated the American model. Inspired by Grundtvig's inclusive views, the Danes ultimately settled on a hybrid model, which privileged the country's cultural affinity for evangelical Lutheranism without establishing an official state church, while also making legal room for alternative independent religious groups within Danish society.

The Religious Reformer N. F. S. Grundtvig

Alongside D. G. Monrad, N. F. S. Grundtvig was one of the most influential figures in the promotion of religious freedom in Denmark in the nineteenth century. Unlike Monrad's, however, Grundtvig's name is known for good in every Danish household as the father of Danish Lutheranism. His influence on both the institutions and self-perception of the Danish state and church today is indelible. Religious historian Jes Fabricius Møller cautions that the branding of Denmark as Grundtvig's birthplace is a fairly recent phenomenon, which relies on a rhetorical image of Grundtvig as a metaphor for the specifically Danish aspects of Denmark.[38]

Nevertheless, although relatively few of Grundtvig's many works have been translated into English and his name is not as well known internationally as, for example, the philosopher Søren Kierkegaard's, Grundtvig was undeniably a seminal figure in the articulation of Danish national, cultural, and religious identity in the nineteenth century. His many contributions include the 1,500 songs he wrote, many of which are still included in the Danish hymnal, as well as the folk high school system he designed, which flourishes in Denmark and other Nordic countries to this day, with American offshoots established by Scandinavian immigrants from Minnesota to California. Like D. G. Monrad, Grundtvig suffered from manic-depressive disorder; like Søren Kierkegaard, he spent most of his life in and around Copenhagen, traveling just four times to England (each summer from 1829–31 and in 1843), once to Jutland (in 1844), and once to Norway (in 1851). Grundtvig continues to be a leading figure in Danish cultural history, not just as the architect of the modern Danish church and a pioneer in the struggle for religious liberalism, but also as the most ardent defender of Danishness the country has ever had.

It is challenging to convey just how multifaceted and gifted a thinker, scholar, and poet N. F. S. Grundtvig was. Grundtvig's interests were wide ranging, his energy unflagging, and his publications over a writing career of approximately seventy years almost too numerous to count. Born in 1783 to a Lutheran pastor and his wife in Udby, near Vordingborg on the southern end of the island of Zealand, Grundtvig lived in Copenhagen for sixty-three years until his death in 1872 at age eighty-nine. He earned a degree in theology from the University of Copenhagen in 1803, but worked in many different intellectual and professional fields over the course of his life. Biographer Kaj Thaning explains:

He studied theology, but never became a professional theologian. His inclination was toward history, but even though he made significant contributions to historical research, he placed his historical knowledge first and foremost in the service of enlightening the people. He is best known abroad as the creator of the folk high school, but his views of popular education were shaped by the fact that he was not just a historian, as well as a contemporary historian and cultural philosopher, but also a poet. He described his "life-enlightenment" as "historical-poetic." At the same time, he was a scholarly researcher into the Anglo-Saxon language— and internationally known within that field, a skilled Latinist, and translator of Old Norse literature, but also a Danish language reformer with deep knowledge of the Danish language in the past and present, who had grown up with both the Zealand and Jutlandic dialects.[39]

FIGURE 1.2 *N. F. S. Grundtvig* (1843), painting by Christian Albrecht Jensen. The scholar, poet, pastor, and statesman was a driving force behind the reform movement within the Danish Lutheran Church in the nineteenth century, as well as the author of many of the songs in the Danish hymnal. Reproduced courtesy of the Hirschsprung Collection, Copenhagen.

Despite his impressive academic accomplishments, however, Grundtvig's most lasting legacies for Danish culture and society came about
through his poetry, political activism, and leadership of a reform movement within the Danish Lutheran Church.

After becoming disaffected with religion during his university studies and work on the book *Nordens Mytologi* (*Northern Mythology*, 1808),
Grundtvig experienced a spiritual awakening around 1810 that motivated
him to pursue a career in the church, albeit as a crusader for reform.
He worked as curate for his father, Johan Grundtvig for a few years, but
his public criticism of the rationalist tendencies in Danish Lutheranism
blocked him from being given a parish of his own until 1821, when he
was called to Præstø before being transferred to Copenhagen the following year. He attracted attention in 1825 through his involvement in
a public dispute with Copenhagen University professor of theology H.
N. Clausen over the way in which Christianity should be understood.
In response to Clausen's 1825 book, *Catholicismens og Protestantismens
Kirkeforfatning, Lære, og Ritus* (*Catholicism and Protestantism's Church
Constitutions, Teachings, and Ritual*),[40] Grundtvig published a pamphlet
titled *Kirkens Genmæle* (*The Church's Reply*), in which he accused Clausen
of treating Christianity as a philosophical idea rather than an historical
fact and demanded that Clausen be fired from his position.[41] For his part,
Grundtvig defined Christianity as an unbroken chain of sacraments from
the time of Christ to the present day. On the same day Grundtvig's book
appeared, the Danish stock exchange was forced to shut down because
of the commotion it caused. Clausen refused to debate Grundtvig but
instead sued him for libel and won.

As a result of the legal judgment, Grundtvig resigned his pulpit and was
subject to state censorship of his writings for more than a decade, but he
simply turned his attention back to Nordic mythology, world history, education, and nationalism, during which time his approach shifted from German romanticism and idealism to English realism. He traveled to England
three times on a fellowship from the king to study Anglo-Saxon manuscripts and published a new, heavily revised edition of *Nordens Mytologi*
in 1832. In his 1838 book *Skolen for Livet* (*The School for Life*), Grundtvig
stressed the need for a national culture-oriented approach to education
instead of a classical model, with a focus on Danish language, Danish history, and Christianity as crucial components of teaching young Danes

about the world and themselves.[42] While his cherished plan to open an academy at Sorø never came to fruition, despite support from King Christian VIII and Queen Caroline Amalie, Grundtvig's ideas about folk education inspired the creation of a network of folk high schools for continuing adult education in precisely the kinds of nationally-oriented subjects Grundtvig advocated.

In 1839, Grundtvig resumed his involvement with the Danish Lutheran Church when he was appointed pastor at Vartov Hospital for elderly women in Copenhagen, but with a radically different approach to his faith. Grundtvig now eschewed the Pietistic emphasis on suffering and hope in the afterlife, preaching instead that Christianity was designed to prepare people to live life now, not just after death. He dismissed the need for historical veracity to legitimize Christianity or the Bible and emphasized instead the need for childlike faith in Christ as well as the oral transmission of doctrine, revelation, and apostolic authority down through the generations. His sermons focused on the mercy of God and man's inability to either strive for or attain salvation on his or her own merits—one could only be saved through the sacraments of baptism and communion received within the community of believers. Grundtvig regarded his new understanding of Christianity as a relief from a heavy burden, explaining, "It is now a pleasure to preach. . . . I was not raised up with the Lord because I had the power to go with Him into death, but only because I had the faith to be saved."[43] This joyful, inclusive approach alienated some of his earlier "awakened" followers, but ultimately appealed to a broad swath of the Danish population.

Although Grundtvig was in many ways a solitary figure who devoted his life to scholarship and writing, his pastoral work gave him the opportunity to spread his views about the need for a renewal of both religious practice and songs of praise in the Danish church. He was a gifted public speaker who appealed to widely different groups, in particular through the composition, translation, and adaptation of hundreds of songs for use in his church services. In the Danish church today, Thaning explains, "services revolve around the hymns and cannot be conceived of without Grundtvig."[44] Among Grundtvig's most memorable songs are a number of beloved Danish Christmas carols, including "Dejlig er den himmel blå" ("Lovely is the Midnight Sky," 1810), "Det kimer nu til julefest" ("The Bells Ring in our Christmas Feast," 1817), "Et barn er født i Bethlehem"

("A Child is Born in Bethlehem," 1820), "Julen har engelyd" ("Christmas Bears the Sound of Angels," 1837), "Vær velkommen, Herrens år" ("Welcome to the Year of the Lord," 1849), and "Kimer, I klokker" ("Ring O Ye Bells, O Ring Out," 1856). In recognition of his contributions to the Danish church, in particular his hymns, Grundtvig was made an honorary bishop in 1861. He gave his final sermon at Vartov, after thirty-three years of service, on September 1, 1872, the day before his death.

Without any apparent intent to do so, Grundtvig gradually became the leader of a reform movement within the Danish church that came to be known as "Grundtvigianism." Already in 1832, a group of his followers had applied for permission to break off from the state church in order to form their own church with Grundtvig at its head.[45] Grundtvig himself opposed the proposal and it came to nothing, but the idea of a Grundtvigian church was thus demonstrably in circulation. This movement coalesced more permanently in the 1840s out of a heterogeneous cluster of reform-minded individuals who agreed with Grundtvig's approach to renewing the Danish church and religious life in Denmark. Historian Claus Bjørn explains,

> It was toward the end of the 1840s that one can trace the beginnings of a Grundtvigian following among the "awakened" circles in the lay population. As the leading figure in the Danish church he seemed for many people, especially among younger people, to have taken the place of the Bishop of Zealand, J.P. Mynster, who had been the primate of the Danish church for the past two decades. Whereas his older like-minded colleagues had been his brothers-in-arms, the next generation was more likely to become his disciples, who strove to implement Grundtvig's religious and social ideas in their own pastoral work, as is illuminated in detail in the correspondence between Grundtvig and Peter Rørdam in Mern. Grundtvig's son-in-law P. O. Boisen came to function in many respects as Grundtvig's immediate flag-bearer and the person who organized the logistics of Grundtvig's connections to his environment and his growing circle of followers.[46]

In keeping with Grundtvig's own wide-ranging interests, his followers were far from a homogeneous group. As Grundtvig noted in 1847,

"Among the *so-called* 'Grundtvigians,' one praises my sermons or hymns, but despises my interest in mythology, history, or nationalism, or at least my blindness toward the superiority of the godly awakenings and mission societies, while another thinks the exact opposite" (emphasis in original).[47]

This diversity was both a strength and a hindrance to the movement's effectiveness, as even its opponents admitted. In an article published in the liberal Copenhagen newspaper *Morgenbladet* (*Morning Paper*) on the occasion of Grundtvig's one hundredth birthday, politician Edvard Brandes mocks the movement's lack of a clear focus, describing it as "incoherent and entirely too complacent." However, Brandes still prophesies that "the movement will last a long time, because it has such far-flung roots and its doctrines possess a new religion's ability to expand itself and seduce souls by promising a great deal and asking very little."[48]

Grundtvig's disciples and supporters embraced an image of themselves as "Happy Danes," in contrast to the bleaker worldview associated with members of the Pietistic movement *Indre Missionen* (the Home Mission), which placed strong emphasis on personal holiness rather than on the sacraments, for which reason its adherents were often referred to as "Holy Danes". This distinction between subsets of Danish Lutheranism persisted well into the twentieth century, not only in Denmark but also among Danish American Lutherans. While adherents of the Home Mission tended to belong to the conservative United Evangelical Lutheran Church (UELC), Danish American Grundtvigians constituted a special interest group within the more liberal Association of Evangelical Lutheran Churches (AELC), until both groups were subsumed into the Evangelical Lutheran Church in America (ELCA) in 1988.

This kind of reconciliation was exactly what Grundtvig hoped the Danish Lutheran Church could accomplish in the mid-nineteenth century, despite the increasing diversity of religious orientations in the country. Rather than breaking with the church, as his followers had proposed in 1832, Grundtvig focused on achieving freedom within the church for individuals to choose the pastor or congregation they preferred instead of the geographically assigned parishes that were customary at the time. Grundtvig was an outspoken proponent of freedom, in keeping with his mantra: "He who would be free, must allow his neighbor to be free as

well."[49] He did not support unfettered freedom for the individual, however, either in political or religious matters.

While he did not share Bishop J. P. Mynster's view that freedom of
conscience was sufficient to deal with religious difference, Grundtvig
felt that the most harmonious balance between competing individual
claims to freedom could be reached within the protective bounds of society and the church. In addition to the parishioners' freedom, Grundtvig
sought freedom for pastors to choose rituals and doctrines they could
wholeheartedly endorse, rather than requiring them to preach hypocrit-
ically about doctrines in which they did not believe. He advocated for a
"*rummelig*" (capacious) church that would have room for a wide variety
of faiths, similar to the "Big Tent Christianity" approach that became
popular in the United States at the end of the twentieth century. While
acknowledging the specificity of each faith, Grundtvig believed they
could coexist peacefully under the auspices of a civil, ecumenical church.

At the same time, Grundtvig felt strongly about the church's need for
independence from the state. During the Baptist crisis in 1842, Grundtvig objected to Bishop Mynster's insistence on forced baptisms on the
grounds that this intervention by the state violated the church's autonomy. He wanted to bring about the separation of citizenship from church
membership and proposed instituting a kind of civil confirmation that
would allow nonbelievers access to the privileges and responsibilities
of citizenship. He also advocated for the possibility of civil marriage
as an alternative to the religious ceremony. These issues—along with
his passion for cultural nationalism and investment in the preservation
of Danishness in the duchy of Schleswig—motivated Grundtvig to
involve himself in Danish political discussions of religious freedom
and national identity.

Although he was only elected to political office once (after his opponent withdrew rather than compete with the pastor who had confirmed
him), Grundtvig was a highly visible figure in Danish politics by virtue
of his role as an ardent and influential cultural nationalist. Throughout
his life, he regarded Danishness as the basis of public life and the most
effective way to overcome popular tastes for imported ideas and customs,
particularly from Germany. He volubly defended this principle in the
areas of linguistics, mythology, history, education, music, religion, and
politics. His early writings reflect a romantic engagement with the idea

of the "folk," with its primitive but pure national culture. From 1816–19, Grundtvig published a nationalistic newspaper called *Danne-Virke*, which invoked the name of Denmark's defensive fortifications against Germany in order to call upon Danes to intensify their patriotism.

Despite his clash with professor H. N. Clausen in the 1820s, Grundtvig became associated with the National Liberal Party in the 1840s and joined Clausen in campaigning for the implementation of pro-Danish policies in the duchy of Schleswig. In 1844, he was one of the invited speakers at a nationalistic celebration on *Skamlingsbanken* (Skamling Hill), organized by the prominent national-liberal politician Orla Lehmann. Bjørn identifies this speech as both Grundtvig's breakthrough as a public speaker and a major source of inspiration for the pro-Danish movement in the duchy of Schleswig. Grundtvig's speech became the moment when his conception of Danishness, which he had formulated in the preceding years, first gained widespread traction. In essence, Grundtvig defined Danishness—expressed first and foremost through language—as "a living feeling within the individual, which implies that one commits to a shared life and not least to a shared language. Danishness was something that affected the way one lived, not a fixed teaching or a comprehensive philosophy."[50] In the years leading up to the First Schleswig War, Grundtvig increasingly defined Danish identity in opposition to German culture, though he insisted that his hatred for Germanness only extended to the Eider River, which the national-liberals regarded as the natural border of the Danish kingdom.

Although Grundtvig was a loyal monarchist who opposed the idea of a constitution in 1839, when King Christian VIII ascended the throne, his views shifted over the course of the next decade, despite his close association with both the king and Queen Caroline Amalie, who functioned as his protector on several occasions. When Christian VIII died in January 1848, Grundtvig held back from participating in public debates about the need for a constitution until after the king's burial on February 26. By the time the March revolution reached Copenhagen, Grundtvig was ready to support the changes that were coming. At a pro-Danish rally in Schleswig on March 14, Grundtvig explained that he had always been loyal to the king, but he had come to realize that it was no longer enough for him simply to have a king; he wanted to be part of the political process. As Grundtvig put it, he desired "to be a little king and to see crowds of small kings around me, when we have finally mastered the most noble of all arts: the royal art of self-control."[51]

Grundtvig was not an active participant in the meetings at the Casino Hotel leading up to the march on Christiansborg that took place on March 22, as a result of which King Frederik VII agreed to abolish absolutism and accept the role of constitutional monarch, but he was keenly interested in the issues being debated. In the first issue of his weekly self-authored newspaper, *Danskeren* (*The Dane*), which appeared on March 22, he urged "all Danish men and women in the entire kingdom to join together in a society bearing the Danish name and to set themselves the single, popular, peaceful, and innocent goal of awakening, strengthening, and enlightening in all possible ways the Danish love of the fatherland and national consciousness."[52]

Grundtvig used *Danskeren* as a vehicle for publicizing his views about the need for a constitution and what it should contain. His primary demand was that the constitution should protect both physical and intellectual freedoms, including religious freedom. During the run-up to the elections for the constitutional assembly, Grundtvig published "About the Constitution in Denmark" in the August 30, 1848 issue of *Danskeren*. In this article, Grundtvig argued that the new constitution must ensure "freedom to confess one's faith, if one has such, and one's lack of faith as well, if one does not believe."[53] Grundtvig's position on this issue was more radical than most of his peers, but his extensive influence in Danish society gave his opinions disproportionate clout during the constitutional deliberations.

Grundtvig nearly missed being part of the constitutional assembly, however. He lost his initial bid to be elected from Copenhagen's eleventh district and was not appointed as one of the king's delegates. He was finally elected from the district of Præstø on November 6, 1848, after the initially elected delegate, the weaver Hans Hansen, was pressured to withdraw because of rumors about his character. Monrad's draft constitution had been presented to the assembly and a subcommittee established to review it prior to Grundtvig's election, so his involvement was primarily restricted to making minor corrections and suggesting adjustments, such as changing the wording of the requirement in paragraph six that the king must be a member of the evangelical Lutheran church to specify membership in *Folkekirken* instead. When the assembly discussed the provisions of the constitution that dealt with *Folkekirken* and religious freedom, Grundtvig supported Monrad's proposals, but insisted on specifying the greatest possible degree of freedom for the individual and the strictest possible limitations on the state's power to control the free exercise of religion.[54]

While he wanted to maintain the institution of a national church, Grundtvig accepted the need to distinguish between national and religious identity and advocated separating citizenship from religious affiliation:

> The state church is not a church-state, but simply an establishment of the state that the government has the right to discontinue or alter according to its own judgment. No bishop, priest, or professor has the right to complain about it, as long as no infringement is made upon freedom of conscience, which is both the highest maxim of all religion and the irrevocable right of each upstanding citizen.[55]

Throughout the 1830s and 1840s, Grundtvig had argued for radical church reforms. He advocated for the abolition of parish bonds, such that parishioners could seek out priests whose teachings corresponded with their own doctrinal views regardless of their place of residence, as well as for the legal protection of priestly freedom of liturgy and dogma, such that priests could decline to accept into their congregation those whose beliefs did not harmonize with their own.

Although Grundtvig offered his colleagues the tongue-in-cheek assurance that his often excessive need to speak had vanished along with his teeth,[56] the records of the assembly show that Grundtvig was one of the most frequent speakers during the constitutional negotiations. On the whole, however, Grundtvig was apparently frustrated with how little influence he had in the assembly. His informal speaking style aroused the contempt of some of his fellow delegates, including the speaker of the assembly, A. F. Krieger, who protested that "the curious manner of negotiating, which the honored delegate who just spoke, has allowed himself, will not cause me to forget the respect I owe the assembly or the respect I owe Denmark's bard, Nicolaj Frederik Severin Grundtvig."[57]

This antagonism between Grundtvig and his fellow delegates limited his influence on the text of the constitution and resulted in his refusal to support it. Most of Grundtvig's proposed amendments, including his revision of paragraph six, were voted down by large majorities. Regarding the other provisions about religion, Grundtvig declared, "The less there stands [about it] in the constitution, the better!"[58] When it came to the final vote on the constitution, Grundtvig was one of only five delegates to vote against it, but he later explained in *Danskeren* that he could not have voted either against or for it with a clear conscience, given both the valuable freedoms it guaranteed and its failure to accommodate "the tastes of the Danish people."[59]

Despite his overall ambivalence about the constitution, the final shape of the Danish church established by the June Constitution—a *Folkekirke*, or people's church, administered by the state instead of an ecclesiastical council or the like—met Grundtvig's expectations as "a completely secular and legal concept, that encompassed every faith— Christian, Jewish, Turkish, or pagan."[60] In theory, all Danes were now equal before the law, regardless of their religious beliefs. As Grundtvig explained to his critics,

> I have fought openly so that all *Danish people* who so desire can retain the church's *baptism, confirmation,* and *marriage ordinance* in their old Christian form, but also so that all Danish people who so desire can be *free* of infant baptism, confirmation, or church marriages, even though this may assign me to the ranks of the "ungodly" or the "religious freelancers" who have no sense of "community life" (emphasis in original).[61]

However, Grundtvig did have some concerns about the possible weakening of the Danish Lutheran Church as a result of these new freedoms. He was concerned that people whose faith was weak would have difficulty making good choices about which church to join if they lost the predictability of the state church. A law passed in 1868 allowed members of the state church to choose their own pastors and form their own congregations, leading Grundtvig to warn against the formation of "free churches" outside the confines of the national church, as such divisions had historically led to "the same subtle but inevitable degeneration that destroyed the apostolic congregations."[62] Grundtvig also worried that people who chose to leave the church would feel they had an exclusive claim on Christianity, foreshadowing one of the issues that would arouse

FIGURE 1.3 *The Constitutional Assembly* (1861–64), painting by Constantin Hansen. This monumental painting of the assembly charged with transforming Denmark from an absolute monarchy to a parliamentary democracy was not painted from life, but rather from a series of individual portraits of the delegates. The final painting, depicted here, includes D. G. Monrad, who was not actually a delegate. Reproduced courtesy of the Museum of National History in Frederiksborg Castle, Hillerød.

antagonism toward Danish Mormons less than a year after the constitution was adopted.

Establishing Religious Freedom in the Constitution

The Danish constitutional assembly convened on October 23, 1848, with a mandate to produce Denmark's first democratic constitution. Their final document, after more than six months of debate and revision, was ratified on June 5, 1849, and may seem by today's standards quite conservative in many respects—for example, it gave the king the right to choose his own ministers without parliamentary approval. Yet the June Constitution's very existence and basic structure laid the groundwork for modern Danish government by abolishing absolutism and establishing a constitutional monarchy with a bicameral legislature. It also greatly expanded male (though not universal) suffrage, established a separation of powers within government, and enshrined a wide range of civil rights for common Danes, including freedom of speech, freedom of the press, and limited freedom of religion. In proposing these rights, Monrad drew heavily on the U.S. Constitution, in particular the Bill of Rights, for inspiration. The guarantee of religious freedom for all Danes was one of Monrad's signature achievements, accomplished over the objections of many prominent Danish clergymen, in particular Bishop Mynster, but with the support of many Danish liberals, including Grundtvig.

Paragraph eighty-one of the June Constitution[63] decrees that "citizens shall have the right to gather together in communities to worship God in the manner consistent with their convictions, as long as nothing is done that contravenes civic order and common morality." Although the assembly decided to omit the first few words of Monrad's proposal, which declared explicitly that "religious freedom is hereby granted," the inclusion of de facto religious freedom represented a significant step beyond the almost complete lack of religious liberty in Denmark up to that point. Yet paragraph eighty-one was much more than an official acknowledgment of the validity of the rationalist philosophical principle that religion is an inherently personal matter, between man and God—it was also the opening salvo in a battle over Danish cultural identity that has raged ever since.

Rather than establishing a level playing field for all religions, the June Constitution simply legalized the existence and activities of other religious communities in Denmark while preserving the dominant position of *Folkekirken*, which, in a certain sense, was created by the constitution. Prior to 1849, the Danish Lutheran Church did not exist as an independent entity. It was simply part of the bureaucratic apparatus of the absolutist state, the institutional manifestation of "the king's religion." Paragraph four of the June Constitution refers to *den danske Folkekirke* (the Danish People's Church), a name proposed by Peter Christian Kierkegaard, and gives it a privileged position as the official church of Denmark with funding from the state. The description of the relationship between church and state was, however, left deliberately ambiguous. The relevant passage simply declares: "The evangelical Lutheran church is the Danish

People's Church and as such is supported by the state." Although the commentary attached to the original legislation explains that this sentence is to be read descriptively—that is, that the evangelical Lutheran Church is supported by the state because it is the church to which the Danish people belong—many leading figures at the time advocated for interpreting it prescriptively—in other words, if an individual is a part of the Danish people, then he/she should belong to this church, which is supported by the state.[64]

Unsurprisingly, most leaders of the Danish People's Church were proponents of the latter interpretation, which equates Danish identity with Danish Lutheranism. Bishop H. L. Martensen, who became primate of the Danish People's Church in 1854, noted in his memoirs that it was "certainly of great significance that Church and State should continue to be united, and that there should continue to be a State Church, even if it was called a People's Church."[65] Martensen's support for this view, though firm, was surpassed by the enthusiasm of his predecessor, Bishop J. P. Mynster, who objected to the term "state church" and embraced the term *den danske Folkekirke* as a symbol of the voluntary and essentialist nature of the Danish community it described. In a sermon in 1852, Mynster declared:

> The Church's enemies have tried to make use of it [the term "state church"] to serve their purposes, namely to imply that it was the worldly authorities who used compulsion to maintain among the people a confession to which they would otherwise be indifferent, or which they would abandon. Therefore, let us hold fast to the beautiful, living term "People's Church"; it signifies that this is the Church to which the people cling, the Church whose confession is rooted in the people, the Church which is one of the strong bonds which holds the people together, and which connects the generations that follow with those that have gone before. Praise and thank God that we still have such a People's Church that binds together the vast preponderance of the people, so that those who deviate from it can be quickly added up. There are indeed people living among us who confess another faith . . . but everyone feels that they are in many respects guests and foreigners and that in essential ways they are not a part of our people.[66]

Thus, although no longer an indistinguishable part of the state, *Folkekirken* still occupied a position of protected privilege within the Danish state and psyche—as Mynster noted, confessing another faith was tantamount to excluding oneself from the national community. H. N. Clausen also supported this view of an essential, almost biological connection between Danish Lutheranism and Danish national identity, explaining that "it is virtually the pronouncement of an historical fact, namely that a certain church, a certain type of confession, stands in a certain peculiar relationship to the people who inhabit and work in the land, that the great majority of people feel drawn to it."[67] The Danish People's Church was thus, at least in Clausen's opinion, a specifically Danish phenomenon.

The June Constitution reinforces this association between church and state in several ways. The June Constitution does not establish any self-governance for the church, but merely states in paragraph eighty that "the administration of the People's Church will be ordered by law." Although many church leaders at the time, including Monrad, expected that a law providing a synodal constitution for the church would eventually be passed (in consultation with the Danish clergy), others, notably Grundtvig, were concerned that such a law would give the state too much control over the church. The failure of both the Danish Parliament and the various parties within *Folkekirken* to reach a consensus about how the church should be governed meant the phrase "ordered by law" has come to imply "ordered by laws," namely the individual pieces of legislation regarding the Danish People's Church that have been passed by the Danish Parliament since 1849. The Danish monarch is still the nominal head of the church and the government maintains a minister for church affairs. After much debate, the constitutional assembly did agree that the constitution should mandate that the Danish monarch must be a Lutheran. Although it technically does not specify to which Lutheran church he or she must belong, every Danish monarch since 1849 has been affiliated with *Folkekirken*. This expectation prompted Australian Mary Donaldson to convert from Presbyterianism to Lutheranism when she married Crown Prince Frederik in 2004. The assembly's decision to use the constitution to maintain a close connection between church and state ensured that religious freedom in Denmark would not establish equality among religious groups, but would simply create an official atmosphere

of benign tolerance for religions whose views diverged from the dominant religion. Yet even this relatively modest concession was the product
of intense debate and the cause of considerable social unrest.

Declaring religious freedom on paper and implementing religious
freedom in practice turned out to be very different endeavors. The process of determining the extent and implications of religious freedom
relative to other freedoms in Denmark continues to this day, as the 2005
public relations crisis over the publication of several cartoons depicting the Muslim prophet Mohammad vividly illustrated. The immediate
consequences of the establishment of religious freedom in Denmark
included determining precisely what Danes were now free to do or not
to do regarding religious matters. A person could choose to convert to
a faith other than evangelical Lutheranism, for example, but he or she
was not permitted to simply disavow religion altogether. Habits and attitudes shaped by centuries of state control of religious practice could not
be changed overnight, nor did everyone approve of the radical societal
changes that followed in the wake of the constitution.

The legal dissolution of the fusion of religious and national identity
meant that being Danish no longer automatically or exclusively meant
being Lutheran. This was in itself disruptive, as was the fact that Danes
were no longer required to accept long-established social hierarchies
reinforced by the state church. Many of the most disadvantaged members of Danish society, who had also been the strongest supporters of the
"godly awakenings" and the Baptist movement, were quick to recognize
the emancipatory potential of religious freedom and threw in their lot
with new religious movements, including the Church of Jesus Christ of
Latter-day Saints.

In light of the controversy surrounding the question of same-sex marriage in the United States in the early twenty-first century, it is interesting
to note that one of the unexpected consequence of religious freedom in
nineteenth-century Denmark, was the need to resolve the question of
how and where marriages should be performed, particularly for people
who did not belong to *Folkekirken* or another state-recognized religion.
In November 1850, N. M. Spandet proposed a law designed to institu-
tionalize "as complete a freedom of belief as reason and Christianity
demand and as the Constitution allows" by permitting civil marriage for
all citizens, granting parents the right to decide their children's religious

affiliation, and allowing individuals to disassociate themselves from organized religion.[68] Spandet's proposal was supported by Grundtvig, but opposed by a majority of parliament, who felt such freedoms went too far toward eroding the Christian basis of the Danish state. Clausen functioned as the spokesman for the opposition, warning against the "weakening, possibly even the gradual dissolution of every religion," *Folkekirken* in particular, that must inevitably result from Spandet's law.[69]

Following Clausen's lead, the Danish Parliament passed a much narrower law in April 1851 that granted the right of civil marriage only to members of nonrecognized religious communities—such as Baptists, whose priests did not have the legal authority to perform marriages— or in cases of mixed couples in which one of the parties belonged to a nonrecognized religion. However, members of *Folkekirken* and other state-recognized religions, such as Catholics or Jews, were not granted the right of civil marriage until 1923.[70] Incidentally, the first civil marriage performed in Denmark took place on July 14, 1851, in Copenhagen between the journeyman tailor Christen Christensen and Christine Marie Bruun, both of whom had recently joined the Mormon Church.[71]

The Initial Reception of Mormonism in Denmark

In stark contrast to the religious homogeneity that had defined Danishness for so long, the introduction of religious freedom in Denmark in 1849 opened the door to more heterogeneous interpretations of Danish cultural identity. The early reception of Mormonism in Denmark illustrates that neither the Danish elites who had promulgated the constitution nor the general public were prepared to deal with this new cultural diversity. This period is characterized by the initial rejection of Mormon doctrine and the cultural upheaval it caused. This rejection took the form of both violent opposition and isolated but sincere attempts at practicing tolerance, despite differences in religious belief.

The first missionaries of the Church of Jesus Christ of Latter-day Saints arrived in Denmark from America in the spring of 1850, eager to win converts, as their fellows had already done—with impressive success—in the United Kingdom, Canada, and Germany, among other places. Having finally established a safe haven for itself in the Utah Territory, the LDS Church embarked on an ambitious plan to expand Mormon evangelization across the globe in order to both spread the gospel of

Jesus Christ and attract settlers to build God's kingdom on earth. Sending missionaries to Denmark in 1850 was one element of this larger program, and it paved the way for missionary endeavors throughout Scandinavia. Mormon missionary work in Norway, conducted primarily by Danish converts, commenced in September 1851, after a Norwegian ship captain was baptized in Aalborg;[72] in Iceland in December 1851, when two Icelanders who had converted to Mormonism in Denmark returned home;[73] and in Sweden in April 1852, if one discounts a brief visit by John Erik Forsgren in July 1850 that was quickly terminated by Swedish authorities.[74] By 1853, LDS missionaries were active in nineteen countries on six continents, from Sweden to South Africa.

While the activity of Mormon missionaries in Denmark was thus comparable in timing and scope to LDS missionary work in other countries, the missionaries' impressive early success among Danes, particularly in comparison to the much slower growth of the church in neighboring Norway and Sweden, makes the Danish situation quite distinctive. This success is closely linked to the June Constitution and the civil rights it guaranteed, as well as the opportunities for cultural identity negotiation that it created. Although early Mormon missionaries encountered suspicion, hostility, harassment, and often outright violence from civic leaders, ecclesiastical authorities, and the general public, they and the people they baptized did in fact benefit from the protection of the Danish authorities to a significant degree. The missionaries had a legal right to remain in the country and, despite the intervention of the occasional overzealous local official, to proselytize and worship freely. Unlike in Norway, where the Supreme Court ruled that Mormons did not fall under the Dissenter Law of 1845, which granted religious freedom to all Christian denominations,[75] LDS missionaries in Denmark were not regularly arrested, fined, or thrown in jail, with one exception—a period in the 1880s and 1890s when some local officials took it upon themselves to banish and/or deport individual LDS missionaries in response to tacit U.S. governmental pressure to contain the "Mormon threat" by restricting the influx of Mormon convert-immigrants.

Another important factor in the introduction of Mormonism to Denmark was the missionaries themselves, who were handpicked for their individual connections to Scandinavia. Led by Erastus Snow, one of the twelve LDS apostles tasked with directing missionary efforts of the church and an experienced missionary who had spent many years proselytizing throughout the United States, the group consisted of Peter Olsen Hansen (1818–1894), a native of Denmark who had joined the church in Boston; George Parker Dykes (1804–1888), who had served as a missionary among the Norwegian settlers in Fox River, Illinois, in the early 1840s; and John Erik Forsgren (1816–1890), a native Swede who was initially sent to his homeland, where he performed the first Mormon baptism—of his brother—in Scandinavia on July 26, 1850, but subsequently joined his fellows in Copenhagen when he was evicted from Sweden. Snow and Dykes were, relatively speaking, long-standing members of the LDS Church, having joined in the 1830s, but Forsgren and Hansen, the only native Scandinavians in the group, were more recent converts. A sailor by profession, Forsgren had embraced Mormonism in Boston in the early 1840s and moved westward with the church, first to the Mormon city of Nauvoo, Illinois, and then, in 1846–47, across the continent to what would become the territory of Utah.

Like Forsgren, Peter Olsen Hansen had also joined the Mormon Church in Boston, but the story of his conversion is somewhat more complex. Hansen was raised Lutheran in Copenhagen, but came to Boston in November 1843 for the express purpose of learning more about the LDS Church, which he had read about in a Danish newspaper account by a Fox River Norwegian convert.[76] Additionally, Hansen's older brother Hans Christian Hansen (1806–1890), formerly a Baptist, had joined the Mormon Church in June 1842. Hans Christian, like his father and grandfathers before him, was a sailor, but he left Denmark to work for an American shipping company based out of Boston. A fellow Dane, Peter Clemensen, who had recently become the first Danish member of the LDS Church,[77] introduced him to the Mormon missionaries there. In a letter to his younger brother in the spring of 1843, Hans Christian announced that he "had become a member of the true church of God, which now had been restored by the power of God."[78] Convinced that he had been called by God to follow his brother's example, Peter stayed in Copenhagen just long enough to earn the money for his passage. Having turned twenty-five and attained his majority, he sailed for Boston, where he worked for the winter until his brother returned from meeting LDS Church founder Joseph Smith in Nauvoo, Illinois. Not quite two years after his own baptism, Hans Christian baptized his brother Peter on

FIGURE 1.4   Peter Olsen Hansen (1874), photograph by C. A. Zehngraf, Aalborg.
The third Dane to join the Church of Jesus Christ of Latter-day Saints, Peter
Olsen Hansen translated the Book of Mormon into Danish and served two missions back in Denmark after immigrating to the United States. Reproduced courtesy of the LDS Church History Library, Salt Lake City, Utah.

March 7, 1844, before returning to Nauvoo to work on the construction
of the Mormon temple.[79]

Peter Hansen was not just an enthusiastic convert—he was also passionate about introducing Mormonism to his countrymen. From the
moment he heard about the Book of Mormon from his brother, Hansen
was eager to make it available to his countrymen by translating it into
Danish. Immediately after his baptism, he bought a copy of the book
for one dollar (half price) from a former Mormon and began translating
it on his own initiative, doing "a little every evening by the light of a
lamp" while still in Boston.[80] Near the end of 1844, approximately six

months after the death of Joseph Smith at the hands of a mob, Hansen joined his brother in Nauvoo, where Brigham Young, who would succeed Smith as president of the church in 1847, encouraged him to continue his translation. Given the very small population of Danes in America at the time and the fact that written Danish and Norwegian were essentially identical in the mid-nineteenth century, Hansen's translation may have been intended for use among Norwegian immigrants in the Fox River settlement in Illinois as well as elsewhere in the United States. However, President Young's support of Hansen's efforts to translate the Book of Mormon into Danish suggests that church leaders may have considered the possibility of sending LDS missionaries to Denmark several years before the country's establishment of religious freedom. Young even counseled Hansen against getting married in the fall of 1846, as he "was going to send me to Denmark and would be gone many years and I had better get me a wife there," as Hansen later recounted.[81]

Hansen's involvement in the Mormon exodus from Nauvoo and journey westward to Utah in 1846–47 interrupted his translation work; he was not able to resume it until he returned to Copenhagen as a missionary in the spring of 1850. Before leaving Nauvoo, Hansen and his brother were adopted by Apostle Heber C. Kimball, in whose company they traveled to Winter Quarters, Iowa, and then on to the Salt Lake valley in the summer of 1847.[82] After spending that winter in Utah, Hansen worked for nearly two years assisting other Mormon wagon trains crossing the plains to Utah before confiding in Kimball, now a counselor to President Young, his conviction that he needed to return to Denmark to preach the gospel. When Kimball conveyed this to President Young, the prophet reportedly replied that "the time has come for preaching of the Gospel to be extended to other nations as well."[83] Accordingly, Hansen, Snow, and Forsgren were called to serve as missionaries to Scandinavia at a general conference of the church in Salt Lake City on October 7, 1849; Dykes, who was already serving a mission in the United Kingdom, met them in England the following spring.

Due to the primitive means of transportation available at the time (the transcontinental railroad wouldn't reach Utah until 1869), the missionaries' journey from Salt Lake City to Copenhagen took more than six months. Departing on October 19, 1849, by wagon caravan, they retraced the steps of the Mormon pioneers who had settled the valley only two years previously, stopping at Ft. Kearney, Nebraska, and St. Louis, Missouri, before embarking for Europe from Boston. They reached England in April 1850 and met up with Dykes. Hansen arrived in Denmark on May 11, 1850, followed by Snow, Dykes, and Forsgren on June 14. They rented a room from Lauritz B. Malling at Bredgade 196 in Copenhagen and commenced their proselytizing efforts. Hansen's father had objected to his son's departure in 1843 so Peter's reception by his relatives in Denmark was not warm. Moreover, he was apparently not a particularly gifted orator and had, according to Snow, forgotten much of his native language.[84] Hansen's fellow missionaries could not yet speak any Danish, although Forsgren and Dykes could speak Swedish and Norwegian, respectively. Despite these handicaps, however, the missionaries found eager listeners in Copenhagen and made dozens of converts, including their landlord and his family, in a very short time.[85]

One key to the missionaries' success was their effective use of print media, which capitalized on high literacy rates and voracious newspaper reading among Danes. Immediately upon arriving in Denmark, Hansen wrote and published three hundred copies of a pamphlet titled *En Advarsel til Folket* (*A Warning to the People*) to distribute in Copenhagen. Upon his arrival a month later, Snow composed a tract called *A Voice of Truth* that Hansen translated for him. The missionaries printed two thousand copies of this tract under the title *En Sandheds Røst*. Hansen also resumed translating the Book of Mormon in June 1850, with editorial assistance from Snow and two Danish assistants, but the process still required seven additional months of intense translation, revision, and proofreading before it could be printed. When it was published by F. E. Bordings Bogtrykkeri in Copenhagen in May 1851, *Mormons Bog* became the first foreign language edition of the Book of Mormon. Snow had to borrow money from missionaries in England to finance the publication, which cost 1,000 rigsdaler (approximately $500 at the time), but the fact that he chose to have one thousand copies of the first edition printed indicates his optimism about its effectiveness as a missionary tool.[86] In October 1851, the missionaries founded a monthly periodical, *Skandinaviens Stjerne* (*Scandinavia's Star*), consisting of sixteen medium octavo pages per issue, to communicate directly with members of the LDS Church in Denmark as well as with interested outsiders. Newspapers had become highly influential in Danish society in the politically turbulent 1830s and 40s and proliferated after the abolition of police control of the media in 1849, reaching a large percentage of the Danish population, particularly in Copenhagen.

Perhaps the single most important factor in the missionaries' initially warm reception in Denmark, however, was the receptiveness of Danish Baptists to the Mormon gospel, which shared some key doctrinal similarities with Baptist theology, including the practice of adult baptism by immersion. The majority of the earliest Danish converts to Mormonism came from Peter Mønster's Baptist congregation in Copenhagen, the Baptist congregation in Aalborg, and other groups of "awakened" Pietists. Two Baptist sailors befriended Hansen on the day he arrived in Copenhagen[87] and Pastor Mønster himself initially welcomed the LDS missionaries as allies in his cause. They attended his meetings regularly, without mentioning Mormonism, and befriended individual members of the congregation.[88] Mønster met with the missionaries on June 17, 1850, and Snow recorded an account of the meeting in his diary:

> Mr. Mønster's visit on Monday was very interesting. He related a short history of his life during the last eight years. He was about fifty years old; his countenance and bearing bespoke intelligence, meekness, and sincerity, and he was the first man in recent years to preach baptism by immersion in Denmark. His persecutions had been similar to those of the Saints in America. He had often been brought before rulers and judges, had been fined, and six times imprisoned—three years in all—and yet he had continued to teach his faith, and some three hundred and fifty had been baptized into the Baptist Church. Had he been a foreigner, he would have been expelled from the country, but being a native, they could only fine and imprison him. Yet the more he was persecuted, the more friends he gathered to his standard, until now, by the late political revolution, his persecutors (the State priests) are restricted in their power, and he now enjoys comparative peace and quietness.[89]

Despite the Baptists' and Mormons' shared belief in adult baptism and mutual experience of persecution, however, Mønster felt betrayed when more than 150 members of his congregation eventually chose to join the

Mormon Church. Disillusioned and alienated from the rest of the Danish Baptist community, Mønster later rejoined *Folkekirken*.

The first Mormon baptisms in Denmark were performed on the evening of August 12, 1850, in the Øresund sea just outside of Copenhagen, across from the lime kilns near Langelinie. The first Dane to be baptized a Mormon in Denmark was one of the two sailors who had befriended P. O. Hansen, a man named Ole Ulrich Christian Mønster (no relation to the Baptist minister Peter C. Mønster). He was followed by his wife, Marie Christine, and thirteen other members of Mønster's Baptist congregation, predominantly married couples. Four days later, another eleven converts were baptized, including Knud H. Bruun, the first member of *Folkekirken* to join the Mormon Church. On August 17, 1850, Snow reported in a letter to church headquarters in Utah that he and his fellow missionaries had baptized twenty-six Germans, Swedes, and Danes.[90] By early September, Snow organized the first Mormon congregation in Copenhagen, with around fifty members.[91] These humble beginnings soon led to larger numbers of converts, and by the middle of 1851 Snow reported that Danish membership in the LDS Church numbered approximately 260 people.[92] Between 1850 and 1904, 23,443 Danes became members of the Church of Jesus Christ of Latter-day Saints, more than half of them prior to 1870.[93]

Due in part to tensions between Snow and Dykes, the missionaries expanded their operations to Jutland in early October 1850. Dykes established himself in Aalborg and converted many within the sizeable Baptist community there. Less than three weeks after arriving in Aalborg, Dykes baptized eight people, including Hans Peter Jensen, a foundry owner with more than one hundred employees, his wife Sarah Josephine Katrine Jensen, and three other couples.[94] After seven weeks, on November 25, 1850, Dykes was able to organize a congregation with twenty-three members in Aalborg; by January 1851, membership had increased to sixty people. Dykes, Jensen, and other new converts also begin preaching in nearby towns, such as Hals. Northern Jutland remained a stronghold of Mormonism for several decades and facilitated the introduction of Mormonism into Norway, after a ship's captain named Svend Larsen encountered the Mormon missionaries in Hans Peter Jensen's home, accepted their teachings, and was baptized on September 23, 1851.[95]

Early Opposition to Danish Mormonism

Although the Danish state was bound by the 1849 constitution to permit the free exercise of religion as long as no laws were broken and common morality was not violated, the process of incorporating toleration of religious difference into Danish public discourse took many years. In the early 1850s, the Danish Parliament had not yet enacted specific laws supporting the exercise of religious freedom. In the meantime, many local government officials and police officers continued to enforce outdated laws that prohibited proselytizing by religious groups or barred them from participating in public life. When Snow presented a statement describing Mormon theology to the minister of culture on September 15, 1850, in order to officially organize the Church of Jesus Christ of Latter-day Saints in Denmark, his application was approved, albeit with the caveat that church members and missionaries might encounter obstruction from local police.[96] The following year, when Snow petitioned King Frederik VII for protection for Danish Mormons, he received the answer that while the king "was not prepared to grant Mormons special privileges," he was "nevertheless resolved not to throw obstacles" in their way.[97] In 1853, when the Danish Parliament—under pressure from the Lutheran clergy—discussed a bill that would ban Mormonism and expel the Mormon missionaries, the bill's backers could not get enough support to pass it.

Perhaps not surprisingly, the rapid spread of Mormonism in its first few years and the perceived threat it posed to the status quo aroused public antagonism, which manifested itself immediately after the first Mormon converts were baptized. Opposition was particularly fierce in the conservative Aalborg region, where, in December 1850, a group of citizens submitted a petition to parliament in favor of suspending religious freedom pending a popular referendum, on the grounds that the Mormon congregation in Aalborg was growing too quickly.[98] In February 1851, the mayor of Aalborg sent a letter to Elder Dykes asking him to change the time of the Mormon Sunday meetings so as not to conflict with *Folkekirken*'s worship services.[99] The mayor's letter implicitly acknowledges the competition between the LDS Church and *Folkekirken* for attendees, particularly those belonging to the middle classes.

The case of Hans Peter Jensen, the first person to be baptized in Aalborg, illustrates the stakes of this competition. Not only had Jensen been an active Baptist leader for more than a decade, who immediately upon his conversion began to try to persuade his former co-religionists of the error of their ways, he was also a prosperous and prominent member of the community, whose enthusiastic acceptance of Mormonism belied the widespread belief that only impoverished, uneducated peasants would be attracted to this outlandish foreign religion. According to Dykes' diary, "Community leaders, thinking it incredible that a man of Jensen's stature would join the Mormons, circulated rumors that Mormons planned to undermine the Danish nation itself and bring on a state of war and confusion. A pillar of society had been 'swallowed up' by Mormon propaganda, and forces of reaction rushed in to repair the hole in the dike."[100] Despite the fact that the Baptist movement had, as little as a decade earlier, been regarded as a serious enough threat to the moral fabric of Danish society to warrant the forcible baptism of Baptist children into the Lutheran Church, the rapid conversion of large numbers of Baptists to Mormonism was interpreted as an attack on "the Danish nation itself."

The missionaries' message—which emphasized the imminent second coming of Jesus Christ, outlined the torments that awaited the ungodly, and described Lutheran theology (in particular infant baptism) as erroneous and apostate, even as "the work of the devil"—offended many of their listeners, nearly all of whom were members of the Danish Lutheran Church.[101] Dykes was particularly fanatical in his style of preaching, which was compounded by his long hair, flowing beard, and emaciated appearance.[102] Bishop Fogtman in Aalborg complained to the Ministry of Justice in 1851 that "the so-called Mormons here in town are made up for the most part of the dregs of the population, and yet they disdain and mock their fellow citizens, whom they call heathens, and call themselves the true Christians."[103] As new converts, particularly those from the lowest socioeconomic class, adopted this rhetoric and exhibited an attitude of chosenness, they further provoked the antagonism of their neighbors as well as the Lutheran pastors charged with the spiritual well-being of the Danish people.

Just as the missionaries used print media to announce their meetings and articulate their doctrinal positions, most of the formal attempts by Danish clergy to combat the spread of Mormonism in Denmark were disseminated the same way. Knowledge of the Mormon movement preceded the missionaries by means of newspaper coverage of events in the

United States and England. Anti-Mormon newspaper articles from the United States provided material for the earliest Danish critiques of Mormonism, well before the movement had had any noticeable effect on Danish society. Shortly after the arrival of Hansen, Snow, and Forsgren in May 1850, Bishop Mynster published a short book, titled *Grundlovens Bestemmelser med Hensyn til Religiøse Forhold i Danmark* (*The Provisions of the Constitution with Regard to Religious Conditions in Denmark*).[104] In this text, he cites the Mormons as exemplary of the dangers inherent in unrestricted religious freedom, although he acknowledges that the only information he has about them came from foreign news outlets. Nevertheless, he advocates opposing Mormonism by any means necessary, including violence. Mynster's treatise set the trend for clerical opposition to Mormonism in Denmark, particularly among those who had opposed the constitutional establishment of religious freedom in the first place. Danish historian Jesper Stenholm Paulsen explains that Mynster had suffered a tremendous loss of prestige, influence, and political capital during the constitutional convention. He was widely regarded as representative of the old, undemocratic system,[105] which lends a note of desperation to his rearguard attempts to maintain a status quo that had already been abolished.

Following Mynster's example and the recommendation from the Ministry of Religion that pastors should inform their parishioners about the dangers of Mormonism,[106] Danish clergymen were particularly energetic in their efforts to discredit the Mormon missionaries. According to American historian William Mulder, "the priests could see dwindling tithes, emptier pews, a breakup of a snug and time-honored village order in which their estate had been secure. It was an economic threat, and, for those genuinely interested in the cure of souls, a still more serious spiritual one."[107] Several prominent Lutheran ministers and theologians, including Carl Fog and H. C. Rørdam, published more than three dozen articles denouncing the Mormons as false prophets and swindlers between 1850 and 1853,[108] many of them direct translations of anti-Mormon articles previously published in American newspapers.

L. D. Hass's article "The Teachings, Origins, and Progress of the Mormons," which was published in 1851 both as a newspaper article and later as a pamphlet, exemplifies the tone of these articles, which underscored the foreignness of Mormonism. Hass cautions, "People who come from far away have no trouble lying. It has therefore in all times been an easy thing for those who come with news and innovations from both far and near to make the simple people sitting at home believe all manner of lies. . . . Let us now discuss . . . ONE OF OUR CENTURY'S GREATEST AND IN ITS OWN ORIGINS SELF-DECEIVING LIES, NAMELY MORMONISM" (emphasis in original).[109] In light of the Mormons' demonstrable success at winning converts, a smattering of newspaper articles, however vituperative, might seem like a tame response, but it was only the beginning of a period of intense anti-Mormon persecution that turned violent on several occasions in the early 1850s. It is important to note that although the Mormon practice of polygamy featured prominently in many later popular cultural depictions of Mormonism, the fiercest anti-Mormon activity in Denmark took place before the doctrine of polygamy was publicly acknowledged in Scandinavia by mission president John van Cott in 1853 (which accordingly will not be discussed until chapter 3, together with the relevant texts denouncing it).

The failure of the written word to dissuade their parishioners from attending Mormon meetings and adopting this new faith prompted some, though certainly not all, Danish ministers to advocate more severe modes of opposition. They instructed their parishioners not to feed or house the missionaries, cut off financial assistance to people who embraced Mormonism, advised farmers to blacklist any farmhands who converted, and offered preferential treatment to converts who changed their minds.[110] Although the clergy rarely initiated or directly organized physical attacks on Mormon congregations, their vocal opposition, along with the passivity of government and police authorities, effectively encouraged the violent disturbances. In particular, the practice of reading from the pulpit the names of people "lost to Mormonism . . . [seemed] to the Mormons a fiendish device for identifying converts and setting neighbor against neighbor, a call to ostracize, to boycott, and to persecute."[111]

Disruption of Mormon worship services was common in the 1850s, with sporadic incidents of mob violence, destruction of property, and attacks on both missionaries and converts, particularly in larger cities such as Aalborg, Roskilde, and Odense. Snow wrote in his journal that Lutheran ministers in Copenhagen began to hold evening meetings coinciding with the Mormon gatherings, but that,

When this [measure] did not have the desired effect, they then attempted to inflame the students to lead the craft apprentices and journeymen to disrupt and disperse our meetings. . . . We tolerated their interruptions, audacity, and mocking in our hall on several evenings, and strove to dissuade them with patience and persuasion. We besought protection from the magistrate and chief of police, but the police administration turned a blind eye to the mobs, . . . and while they made us promises that they never fulfilled, they apparently provided the mob with secret support in their lawlessness.[112]

The mob violence Snow describes began in the fall of 1850, when Mormon meetings in Aalborg and Odense were disrupted by angry crowds who destroyed the Mormons' apartments and meetinghouses and attacked Mormon converts. It is worth noting, however, that many accounts of violence against Mormons during this period also mention attempts by other Danish citizens to prevent or at least protest the attacks against their neighbors. For example, on January 24, 1851, after openly condemning the Lutheran clergy, Dykes found himself surrounded by a crowd of drunken fishermen intent on delivering a beating, only to be protected by a group of women "who formed a human ring around him" until he could be smuggled out of the city by his defenders.[113]

Mobs repeatedly interrupted Mormon meetings in Roskilde in early 1851 as well, though their intent was apparently more mischievous than malicious and some of the local population disapproved of their actions. The missionaries generally advertised their worship services in the newspaper, making it easy for unruly crowds to attend and drown out the speakers with laughter, swearing, insults, rowdy songs, knocking over furniture, and the "explicit expression of their desire to demonstrate loyalty to 'the inherited faith of our fathers'—in a violent way," as a local newspaper phrased it.[114] These disturbances prompted the missionaries to make their escape, but the article also notes that they were escorted safely home by concerned local citizens. The mob dispersed but reformed in time for the advertised evening meeting. When that did not take place, the mob gathered around the missionaries' apartment, despite their landlord's protestation that they were not at home. Shouting "out with the

Baptists, out with the prophets," they threatened to search the house before contenting themselves with pranks such as breaking windows, ringing doorbells, and singing loudly until the night watchman managed to get them to leave at around ten o'clock. One of the missionaries was caught by the mob, but a few cooler-headed citizens extracted him from the crowd with promises to have him arrested, whereupon they brought him to safety at the town hall. On January 25, 1851, an anonymous citizen published a note in the local paper criticizing the town's police force for failing to intervene against the mobs.[115]

Violent anti-Mormon agitation peaked in Aalborg in June 1851, when the local congregation of Mormons was harassed by mobs for more than a week. As Mormon convert Hans F. Petersen's diary records, an attempt to perform adult baptisms at a public beach in the Limfjord on June 22, 1851, was disrupted by a crowd of several hundred people who shouted obscenities and physically abused the Mormons present.[116] When Hans Peter Jensen warned the assembled crowd to "flee from the church of the devil," the crowd attacked the meeting hall, where, as Dykes recorded in his diary, they "broke up all the benches and destroyed all of the furniture in the house, . . . shamefully abused the brethren, casting them down and treading on their necks."[117] Some townspeople intervened and called the mayor, who initially dismissed the danger but was finally persuaded to call out the city watch. However, the violence, particularly against the windows, continued "about every night after for a week to a limited extent."[118] The situation was not defused until Jensen and Dykes, the most prominent Mormon leaders in Aalborg, left town.[119] Similar episodes took place in Hals, on the island of Bornholm, and in Brøndbyøster, where twelve Mormons were stoned and beaten with sticks by a large mob.[120]

News of the rioting even made the Copenhagen newspapers. This kind of widespread public rioting was as unusual in Denmark then as it would be today and aroused public criticism. Despite general antipathy toward the Mormons, the majority of the blame was directed toward police chief John Johnsen, who lived close to the Mormons' buildings and yet did nothing to stop the disturbances. One newspaper article denounced "the crowds, disorder, and violent acts for which our town has been the stage for several evenings and which have disrupted moral and civil order to an extent we have rarely, God be praised, seen the like of in this country."[121]

It is important to remember, however, that these disturbances did not arise in a vacuum. As in neighboring Norway, where Mormonism came to be associated with the political radicalism of labor activist Marcus Thrane, anti-Mormon protests in Denmark were closely related to both the social unrest that had begun to manifest itself among poverty-stricken urban craftsmen in the 1840s and the unsettling effect of the new democratic constitution, with its array of civil rights inconceivable under the earlier absolutist regime. The majority of those involved in the mob violence against the Mormons were craftsmen and day laborers, groups that had benefited the least from land reforms of the late eighteenth and early nineteenth centuries that gave rise to a middle class of landowning farmers. The arrival of the Mormons in Denmark thus coincided with a period of significant social and cultural upheaval, which the Mormons' unfamiliar doctrines and energetic, judgmental proselytizing exacerbated.

The widespread, vocal, and often violent opposition to Mormonism in Denmark reflects the Danes' apparent distress over the fact that their neighbors who joined the Mormons seemed to be choosing to reject not only Danish Lutheranism, but also Danish social order and—once the Mormon emigration from Denmark began—even Denmark itself. Violence against the Mormons gradually abated over the course of the 1850s, but the Mormon movement was still perceived as a destabilizing force within Danish society for two main reasons. First, the Mormons drew the majority of their converts, though by no means all, from the poorest classes of Danish society, who found in the LDS Church not only an empowering theology but also the hope of improving their social situation. Their subsequent refusal to accept their formerly subordinate social position disrupted well-established class hierarchies.[122] Second, conversion to Mormonism almost always entailed immigration to the United States, accounting for around seventeen thousand Danish Mormon emigrants between 1852 and 1900. Nearly 80 percent of all Danes who converted to Mormonism before 1890 immigrated to America. During the 1850s and 1860s, Danish Mormon converts made up nearly half of the total emigration from Denmark.[123]

Folkekirken's clergymen were acutely aware of the long-term threat these twin trends posed, and they kept close tabs on the growth of the Mormon movement. In 1854, the newly appointed bishop of Zealand, Hans Lassen Martensen, solicited reports from ministers across the island about the status of the "Mormon problem" in their parishes. Christian Abraham Mølmark, pastor of Sørbymagle and Kirkerup parishes, reported matter-of-factly that very few parishioners had gone over to the Mormons since their initial successes in 1851, a development that he attributed, at least in part, to his own energetic efforts to protect his parishioners from apostasy.[124] Martensen later admitted that of all the dissenting religious groups that emerged in Denmark in the late nineteenth century, Mormonism "was the most repulsive to me."[125] However, when his survey produced no evidence that the local Mormon converts were contravening the law, Martensen simply filed away the results and undertook no further action against the LDS Church in Denmark.

Conclusion

In Denmark today, the revolution of March 1848 is not publicly commemorated, nor is the violent opposition to Mormonism in the 1850s common knowledge. Instead, Constitution Day (June 5) is a national holiday and Danes generally regard themselves as having always been a peaceful, tolerant people. Even if its consequences have become so ingrained in Danish society as to be invisible today, however, the social and cultural significance of the writing of Denmark's first constitution by forward-thinking individuals like D. G. Monrad and N. F. S Grundtvig can hardly be overstated. Claus Bjørn reminds us that "the June Constitution of June 5, 1849 was the result of struggles and compromises, born out of the contemporaneous Danish society's competing interests and conflicts—interests and conflicts that were in the process of sloughing off old concepts of class."[126] The social hierarchies and cultural conformity represented by the complete unity of church and state in Denmark prior to 1849 did not crumble immediately with the introduction of religious freedom. However, they were weakened enough by the separation of church and state that large-scale social movements like Mormonism could render the changing nature of Danish cultural identity visible. There is, of course, considerable continuity between pre- and post-1849 Denmark, but the egalitarian social welfare state of modern Denmark is rooted in the civil rights and political equality guaranteed by the June Constitution.

The transformation of a culturally and religiously homogenous, semi-feudal, absolute monarchy into a culturally diverse, participatory, parliamentary democracy did not and could not happen overnight, but the June Constitution marks the turning point when these as-yet embryonic changes were codified into law. The Danish encounter with Mormonism illustrates the stages in the process of learning to accept religious difference as a negotiable component of Danish cultural identity. It took more than half a century for the political changes wrought by the constitution to take full effect in Denmark, as the king continued to rule in tandem with prime ministers appointed from *Rigsdagen* (the upper house of the Danish Parliament), and even longer for the civil rights guaranteed by the constitution to be internalized by the Danish people. The first Danish prime minister to represent the majority party in *Folketinget* (the lower house), was not appointed until 1901, and the struggle for social equality for both working-class Danes and women continued well into the twentieth century. The social changes that began in Denmark in the late nineteenth and early twentieth century—which reflect general processes of urbanization, industrialization, secularization, and modernization—are difficult to quantify on an individual level, but the evolving reception of Mormonism in Danish society illustrates the various ways in which the Danish public came to terms with the exercise of religious freedom and their altered cultural identity.

2

A Tale of Two Kierkegaards

Responses to Mormonism by Denmark's Cultural Elites

The initial phase of Danish reactions to Mormonism falls into two distinct categories: the visceral, often violent, opposition of the crowds described in chapter 1; and a more philosophical, measured evaluation by Denmark's educated elites that is the subject of this chapter. This division reflects a pervasive tension over who decides what it means to be Danish that was present during the drafting of the June Constitution and came to dominate Danish political discourse in the 1850s and early 1860s. During that time, various nationalist parties promoted competing conceptions of Danish cultural identity—based on language, geography, history, and religion, and so on—in order to support their respective agendas for Denmark's relationship to the duchies of Schleswig and Holstein. Behind these political debates, which led to the outbreak of war with Germany in 1864 and the decimation of Denmark's self-image, lies the more existential issue of how and by whom a national cultural identity can or should be determined.

In the early nineteenth century, following the example of Johann Gottfried von Herder and the German romantics, many Danish authors and intellectuals venerated folktales and folk culture as the source of authentic cultural identity. Even while elevating the idea of the "folk," however, Denmark's cultural elites, known as the *dannelsesborgerskab* (educated bourgeoisie), exercised nearly exclusive control over Danish "high culture," from literature to theater to art. It wasn't until the second half of the nineteenth century that common people were able—as we will see in chapter 3—to play a more central role in creating and consuming Danish popular culture. This change was due in part to the increasing accessibility of technologically assisted mass culture productions, from street ballads to silent films, that made "culture" cheaper to produce and distribute.

This power dynamic privileging the upper class's interpretation of Danish culture meant that, in the first decade after the arrival of the Mormons in Denmark, textual and visual depictions of Mormonism were primarily the province of Denmark's classically trained artists, philosophers, and theologians. While such representations of Mormonism's reception in Denmark do not tell the full story, in particular how the general public viewed this new religious movement, they do illuminate the ways in which Denmark's cultural elites attempted to control the public narrative about Mormonism's relevance (or lack thereof) to Danish culture. Despite the fairly homogenous background and education of these cultural elites, as well as their shared concern about the theological heterodoxy of Mormon doctrines, their representations of Mormonism are surprisingly diverse and illustrate a wide range of opinions about the relationship between religion and national identity.

This chapter examines several different high culture responses to and portrayals of Mormonism in Denmark during the 1850s in order to demarcate the scope and character of public discourse about the Mormon movement among Danish intellectuals. First, an iconic painting by realist painter Christen Dalsgaard that captures the early Mormon missionaries preaching to the Danish peasantry offers a unique visual perspective of their reception. Second, an encounter between some of these same missionaries and a prominent Danish Lutheran minister, Reverend Dr. Peter Christian Kierkegaard, resulted in the latter's publication of the critical but thoughtful treatise *Om og mod Mormonismen* (*About and Against Mormonism*) in 1855. This was the same year that Reverend Kierkegaard's estranged brother, the philosopher Søren Kierkegaard, published most of the articles that make up his so-called *Attack on Christendom* (1854–55), in which he criticizes the Danish Lutheran Church for its self-complacency. Contrasting these concurrent publications allows us to compare the views of these two prominent and influential Danish thinkers on the topic of religious difference.

Finally, a remarkable, but never published, manuscript about Mormonism by Elise Stampe—a member of the Danish nobility and a devout disciple of the Danish religious reformer N. F. S. Grundtvig—offers a highly personal and impassioned view of Mormonism in Denmark in this period. Not only does Stampe articulate a rare female view of the matter, but her empathetic and highly detailed engagement with the topic of Mormonism, despite her personal disagreement with Mormon doctrine, exemplifies the most positive aspects of Grundtvig's view of religious freedom.

Each of these texts offers a unique window into how the arrival and spread of Mormonism in Denmark in the 1850s intersects with discourses of Danish religious and cultural identity in a time of transition away from homogeneity. Although none of the authors endorses Mormonism, each makes it clear that some aspects of Mormon doctrine and practice resonated with the intellectual preoccupations of Denmark's cultural elites, despite the fact that Mormonism enjoyed relatively little success among the Danish bourgeoisie. Although, or perhaps because, the upper classes were less directly affected by the wave of conversions, the rapid spread of Mormonism among the common people in Denmark lent urgency to the need to define Danish cultural identity in terms other than religious affiliation. Each of the texts discussed in this chapter, whether visual or written, represents an attempt to articulate the role of Lutheranism in defining and circumscribing Danishness. In general, these texts deal with Mormonism on the level of professed doctrine, not lifestyle, which presents a marked contrast to the popular cultural texts discussed in chapter 3 that focus almost exclusively on polygamy and emigration as the distinguishing features of Mormonism.

A Window into Danish Homes and Hearts

In 1856, the Danish realist painter Christen Dalsgaard submitted a painting to the Charlottenborg Exhibition that bore the unwieldy title *Two Mormons have, in the course of their wanderings, entered the home of a country carpenter, where they seek to win new followers by means of preaching and exhibiting various of their sect's scriptures* (hereafter simply *Two Mormons*).[1] Even before the exhibition opened, the painting was purchased by N. L. Høyen, on behalf of the Society for Nordic Art, which espoused the mission of cultivating "the works of Danish artists that represent Nordic history, Nordic nature, and Nordic folk life."[2] This painting is widely acknowledged to be Dalsgaard's breakthrough piece, an argument supported by the fact that the painting has been part of the permanent

FIGURE 2.1 *Two Mormons Visiting a Country Carpenter* (1856) by Christen Dalsgaard. The scene depicted here is highly realistic, both in terms of its setting in a Jutlandic craftsman's home and in the varied responses, from skepticism to transcendence, manifested by the missionaries' listeners. Reproduced courtesy of Statens Museum for Kunst (the National Gallery of Denmark), Copenhagen (www.smk.dk). © SMK photo.

collection of the National Gallery of Denmark in Copenhagen since the dissolution of the Society for Nordic Art in 1871.

On an aesthetic level, Dalsgaard's painting is an elegantly realistic representation of the home and family of a rural Danish carpenter in the mid-nineteenth century. The scene is highly detailed, with vivid colors, deft use of lighting, and the inclusion of many small details such as wood shavings, everyday household implements, and folk costumes, which give the scene a stamp of authenticity and meet Høyen's criteria for depicting "Nordic folk life." In 1937, the Danish author and critic Johannes V. Jensen argued that the value of Dalsgaard's paintings lay precisely in their richness as culture-historical source material: "It is the clothing, the characters, the room, and the period-specific attitude toward life that modern viewers will pay attention to."³ All of these features make the painting a complex and satisfying visual scene—so satisfying, in fact, that a version of the painting from 1855 exists in which no figures are present, just the workshop itself.⁴

On a thematic level, however, Dalsgaard's painting gains additional significance as an authoritative representation of "Nordic history." It provides a rare but intimate glimpse into the homes and hearts of the Danish peasantry amidst the social turmoil created by the arrival of the Mormons in Denmark six years earlier. With nearly photographic precision, Dalsgaard captures a scene of two Mormon missionaries presenting their message of apostasy and restoration to a Danish carpenter and his family, friends, and neighbors. Although nothing is known about the circumstances accompanying the painting's creation, particularly whether Dalsgaard witnessed such an encounter for himself, the realistic detail and historical veracity of the scene suggests it could be an eyewitness account.

The image of Mormon missionaries going door to door and preaching in private homes has long been an iconic symbol of the LDS Church and continues to be so today, as demonstrated by the use of missionaries as the protagonists of the Broadway musical *The Book of Mormon* (2011). Unlike the satirical American musical, however, Dalsgaard's painting is not a caricature, nor does it overtly denounce Mormon doctrine, as many contemporaneous Danish texts about Mormonism do. Instead, it depicts an apparently genuine moment of communication between missionaries and potential converts. Although it postdates the printed texts discussed later in this chapter by a year or two, Dalsgaard's painting offers a useful starting point for the exploration of what Danish intellectuals's inquiries into the necessity and value of religious freedom, particularly as exemplified by the success of Mormonism in Denmark, can reveal about the issues at stake in Danish religious, cultural, and national identity in the years immediately following the adoption of the June Constitution.

In a considerate gesture to modern scholars, Dalsgaard wrote a "reading guide" to the painting for Høyen in 1856, in which he explains the thoughts and emotions he attributes to each of the figures in the scene. Dalsgaard's narration of the painting's psychological subtext reveals his awareness of the attractiveness of the Mormon teachings to certain segments of Danish society, whose curiosity about Mormonism provides the basis of the scene. It also exemplifies one way in which Denmark's intellectual elite attempted to account for the popularity of Mormonism among Danes during this period, but without resorting to obvious slander, scandalous gossip, or lies.

Dalsgaard explains that the two Mormon missionaries depicted in the painting—"the one young, convinced of the truth of his teachings, and fanatically enthusiastic; the other old, hardened, sly, an altogether bad person"⁵—had previously met the young blind girl (at the center of the painting). She has now brought her father with her to hear them in the carpenter's house and convince him of the truth of their teachings. Dalsgaard attributes the girl's interest in the Mormons to her blindness and physical weakness. Their promise of healing has captivated her completely, but her father is more cautious, though the hope that his daughter could be healed does tempt him. He is impressed by the Mormons' energy, which contrasts favorably with "the lassitude of habitual Christianity," but, Dalsgaard assures his readers/viewers, "like the five wise virgins, he has managed to preserve the true oil in his lamp."

Despite the harmony of the scene, the reading guide reveals undercurrents of hostility and anger among the characters inside the frame. According to Dalsgaard, the girl's father finds the unfamiliar Mormon faith "unethical and worldly," and so disruptive to his Lutheran views that he almost hates the missionaries. By way of contrast, Dalsgaard describes the carpenter, in whose home the Mormons are preaching, as "too healthy a nature to want anything to do with this sect, without even really knowing why."⁶ The rest of the figures in the scene—the woman at the window and the children in the room, as well as their mother in the back room—are, respectively, merely curious, indifferent, or annoyed. Mormonism is thus shown to be of interest primarily to the weak, the sick, or the revivalists, to which latter group the girl's father may belong.

As well as being the visual focal point of the painting, the blind girl's father is the most important figure in the scene in terms of his sociopolitical significance. His inner turmoil over the Mormon teachings reflects the volatility of Denmark's religious climate in the 1850s and encapsulates many of the fundamental issues under debate after the June Constitution was ratified. His disillusionment with "the lassitude of habitual Christianity" echoes the widespread dissatisfaction with the passivity of the Danish Lutheran Church, which thinkers as ideologically diverse as Søren Kierkegaard and N. F. S. Grundtvig openly criticized in the 1840s and 1850s. The father's antipathy toward the Mormons, however, calls to mind the rioting crowds that had attacked Mormon congregations in Odense and Aalborg a few years previously, as mentioned in chapter 1. The father's choice, as Dalsgaard frames it, is essentially the same one that faced many Danes of the period: whether to embrace a foreign religion with its unfamiliar doctrines and grandiose promises or to remain faithful to traditional Danish Lutheranism, despite its shortcomings.

Early Mormon Missionary Work in Denmark

The scenario that Dalsgaard depicts in *Two Mormons* was one that repeated itself in homes and cottages across Denmark countless times throughout the second half of the nineteenth century. One of the distinguishing features of the LDS Church from its earliest beginnings has been its active involvement in missionary work to fulfill the biblical injunction (as outlined in the New Testament Gospel of Matthew) to "teach all nations, baptizing them in the name of the Father, and of the Son, and of the Holy Ghost."[7] While this belief is one that many other Christian denominations share, the central thrust of European and American non-Mormon missionary efforts in the eighteenth and nineteenth centuries was directed at non-Christians living in developing nations in the Pacific, Asia, Latin America, South America, the Middle East, and Africa, as well as some Protestant missions to Catholic Europe.[8] By contrast, the Mormon conviction that the true gospel of Jesus Christ had been corrupted by apostasy in the Dark Ages and restored to the earth by Joseph Smith in 1830 led the LDS Church to focus its early missionary efforts primarily on Christians in the Western world. The Mormon missions to Protestant Europe were thus unique in both their target audience and their claim to represent the literal church of Jesus Christ that had been restored to the earth.

In the early years of Mormon activity in Denmark, most missionaries were drawn from the pool of recent converts, unlike in later decades, when the missionaries (most of whom were Danish convert-emigrants or their descendants) were sent over from Utah. The efforts of the first four Mormon missionaries who arrived from Utah in the spring of 1850 (as discussed in chapter 1)—Erastus Snow, P. O. Hansen, John Forsgren, and

George Parker Dykes—were soon supplemented by the energetic assistance of new Danish Mormon converts from Copenhagen and Aalborg, who were commissioned to share this new gospel not only with their friends and family, but also in far-flung parts of the country. In Copenhagen on March 3, 1851, for example, recent converts Christian J. Larsen and his brother Johannes Larsen were "appointed to go to Jutland as missionaries, to assist Elder George P. Dykes," as Andrew Jenson reports in his *History of the Scandinavian Mission*.[9] Despite the relatively small size of Denmark by modern standards, the primitive state of transportation at the time meant traveling from Copenhagen to Jutland was the sort of journey most Danes undertook only once or twice in their lives.

Having no paid clergy, the entire organization of the nineteenth-century Mormon Church depended on volunteer labor, including its missionary force in countries around the world. Willingness to serve was the primary qualification, rather than education, training, or financial means. In the 1850s, Mormon missionaries were laymen of all ages who had been appointed by church authorities in Salt Lake City to take unpaid sabbaticals from their employment and family responsibilities in order to preach, at their own expense, for periods ranging from several weeks to many years. Reid Neilson describes these early missionaries' evangelizing strategies:

> This corps of nonprofessional missionaries preached wherever they could be heard. They evangelized in both public and private spaces. Town squares and street corners, as well as barns and cabins, became the sites of Mormon preaching. Untrained by the Protestant divinity schools of the East Coast, they preached a homespun message, noteworthy for its simplicity. . . . The men spent much of their time tracting or canvassing neighborhoods and busy streets while handing out printed leaflets or other literature on Mormon subjects. They would either sell or loan the pamphlets to interested persons and then try to arrange a teaching meeting to discuss unique LDS doctrines.[10]

Although they also held formal meetings advertised in local newspapers, much of the missionary work was done on an ad hoc basis, wherever the missionaries could find someone to listen to them. The informality of their preparation and their style of proselytizing made it unlikely that they would come into contact with—or that their approach would appeal to—members of the upper classes in Denmark. Few Mormon missionaries of that time would have been able to debate subtle theological points or make scholarly arguments about the relative merits of different Biblical interpretations. Their main goal was to introduce people to the LDS doctrine of the apostasy and restoration of Christ's church, followed by the urging to gather to Zion in Utah to await the millennium together with the rest of the Latter-day Saints. In pursuit of this goal, enthusiasm generally counted for more than erudition.

The missionaries thus aroused opposition among the Danish bourgeoisie not only because of their provocative message of apostasy and restoration, but also because of their lack of formal education and professional training. J. P. Mynster, the bishop of Zealand and primate of the Danish Lutheran Church, found the Mormon practice of sending recent converts out to preach a particularly galling contrast to the careful, extensive training that Lutheran pastors received. In a small book called *The Provisions of the Constitution with regard to Religious Conditions in Denmark*, published in June 1850 and discussed briefly in chapter 1, Mynster argues that lay preachers are unqualified to teach Christian doctrine or administer the legal formalities of church administration, whereas Lutheran pastors have been appointed by the king, "contingent upon possession of the necessary insight and education. They are bureaucrats who stand by their actions according to the responsibility of their office and under the supervision of the relevant authorities."[11] Although Mynster was, by his own account, not personally familiar with Mormonism, nor had he encountered any Mormon missionaries, it seems likely that he based his critique on his knowledge of the lay preachers who were a driving force behind the "godly awakenings" of early nineteenth-century Denmark.

Many other Danish Lutheran pastors did have direct personal contact with Mormon missionaries, as evidenced by the survey of pastors on the island of Zealand (commissioned by Bishop Hans Lassen Martensen in 1854) that was discussed briefly in chapter 1. In that survey, various pastors reported meeting Mormon missionaries in their parishes and speaking out against Mormonism both in their congregations and in conversations with individual parishioners. In addition, a large percentage of the anti-Mormon publications that appeared in Danish newspapers in the 1850s were authored by Lutheran pastors intent on countering the missionaries' apparent effectiveness among their parishioners, notwithstanding the missionaries' lack of training or education.

Peter Christian Kierkegaard Meets the Mormons

One prominent Danish Lutheran pastor who personally encountered the Mormons and published an account of the experience was the Reverend Dr. Peter Christian Kierkegaard (1805–1888). At the time, P. C. Kierkegaard was the pastor of the parishes of Pedersborg and Kindertofte in the western part of Zealand, near Sorø, a position he had held since 1842. Guided by his mentor N. F. S. Grundtvig (who was, incidentally, also the uncle of P. C. Kierkegaard's second wife, Sophie Henriette Glahn), Reverend Kierkegaard was one of the most prominent Danish clergymen to refuse to perform forcible baptisms of Baptist children in his parish, for which stance he nearly lost his position and had to present himself to the king to account for his recalcitrance.[12] He was also an active participant in the Lutheran clergy's attempts to influence the Danish constitution in 1848–49, as well as in the Danish Lutheran Church's transition from an arm of the state to the people's church—he even coined the term *Folkekirken*. He played a number of prominent roles in Danish politics: as a member of the *Landsting*, the upper house of the Danish Parliament in the early 1850s; as minister of culture in the 1860s; and as bishop of Aalborg from 1856 to 1875. He was also the older brother of philosopher Søren Kierkegaard, whose final work, which questioned the legitimacy of the Danish Lutheran Church, will be discussed later in this chapter.

Reverend Kierkegaard may well have become aware of the Mormons within the first year of their arrival in Denmark in 1850, both as a result of the public disturbances and media debates surrounding them and in his capacity as a member of the Danish Parliament, to which a group of Danish Mormons submitted a petition for protection against mob violence in 1852.[13] Given the location of his parish, he would most likely have received Bishop Martensen's survey about the spread of Mormonism in the diocese of Zealand in early 1854, but no response from him was recorded. No evidence exists of P. C. Kierkegaard's involvement with or against the Mormons until the summer of 1854, when he mentions in his diary, "There will also be a great deal to do in Pedersborg in

FIGURE 2.2 Peter Christian Kierkegaard, depicted here (ca. 1870) wearing his pastoral robes, was a highly respected public figure who served his country vigorously in many capacities, but suffered many challenges and disappointments in his personal life. Photograph by J. A. Schultz. Reproduced courtesy of the Danish Royal Library, Copenhagen, Department of Maps, Prints, and Photographs.

the coming months: the Mormon upheaval has come to Pedersborg."[14] In August 1854, he goes into greater detail about his contact with the Mormons, explaining:

> On the 4th or 5th, I learned that Mormons had come to Ped-
> ersborg and Kindertofte. I spoke with one who was visiting in
> Pedersborg town. Spoke with [Mathias C.] Hemerdt, who was
> with them and who has visited their meetings elsewhere (for
> a long time?). With many at his home, all of whom had been
> rebaptized in Haugerup. On the 13th, I attended their meeting in
> Haugerup at Hemerdt's home and testified against them, God
> be praised, with noticeable effect.[15]

Upon discovering that the Mormons were proselytizing in his parish, Kierkegaard was alarmed enough to research the matter. He discovered that Lars Wilhelmsen, the son-in-law of his parishioner Mathias C. Hemerdt, had joined the LDS Church in 1852 and had invited the missionaries to teach his relatives in Pedersborg. As reported in his diary, Kierkegaard apparently spoke with one of the missionaries and then attended a Mormon meeting at Hemerdt's home in the village of Haugerup (now spelled Haverup). At that meeting, he was apparently given (or requested) the opportunity to speak in order to counter the missionaries' claims.

Unlike the violent anti-Mormon demonstrations that took place in various Danish cities in the early 1850s (described in chapter 1), Reverend Kierkegaard's strategy of witnessing against the Mormons conforms to the recommended methods for *Folkekirken*'s pastors to counter the Mormon threat. In a letter published by the national-liberal newspaper *Fædrelandet* (*The Fatherland*) on February 1, 1851, Pastor L. D. Hass in Hals protests the mistreatment of Mormons in the city of Aalborg, in particular the attempts to deny them the right to hold worship services. Pastor Hass was not sympathetic to Mormon doctrine, as his 1851 article "The Teachings, Origins, and Progress of the Mormons" demonstrates, but he explains in this letter that he felt obligated "to lodge a formal protest in the name of the enlightened and broad-minded Lutheran clergy."[16] Rather than attempting to deny Mormons their constitutional right of assembly, Pastor Hass recommends attending their meetings and bearing witness against them, which is precisely what Reverend Kierkegaard did on August 13, 1854.

Contemporaneous accounts indicate that P. C. Kierkegaard was a highly trained, well-educated, and compelling speaker. He held doctoral degrees in both theology and philosophy and, while a student in Germany, earned the sobriquet "the debating devil from the North"[17] for his masterful debating skills. His contemporary, Pastor H. C. Rørdam, described him in a newspaper article in May 1854 as "peerless among younger theologians in terms of his competence and knowledge," and said he is "in possession of a rare gift for awakening, challenging, and motivating his listeners to independent spiritual activity."[18] He was, in short, a formidable opponent for any credentialed theologian or scholar, to say nothing of earnest but uneducated laymen.

For the Mormon missionaries in Haugerup, therefore, the experience of having the Reverend Dr. Kierkegaard attend their meeting and refute their claims must have been a harrowing experience. Kierkegaard did not record the names of the three Mormon missionaries who spoke at the meeting. Given the scarcity of missionaries from Utah during this period and the resulting reliance on recent converts, the missionaries in Haugerup in 1854 were most likely local men, perhaps craftsmen or farmers, with at best a few years' membership in the Mormon Church. New converts were regularly recruited to preach to their friends and neighbors, despite their lack of training in theology or public speaking. William Mulder explains that, during the 1850s in Denmark, such "tenacious laymen . . . did not merely dominate the scene down to 1859; they were the scene, some of them serving six and seven years before emigrating. During that first decade, Utah itself sent only thirteen missionaries to Scandinavia, and six of these were Scandinavians who had joined the church in America."[19] One impressive example of an early Danish Mormon missionary is Christian Daniel Fjeldsted (1829–1905), a harness maker from Sundbyvester (on the outskirts of Copenhagen) who joined the church in February 1852, along with his wife Karen. Not long after his baptism, he was fired for preaching Mormon doctrine to his coworkers.[20] In 1855 he was called to serve as an itinerant missionary, a task he performed throughout Denmark until he emigrated in 1858. Fjeldsted later returned to Scandinavia six more times as a missionary, spending a total of seventeen years representing the Mormon Church in his native land.[21]

Although some critics complained about the Mormons as a source of pernicious foreign influence, the fact that so many missionaries were native Danes proved to be even more offensive to many Danish clergymen, who "saw these elders, these farm hands and artisans who were their own parishioners, as upstarts, ignorant fanatics, perverting Scripture and unsettling the minds of their fellow villagers."[22] Missionary activity was reminiscent of the revival movement earlier in the century, which had also been a source of irritation for some of the clergy, but while the "godly awakenings" had merely advocated a more emotional, individualized view of standard Lutheran theology, the doctrines taught by the Mormons were far more radical and disruptive to the status quo. Moreover, since religious difference was now legal under the new constitution, neither law enforcement nor the judiciary could legally intervene to silence lay preachers with fines or the threat of imprisonment. Instead, the task of combating perceived heresies fell to the clergy themselves.

When he attended the Mormon meeting, Reverend Kierkegaard must have been aware of the missionaries' lack of training, but he evidently felt that his responsibility for his parishioners' spiritual welfare obligated him to take on such humble, though not completely unprepared, opponents. Since Mormon missionaries in the nineteenth century were generally devout Christians prior to their conversion, they tended to be well-versed in the Bible and used it effectively to support their message of restored Christianity. In his study of the nineteenth-century Mormon missionary, Rex Price argues,

> The Elders took pride in their "rational" religion and a method-ological approach grounded in the notion that true religion could be "proved" by argument and logic. The Elders' arguments proved almost unassailable, grounded as they were in Biblical literalism. They surprised many a cleric, as well as "stranger," with able defenses of the absolute need for baptism by immersions, con-tinuing revelation, a primitive polity with prophets and apostles, and the ancient gifts of the Holy Spirit, including tongues, heal-ings, and prophesyings.[23]

Despite this general tendency toward Biblical literacy among Mormon missionaries of the period, Reverend Kierkegaard criticized the missionaries he debated for quoting scripture from memory rather than reading it from the Bible. Before beginning his rebuttal, Kierkegaard produced a Bible and asked a member of the audience to hold it in order to verify the accuracy of any scriptural references he might make, since, as he explained, "one can easily obtain the appearance of proving by the scripture whatever is at stake if one dares to be satisfied with occasionally quoting a few random words, which, while the speaker continues on, sound to a casual listener approximately like what is actually found in it."[24] During his remarks, he occasionally takes the missionaries to task for factual errors in their presentation—for example, a reference to Catholic popes five hundred years before the office had been created. He cautions, with apparently amused disdain, that such errors come from allowing "one's mouth to direct one's thoughts instead of the thoughts the mouth, and when one who could perhaps be an attentive listener prefers instead to be a confused teacher."[25] Reverend Kierkegaard's condescending attitude toward the missionaries exposes the social hierarchy entrenched in Danish society at that time, which Mormonism destabilized. According to that hierarchy, members of the working class to which the lay missionaries belonged were expected to remain subservient to their intellectual "betters."

Moreover, Kierkegaard's veiled allegation that the missionaries misquote scripture to serve their particular agenda illustrates his general view of both the missionaries' moral character and their nonstandard interpretations of Christian theology—to say nothing of the new teachings unique to Mormonism—as untrustworthy. In the introduction to the printed version of his remarks, Reverend Kierkegaard explains that he chose to respond only to points of doctrine that the missionaries themselves discussed at the meeting rather than pursuing a more wide-ranging theological discussion. The apparent magnanimity of this gesture is undermined by his subsequent accusation that the missionaries would otherwise have denied knowledge of Mormonism's radical doctrines or the history of the LDS Church itself:

> I knew well that, first, some of these itinerant Mormon preachers
> are themselves ignorant of their party's actual radical doctrines,

so that the whole thing often becomes for them just a sort of revivalist speech without any particular dogmatic content, and that, second, they claim unfamiliarity with the most flagrant Mormon delusions and denounce as lies the evidence from the religious-historical records that demonstrate their errors, thereby causing the common people develop doubts about such proofs. For these reasons, I decided to strive to challenge only those delusions taught by their sect which the speakers themselves had chosen and publicly presented, and which they thus could neither avoid nor claim to be ignorant of.[26]

Whether or not Reverend Kierkegaard had firsthand experience with these alleged evasive tactics is unclear, but his mistrust of the missionaries' willingness or ability to discuss the more unusual doctrines of their new faith is unmistakable.

Without firsthand accounts by those in attendance to draw upon, it is difficult to know exactly what effect the missionaries' debate with Reverend Kierkegaard had on the people in attendance. The disparity between Kierkegaard's scholarly erudition and the missionaries' evangelical fervor, as well as the clear class distinctions between the upper-class clergyman versus the working-class missionaries, may well have generated sympathy for the missionaries' cause among a group of devout farmers and craftsmen, as was often the case in Great Britain during the same period. In any case, Reverend Kierkegaard's diary entry from August 1854 indicates that he felt his comments at the Mormon gathering had "noticeable effect" on those present, most of whom were his own parishioners. As Mormon records indicate, and as Reverend Kierkegaard also noted later in his diary, however, the parishioners who hosted the meeting, the cooper Mathias C. Hemerdt and his wife Christine, were baptized into the Mormon Church two weeks after the meeting, and the missionaries continued to hold meetings in the area. Reverend Kierkegaard apparently visited Hemerdt after the latter's baptism, but could not persuade him of the error of his ways. Instead, Hemerdt and his wife emigrated in 1855 to join the Mormons in Utah. Enough other residents of Pedersborg and the surrounding villages, some of whom Kierkegaard mentions by name in his diary,[27] were receptive to the Mormon message that a LDS congregation was organized in Haugerup in June 1855.[28] It was not until

1858 that Reverend Kierkegard was able to log, "The Mormon upheaval has tapered off."

Perhaps because of his apparent failure to arrest the spread of Mormonism in his parish, Kierkegaard's encounter with the Mormons in Pedersborg seemed to convince him of the necessity of intervening in public discourse about religious freedom in Denmark. In the fall of 1854, he took his anti-Mormon message to a wider audience. He turned his impromptu remarks from the cottage meeting in August into a full-length lecture that he delivered at the schoolhouses in Pedersborg and Kindertofte on October 6, 1854, using the title "About and Against Mormonism" for the first time. His remarks are scholarly, incorporating extensive scriptural exegesis, Latin terminology, and references to serious theological debates, but also entertaining, liberally laced with humorous comments and allusions to well-known folk and fairy tale figures (such as Baron Münchhausen[29] and Lying Hans) that would appeal to a less academic audience. In his diary, he mentions these lectures with the comment, "well-attended and a great deal of interest."[30] He published his speech, under the same title, first in the *Dansk Kirketidende* (*Danish Church News*) in January and February 1855, and then in book form in the summer of 1855.[31]

Reverend Kierkegaard's refutation of the doctrines taught by the Mormon missionaries at the cottage meeting in Mathias Hemerdt's home in August 1854 contains a valuable snapshot of the theological and social objections of the Danish Lutheran establishment to Mormonism in this period. Reverend Kierkegaard's comments can be divided into two parts. In the first section, which he describes as being of secondary importance, he discusses the uniquely Mormon doctrines introduced by the missionaries, including: Jesus Christ's alleged visit to the American continent after his resurrection, Joseph Smith's claim to angelic visitations and subsequent translation of a book of scripture inscribed on gold plates, and the belief that the Native American tribes are descendants of a Semitic tribe that inhabited the Americas more than five hundred years before the birth of Christ.

Since such claims could neither be proved nor disproved, Kierkegaard tends to try to render them ridiculous. For example, he asks somewhat disingenuously how the "stick of Joseph and the stick of Judah," which are mentioned in Ezekiel and interpreted in Mormon theology as representing the Book of Mormon and the Bible, could have been transmuted into golden plates in America. "If this thing happened by natural causes," he continues, "it would be completely understandable that all those people, who, like King Midas among the heathens of ancient times, want so much to see everything they touch turn to gold, yearn for America, where presumably even a hazel staff that they happen to bring along can be hammered into plates of ducat gold."[32] In this sentence, Reverend Kierkegaard's insistence on a literal interpretation of a symbolic representation shifts from a critique of Mormon doctrine to a general disparagement of emigrants who set off to seek their fortune in America. This association underscores the connection between conversion and emigration, both of which are made to appear irrational and self-delusional.

The second, more strictly theological part of Reverend Kierkegaard's response concerns itself with the fundamental ways in which Mormonism diverges from his own understanding of evangelical Lutheran Christianity. This section tackles such questions as the true nature of God, the line of authority from Christ to his church on earth, the designation "Christian," the proper form of baptism, the possibility of establishing Zion on earth, how to discern between faith and reason, how to determine the validity of revelation, and the duties of a Christian. Although Reverend Kierkegaard does not explicitly discuss how Lutheran Christianity contributes to defining Danishness, his treatment of some of these topics has implicit bearing on the question of the intersection of Danish religious and cultural identity, particularly regarding the legitimacy of the (mutually disputed) Lutheran and Mormon claims to being Christian.

In response to the missionaries' assertion that the true church of Jesus Christ had been corrupted after his death and was hence in need of restoration, Reverend Kierkegaard proclaims that every heretical group since the Manichees in the second century has made the same charge of apostasy as the basis for their own claim to unique divine authority. He groups the Mormons together with other alliterating heretical religions—such as the Montanists, Manichees, Monophysites, Monothelites, Muslims, and Mennonites,[33] as well as the Quakers and Cathars—in order refute their claim to an exclusive authority that could challenge the legitimacy of mainstream Christianity in general or Danish Lutheranism in particular. Reverend Kierkegaard seems to be saying, in other words, that the Mormon "restoration" is nothing new, a fad that will pass, while Danish Lutheranism is solid and unshakeable.

Even more important, in Reverend Kierkegaard's view, was the fact that the Mormons' belief that Christ was not able to ensure the survival of the very church he founded discredits Christ's own divinity. Since Christ promised to be with his church—the holy, universal church—until the end of days, he argues, "it causes our reverence for the Lord to suffer, or, more correctly, *destroys our faith* in him *if* we let ourselves be seduced into believing that the Church he founded has been *destroyed*" (emphasis in original).[34] To undermine the divinity of Christ in this way, he warns, is fundamentally incompatible with the designation Christian, such that no dissident groups, whether Mormon or Manichean, who postulate apostasy within Christ's church can rightfully call themselves Christians. Therefore, Reverend Kierkegaard argues, the Mormon claim to represent a restoration of Christ's original church is tantamount to claiming that God has "broken His promise and did not remain with the Church until the end of the world, and was therefore forced at some point in time to make up for this neglect by sending an angel to a treasure-hunter in America. But in that case it would be idolatry to believe in such a Lord, who forgets to keep His word and then has to correct His own mistake."[35] If this were the case, he declares, all those who have called themselves Christians from the days of the ancient church until the present must be regarded as "hypocrites and liars." Since this is naturally not a view he would be willing to endorse, he concludes that it is the Mormons themselves who are not Christian.

Peter Christian Kierkegaard's experience debating the Mormon missionaries led others to ask his advice on the matter, as a series of letters from Reverend Christian Anker Winther, a Lutheran pastor married to Kierkegaard's sister-in-law, attests. In October 1854, Winther wrote to Kierkegaard asking for advice on how to handle the Mormons who had begun proselytizing in his parish. For whatever reason, although he acknowledged receipt of the letter in his diary with the comment "Christian A. Winther has Mormon visitors,"[36] Reverend Kierkegaard apparently never replied. Winther wrote again, in January 1855, expressing disappointment in his brother-in-law's silence and outlining the actions he had ultimately taken to combat the Mormon incursion. After a period of painfully paralyzed indecision, Winther decided to speak to his parishioners "as independent people who had the right to choose. I just tried to make them aware of the fact that one cannot be a Mormon and a

Christian at the same time, that the Mormons are not, as they would of course like to be known, better Christians, but heretics and apostates."[37] This distinction between Mormonism and Christianity echoes the main point Kierkegaard tried to make in his tract, namely that the Mormon brand of Christianity was, by definition, un-Christian—and, since Denmark legally defined itself as a Christian state, un-Danish as well.

While he does not seem to have debated any more Mormon missionaries, Kierkegaard earned a reputation as an authority on dealing with the Mormons, which may have played a role in his appointment in 1857 as bishop of Aalborg, a city in northern Jutland where the LDS Church had been extremely successful in winning converts. *About and Against Mormonism* appears to be his only Mormon-related publication, however, aside from a letter from a disillusioned ex-Mormon that he forwarded to *Dansk Kirketidende* for publication in November 1855 and a circular he wrote to the pastors in his diocese about the process of rebaptizing Mormons who desired to return to *Folkekirken*.

In Aalborg in February 1866, Kierkegaard undertook a similar type of public newspaper debate with a man named Mogens Sommer (1829–1901). Sommer was traveling around Denmark in the 1860s preaching against the state church and infant baptism, using Søren Kierkegaard's writings as his text and recruiting emigrants to his colony in the United States. In his rebuttal of Sommer's claims, Bishop Kierkegaard asserts that freedom of religion includes confessing one's faith but not insulting other religions nor, as he accused the Mormon missionaries he had met a decade earlier of having done, "rushing around to recruit people, spiritually for apostasy from every Christian faith and confession, and physically to become colonists in America, where they are given hope of finding something that can roughly be called heaven on earth."[38] Just as he did in his remarks twelve years earlier, Kierkegaard warns against the LDS Church in Denmark primarily because of its activities as a emigration agent, luring Danes from their homeland with pie-in-the-sky promises, as well as its divergence from Lutheran doctrine, which alienates its converts from their inherited cultural identity.

The Peculiarly Danish Brand of Grundtvigian Christianity

Peter Christian Kierkegaard's printed remarks about religious freedom and Mormonism are a generally dispassionate rebuttal of specific points of Mormon doctrine as taught by LDS missionaries, in contrast to the scandalmongering that characterized many anti-Mormon texts published during this period. In addition, *About and Against Mormonism* illustrates certain principles of a peculiarly Danish brand of Lutheranism as articulated by N. F. S. Grundtvig, whose biography and political activities were discussed in chapter 1 and who has had a seminal influence on the way Danish Lutheranism is viewed and practiced to this day. In particular, Reverend Kierkegaard's defense of the concept of an unbroken line of authority within Christ's holy, universal church via the oral confession of faith, irrespective of denominational differences, is derived from Grundtvig's teaching that Christians—through reliance on the oral transmission of covenants and the confession of faith—could bypass Luther, so to speak, and arrive at the ancient foundation of Christ's church. Grundtvig's expansive, undogmatic, communal interpretation of Lutheran Christianity was regarded as radical in the early nineteenth century, but gained traction around the middle of the century. This was due in part to Kierkegaard's efforts to introduce Grundtvig's views into Danish theology, particularly his defense of the validity of the living oral tradition and transmission of the baptismal covenant from generation to generation within the church.[39]

Grundtvig's view of Danish national and cultural identity was inextricable from his view of Danish religious identity as Christian, based on the belief that patriotism is predicated on faith. Flemming Lundgreen-Nielsen formulates Grundtvig's self-conception as being a "Dane first, then human, finally Christian."[40] Grundtvig regarded Christianity and Danishness as existing in a mutually beneficial, almost symbiotic relationship. Claus Bjørn explains,

> He [Grundtvig] seemed to have reached a conclusion about the relationship between the natural human life and Christianity, with repeated emphasis on his side of the *Danish* natural human life. The natural individual and people's life was the prerequisite for Christianity. And when natural life developed according to its destiny, it would prepare the way for salvation through Christianity. Grundtvig believed in an interplay between the two—Christianity should not suppress the national, but rather serve and promote it; and on the other side all of the national institutions,

especially school, should essentially serve Christianity. Public life
and schools could and should prepare the people for the word of
God (emphasis in original).[41]

This close association between Christianity and Danishness derives from
Grundtvig's view that human life depends on a sense of belonging to a
certain people, to a certain nationality. According to Grundtvig, a people
must be aware of itself and its own characteristics before its members
can fully embrace Christianity. As Bjørn phrases it, Grundtvig believed
that "Danishness, which dwelt within the individual, was a prerequisite
for both mortal and eternal life."[42] In a January 30, 1848, article in *Dansk
Kirketidende*, Grundtvig asserted that post-Reformation Christianity
could only benefit those who were conscious of their national identity.
Accordingly, Grundtvig stressed the development of a national faith
community as the means of both binding the nation together and ensuring Danes' salvation.

Despite his insistence on the close relationship between Danishness
and Christianity, however, Grundtvig was also an influential advocate for
an inclusive view of religion and tolerance of a wide range of religious
views. He objected to state control of the Danish Lutheran Church and
fought for the freedom of Lutheran pastors to preach their own interpretations of the Christian gospel, as well as for members to have the right
to choose which congregation to attend based on the compatibility of
the pastor's views with their own. The so-called "freedom laws" of 1855
and 1868 enshrined both of those rights in law. Grundtvig's insistence
on inclusivity was not a result of indifference to religious doctrine—his
voluminous writings on theology make it clear that he had very strong
opinions about Christian doctrine—but was rather an outgrowth of his
conviction that because religion is what concerns man the most, he must
have the freedom to choose it for himself.[43]

Rather than ascribing to the church an exclusive claim to truth and
authority, Grundtvig regarded it as a "living, sacramental community
with focus on baptism, communion, and the creed. It is an inclusive community that puts emphasis on Christianity as a way of life instead of a
doctrine."[44] In the service of that ideal, Grundtvig conceived of the state
church as a civic institution that could function as an umbrella organization over a range of independent or "electoral" Christian congregations

that (unlike evangelical Lutheran "free congregations") remain within *Folkekirken*. Initially, it was primarily reform-minded Grundtvigians who established their own congregations, but it soon became common among more conservative factions of the church as well, such as adherents of *Indre Missionen* (the Home Mission). Reflecting the potency of Grundtvig's legacy, *Folkekirken* functions today not only or even primarily as a faith community, but as a cultural and societal signifier for membership in the national community.

Although Grundtvig never expressed himself publicly on the subject of Mormonism, his influence on the structure of *Folkekirken*, his position as an ideological leader, and his prominence as a Danish cultural nationalist make his views of religious identity, religious freedom, and religious difference relevant to any discussion of Danish Mormonism. Private comments in letters reveal that he personally had little interest in or respect for Mormonism, but he never spoke out or published anything against it. However, discussions of Mormonism by his close associates and disciples, including Peter Christian Kierkegaard (discussed above) and Elise Stampe (discussed below), can provide some insight into the relationship between Grundtvigian Christianity and Mormonism in Denmark. While such texts cannot simply be equated with Grundtvig's own opinions, of course, they demonstrate how Grundtvig's ideas permeated Danish religious thought and culture and how this particular conception of Danish Lutheranism informed nineteenth-century Danish intellectuals' responses to Mormonism.

Elise Stampe's Exploration of Mormonism

In the absence of a text about Mormonism authored by Grundtvig, we will instead explore how Grundtvig's views about Christianity and religious freedom informed what is quite possibly the only surviving nineteenth-century Danish text about Mormonism written by a woman. Despite the fact that slightly more Danish women than men, on average, joined the LDS Church, the vast majority of both high and popular culture representations of Mormonism in nineteenth-century Denmark, including those discussed in both this chapter and chapter 3, were created by men. This single rare exception is an unpublished manuscript with the title "Mormonismen" (Mormonism) that was written in the late 1850s by Danish noblewoman Kirstine Marie Elisabeth Stampe

(1824–1883), one of Grundtvig's most devoted disciples.[45] This text not only challenges the widely held notion that Mormonism was an exclusively working-class phenomenon in nineteenth-century Denmark, it also offers a much more tolerant, inclusive view of Mormon doctrine than other contemporaneous Danish texts, although Stampe never subscribed to Mormonism herself.

As the daughter of Baron Henrik Stampe and his wife Christine Dalgas, Elise was raised in the most cultivated and privileged circles of Danish society, toward the end of the Danish golden age. The Stampe family lived on an estate called Nysø, located close to Præstø Fjord near the southern tip of Zealand. Elise's parents were the patrons of renowned Danish sculptor Bertel Thorvaldsen, for whom they built an atelier at Nysø, where he lived from June 1839 until his death in 1844.[46] The Stampe home was a gathering place for artists and intellectuals in nineteenth-century Denmark, with not only Thorvaldsen but also Hans Christian Andersen, Adam Oehlenschläger, H. P. Holst, and N. F. S. Grundtvig, among many other notables and dignitaries, in frequent attendance. Even King Christian VIII and Queen Caroline Amalie paid the Stampes a royal visit when Thorvaldsen lived at Nysø.[47] Their guests would often put on plays, in which the young Elise excelled as an actress, despite the fact, as Thorvaldsen once exclaimed, "She looks as if she couldn't count to five."[48] Elise had a lively intellect and was interested in ideas and debates about current events, but she was also "a quiet and serious child, who thought much more than she spoke."[49] She was not one to seek the spotlight, but she had strong opinions that she defended with skill and sophistication. Her mother's posthumously published memoirs, *Baroness Stampe's Memories of Thorvaldsen*, include an anecdote about a fifteen-year-old Elise arguing with an Englishman about Napoleon while on a trip to Hamburg.[50]

Some of the advantages that Stampe enjoyed as a member of such a prosperous, culturally sophisticated household were the opportunities for international travel, artistic education, and cultural exchange that were rare at the time, which likely contributed to her open-minded view of religion later in life. She traveled abroad for the first time at the age of six, when her family drove their coach down to Italy to visit her mother's relations there and to study art. In 1842, at age eighteen, Stampe traveled

FIGURE 2.3 As a member of Denmark's high society, Baroness Elise Stampe (photograph ca. 1850) was on intimate terms with many of Denmark's leading artists and intellectuals, including the sculptor Bertel Thorvaldsen and N. F. S. Grundtvig. Reproduced courtesy of the Danish Royal Library, Copenhagen, Department of Maps, Prints, and Photographs.

with her parents and Thorvaldsen to Rome, where she interacted with the vibrant group of Danish artists working there, including the painter Carl Christian Constantin Hansen, who would later become one of her most steadfast friends. She also traveled independently later in life. In the early 1860s, she traveled through Scotland and England and wrote a book about her experiences, *Impressions from Abroad* (1863), which deals primarily with the practice of religion in Great Britain.

As she grew up, Stampe's interest in art and theater was gradually replaced by an inclination toward spirituality, especially after a serious illness nearly took her life while in Rome. In 1843, at age nineteen, she became a *Stiftsdame*, a kind of lay nun, at Vallø, a Lutheran convent for women of the Danish nobility that was founded in 1737 by Queen Sophie Magdalena, wife of King Christian VI. In this era, it was still fairly common for wealthy Danish families to purchase their daughters a lifetime place in the order—which cost about 4,000 crowns in 1800[51]—as insurance against the possibility that they not marry. Members of Vallø did not take monastic vows, but dedication to the evangelical Christian faith was required for admission. Although Stampe never lived in the convent, this affiliation afforded her certain rights, an annual stipend, and social rank until her death.

Stampe's inclination toward religiosity was enhanced by her relationship to Grundtvig, which was almost like that of a father and daughter. In a letter to Grundtvig in September 1857, she writes, "I am so excessively fond of Pastor Grundtvig that I dreamt one night of both my own dear father and that Pastor Grundtvig was also my father."[52] Grundtvig's family home at Udby was close to Nysø and he was a close friend of the Stampe family throughout his life. The children of the Stampe household were taught from Grundtvig's *Bibelkrønike* (*Bible Stories*, 1814) and Elise grew up together with Grundtvig's children Svend, Johan, and Meta, with whom she socialized in the mid-1840s. In addition to Meta Grundtvig, Stampe's closest female friends were Susette Dalgas, Georgia Schouw, and Magdalena Købke, who later married the painter Constantin Hansen. The four young women were known collectively as the "four-leaf clover." Magdalena Købke's daughter, Thora Constantin-Hansen, reports in her biography of Stampe that the painter Johan Thomas Lundbye once hung a drawing on the door of the room where the women were gathered, depicting a four-leaf clover with an image on each of the leaves representing one of the women: art for Elise, mythology for Meta, legends for Susette, and song for Georgia.[53] The Danish romantic poet Adam Oehlenschläger immortalized the girls in his poem, "To the Small Girls at Nysø" (1839). Together with her friends and Grundtvig's own children,

Stampe studied with Pastor Grundtvig at Vartov for her confirmation in the Danish Lutheran Church on April 18, 1841, when she was seventeen years old.

Given the intensely patriotic political climate in which she grew to adulthood, it is perhaps not surprising that Elise Stampe was a passionate nationalist. Hans Christian Andersen described her in June 1864 as "a truly Danish soul."[54] She took an intense interest in both the First and Second Schleswig Wars, in which she felt personally invested. Her two older brothers Henrik and Holger—along with her cousins Ernesto, Carlo, and Enrico Dalgas and her friends Svend Grundtvig, Johan Grundtvig, and Johan Lundbye—enlisted as volunteers in the First Schleswig War, known in Denmark as the "Three Years' War" due to the fact that it lasted from 1848–1851. Three of Stampe's close friends and relatives died in the war: Johan Lundbye, Carlo Dalgas, and Ernesto Dalgas.

Stampe was ecstatic at the news of the Danish army's victory at Fredericia in July 1849, but she soon fell into a deep depression over the loss of her friends on the battlefield and the death of a young cousin around the same time. Looking to make a radical life change, she contemplated seeking work as a domestic servant, but was dissuaded from this plan by her family. This was, as Thora Constantin-Hansen notes, fortunate for all involved parties, as Stampe "was not at all gifted in practical matters."[55] She went through a period of extreme spiritual upheaval beginning in 1849 that lasted until the late 1850s, around the time that she wrote her book on Mormonism, which may account for her unusual interest in the subject.

In the aftermath of her spiritual crisis, Stampe became extremely pious. In an era when piety was going out of fashion among the Danish elite, this put her out of step with people of her own age and class. She never married, but instead devoted her life to religion, which was something of a family tradition, despite her parents' preference for art. Stampe's maternal grandfather, Jean Marc Dalgas (1756–1811), was the descendant of French Huguenots who had sought refuge from persecution during the reign of King Louis XIV in the late seventeenth century. Although he died more than a dozen years before Elise's birth in 1824, grandfather Dalgas's calling as a pastor in a French Reformed church in Fredericia remained a source of family pride. The path of the ministry being closed to her by her gender, Stampe instead published

more than a dozen books during her lifetime, most of them self-publi-
cations on religious topics in small print runs that she gave to friends
and family members.

Some of Stampe's longest and most passionate writings deal with patriotism and nationalism, but religion is also a frequent topic. Her books
include, among others, *Alvor* (*Seriousness*) (1850), a volume of religious
poetry; *Venne-Skrivt* (*A Letter to Friends*) (1858); *Guds Levende Ord* (*The
Living Word of God*) (1861); *"O nu Stander Landet i Vaade"* (*"And Now the
Country Is in Distress"*) (1864); *Fædreland og Folkelighed* (*Fatherland and
Nationalism*) (1865); and *Strøtanker af en Navnløs* (*Scattered Thoughts by
a Nameless One*) (1878). They range in length from 2–3 pages—for example, *Et Ord til Retvendelse* (*A Word of Guidance*) (1876)—to 766 pages
(*Fatherland and Nationalism*). At approximately 400 manuscript pages,
handwritten on booklets of blue paper, her treatise on Mormonism falls
in the middle in terms of length, but was composed relatively early in
her authorship. She wrote this treatise only a year or two after *A Letter
to Friends* (130 printed pages), which contains devotional essays about
Christian topics such as the sacrament and the sermon on the mount,
based on scriptural passages and both Stampe's and Grundtvig's interpretation of the same. Stampe's book about Mormonism also focuses on
particular doctrinal issues, with the notable difference that she quotes
extensively from Mormon scriptures—both the Book of Mormon and
the Doctrine and Covenants—as well as writings by contemporaneous
LDS leaders such as Parley P. Pratt and pamphlets published by local
missionaries, including P. O. Hansen and Erastus Snow.

Stampe corresponded frequently with Grundtvig (particularly
between 1856 and 1861), seeking his insight into various religious matters,
such as the ordinance of baptism, and incorporating his suggestions into
her books. Stampe was particularly attentive to Grundtvig's theological
explanations and was able to recite his Sunday sermons nearly word-per-
fect long after they were delivered. Despite her sense of filial piety toward
Grundtvig, however, Stampe was not uncritical of him or his views. Her
biographer, Thora Constantin-Hansen, insists on Stampe's intellectual
independence from Grundtvig. Based on their correspondence, Constantin-Hansen describes Stampe as a "grateful apprentice [to Grundt-
vig], most certainly one of the most apt he ever had, to judge by both
her and his statements—but she was not a blindly adoring follower."[56]

Stampe demonstrated this intellectual independence in her determined inquiry into Mormonism in the late 1850s, although she confesses in a letter to Grundtvig that she had put off writing to him about it out of concern that he would disapprove.[57]

It is unclear how Elise Stampe first came into contact with Mormonism, but her letters to Grundtvig explain that her interest in the subject was connected to her friendship with a woman who had joined the LDS Church. She doesn't explain how they became acquainted, but the relationship was clearly an intimate friendship that mattered a great deal to Stampe. By studying Mormonism, she hoped to be able to persuade her friend of the error of her ways. In a letter to Grundtvig from Nysø on September 14, 1857, Stampe reports that her sister Jeanina had told her "how much Pastor Grundtvig was opposed to my visiting the Mormon woman of whom I am so fond," but she goes on to explain, "I am so happy and peaceful about having had a good talk with her and I am certain that it will prove itself one day not to have been in vain, when the hour of the Lord arrives."[58] Constantin-Hansen, who knew Stampe personally when she was a child and Stampe an older woman, recounts, "circumstances had brought E. St. into contact with a Mormon woman, who awakened her sympathy, which prompted her to study the ideas of Mormonism— and challenge them."[59] While it is clear from her text that Stampe did not endorse Mormon beliefs, Stampe took great pains to treat the matter fairly and found much to admire in Mormon scripture. From a comment in a letter from Grundtvig on October 11, 1858, it appears that Stampe's Mormon friend may have died suddenly. He writes: "I may have wondered a bit over your fascination with the Mormon woman, but I would hardly have let you see that, since matters of the heart are as necessary for us as our eyes. Based on your report, it seems reasonable to me that Our Lord, by cutting her earthly sojourn short so abruptly, has mercifully removed her as a piece of wood from the fire."[60] It may have been sorrow at the loss of her friend and perhaps also distress at the common misrepresentations of her friend's beliefs that prompted Stampe to write her book that same autumn.

Stampe seems to have been aware that any positive treatment of Mormonism would be criticized by the Danish intellectual elites, but she persisted nonetheless. In late 1858 and early 1859, Stampe corresponded with Bishop Peter Christian Kierkegaard, seeking his advice about a book she was writing, presumably her book on Mormonism.[61] Unfortunately, his letters to her have not been preserved, so the surviving conversation is rather one-sided. Although she didn't personally know Kierkegaard,[62] she must have been familiar with him through Grundtvig and she may have read his book *About and Against Mormonism* (1855). Stampe appears to have sent him a copy of her book for critique, most likely because of his prior experience with Mormonism. He apparently made no reply at first, so she asked, in a letter dated December 13, 1858, for the return of her manuscript. He must have replied to this second letter with a negative opinion about it, however, for she responded with the comment, "Of course I am not going to rip my book into pieces, but it must naturally occur to some people that that would be the correct thing to do. The fact that you suggested it is natural and offended me as little as it offends me when the day is done and it becomes night."[63] Bishop Kierkegaard's disapproval may have contributed to Stampe's decision not to publish her book on Mormonism, but, fortunately for posterity, she did not destroy it either.

In the foreword to her book, Stampe acknowledges the widespread prejudices against Mormonism in elite Danish society, but also expresses her determination to approach the subject objectively:

It would be asking a great deal of the reader to digest an entire book about Mormonism. And what would he say to see Mormonism presented as a great spiritual curiosity, even as something extraordinary!—Mormonism, which only attracts ignorant, uneducated wretches with no prospects, which is rarely even mentioned in the civilized world and even those who most fervently oppose false sects and doctrines cannot be bothered to waste more than at most a little, tossed-off pamphlet on! Mormonism! It is said of it that it defeats itself, but even this self-defeat is not worth attending to; Mormonism, which everyone has the right to laugh at and say "God save us!" about without knowing anything about it; Mormonism, which would make a despised social outcast of any person who dared to talk about it with the same interest that one talks of Platonism, Islam, or any religion that might be of interest to learn about. One will find this Mormonism presented here, not just as a highly interesting and enlightening phenomenon, but also as not exactly a theology but rather a combination of doctrines that poses quite serious questions, for which we need to find answers, whether it be in Mormonism itself or somewhere else.[64]

In stark contrast to Bishop Mynster's hostility or Bishop Kierkegaard's superior disdain, Stampe describes Mormonism as "a great spiritual curiosity, even . . . something extraordinary!" Her approach rejects the notion that one can dismiss Mormonism out of hand and criticizes her supposedly intellectually curious peers for their unwillingness to even discuss the topic. She invokes the common preconception that Mormonism appeals only to "ignorant, uneducated wretches with no prospects," but the very existence of her manuscript belies this notion and undermines the widespread assumption that "everyone has the right to laugh at [Mormonism] and say 'God save us!' about without knowing anything about it." She challenges her readers, whomever they might have been, to take Mormonism seriously, to consider the questions it raises, and to make a sincere effort to find answers.

Stampe begins her book by declaring her intention to identify "the strings of truth upon which Mormonism plays"—that is, the elements of commonality between Mormonism and Danish Lutheranism, "that which blinds about Mormonism, which gives it the appearance of truth in the eyes of many seeking the truth." More than any other nineteenth-century Danish commentator on Mormonism, Stampe does not dismiss Danish Mormons as deluded or ignorant, but instead attempts to account for Mormonism's appeal to respectable, intelligent people like her friend. This is her audience, she explains, for it is "with regard to those souls both among the Mormons and the non-Mormons who have some truth in them that this entire book has been written." Stampe defends her decision to look for the truths contained in Mormonism: "Those things that are true in themselves can more easily attract a mind in which there is some truth than outright lies are able to." Her intention, as she states on several occasions, is to show how these leavening elements of truth are distorted or corrupted in Mormon doctrine, but her willingness to admit their existence and their attractive power for truth-seekers is remarkable for her time and place.

With considerable philosophical finesse that reflects both her wide-ranging education and her propensity for discussing theology with Grundtvig, Stampe distinguishes not just between truth and lies, but also between truths that can become untruths in particular circumstances.

She explains, "Although that which is true in and of itself can more easily appeal to what we people would call an honest mind that that which is entirely false, it does not necessarily follow that that which is true on its own merits is therefore always true." For example, even though it is true that the earth needs rain for grain to grow, she says, too much rain at one time can cause seed corn to rot, making the statement "it is good that it is raining, for the earth needs rain for grain to grow" untrue in that context. By the same token, she notes, the fact that something is approved by the world does not make it true, nor does being persecuted by the world make something false: "Even though the world, civilization, and the bourgeoisie's common opinion brand something as despicable, it can still appeal to the truth in a mind that has the courage to defy the world, civilization, and the bourgeoisie."

Applying this principle to Mormonism, Stampe exhibits empathy, even admiration, for the courage it required for her countrymen to convert to a religion as unpopular as Mormonism, whatever its flaws. Such determination, she explains, requires "a conscience that dares to stand against the opinion of all the people in the whole wide world, resting in God." This stance demonstrates the kind of inclusivity that Grundtvig advocated for the Danish church as a whole, although he did not propose extending the "capaciousness" of the Danish church to include Mormons. Stampe seems to suggest that the complete social isolation converts to Mormonism experienced gave them access to powerful spiritual experiences and undermined their peers' attempts to dismiss Mormonism out of hand: "Most people who condemn Mormonism with the most sincere conviction of their entire souls and have never felt a moment's pang of conscience in that regard do so, however, without out the same kind of peace of conscience that . . . comes from having experienced what it is like to have no other witness on your side except God." In Stampe's view, having "no other witness on your side except God" brings with it an inner peace that can actually strengthen an individual's faith, even if that person's beliefs are untrue.

By contrast, Stampe deems reflexive, unconsidered rejections of Mormonism to be inconsistent with a Christian's responsibility to consult with God on matters of faith. Her goal is therefore to show the elements of "absolute truth" contained within Mormonism in order to demonstrate, with the peaceful consciousness of having God on her side, "that the [Mormon] doctrine has nonetheless been weighed and found wanting," in hopes of leading truth-seekers back into the fold of the Danish Lutheran Church.

Stampe's book demonstrates a remarkable familiarity with Mormon scripture and doctrine, despite her own protestation that she had very few resources available to her during its composition. Although she does not identify any of her sources, it is evident that she conducted both textual research and face-to-face conversations with Danish Mormons. In discussing the Mormon claim to a restored gospel of Jesus Christ, she reports: "The first time one meets a Mormon and asks him why he has left *Folkekirken*, one will immediately hear him say: because *Folkekirken* does not believe in revelation. And that is why, he will say, I became a Mormon, because no other church in the entire world except the Mormon church believes in revelation." She explains in great detail the Mormon view that most modern-day Christians, including Danish Lutherans, claim to believe in the revelation contained in the scriptures, but disprove that same belief by failing to accept the renewal of divine revelation as alleged by the LDS Church:

> If one answers him that we others build on the Holy Scriptures, which are precisely the revealed Word, he will say that if we had lived at the time when the words of the Scriptures were revealed, we would not have believed them. . . . The world pretends to believe in revelation but despises everything contemporary that claims to be revelation. . . . If it were true what you say about believing in the New Testament and hoping for its promises, then you would greet us with joy when we arrive with the blessings you claim to expect, we who announce the fulfillment of that which you hope for, we who proclaim the breaking of a new day, whose dawn you claim to await with longing.

In this passage, which takes up nearly two manuscript pages, Stampe allows her anonymous Mormon respondent full freedom to represent his (or her) own views of Mormon doctrine.

Rather than attempting to rebut these claims, Stampe instead elaborates upon them with quotes from Parley P. Pratt's tract, *A Voice of Warning*, which was one of the earliest LDS publications in Danish, as well as from the Doctrine and Covenants, which she describes as "the Mormon Book of Revelation." She is careful to correct the common misapprehension that the Book of Mormon is the Mormons' new Bible, for, as she explains, "Mormons do not regard the Book of Mormon as a newer book, but a very old one, which contains (according to them) the word of God that is just as old as the revelations contained in both our Old and New Testaments." Instead, she chooses to focus on the Doctrine and Covenants—compiled revelations received by the prophet Joseph Smith between approximately 1830 and 1844—because it illustrates how modern Mormon revelation "lives and works within living people." She finds the Doctrine and Covenants to be "a much more tasteful and spiritual application of Biblical style, tone, and character than anything I have found in the Book of Mormon."

Citing several passages of the Doctrine and Covenants she feels are particularly beautiful, Stampe argues that such poetry ought to be acknowledged by Danish educated society, if only on aesthetic grounds:

> Even in the old pagan myths and heretic beliefs, the founders of which died many centuries ago, one can find beautiful elements and bring out something or other as a pleasant thought, such as, for example, Ingemann has done by bringing to our attention Mohammed's beautiful description of the two angels on his right and left shoulders. The fact that the thought occurred to Mohammed did not prevent any of us, although we regarded him as a false prophet, from giving widespread approval to the lovely idea, while now as soon as the conversation turns to the heretic religion that is widely despised by the educated, every thought that it contains is mocked as ridiculous, even as sheer nonsense, even when thoughts are found within in that would be praised to the skies if they had been uttered by one's own poets or in other places.

This line of argumentation recalls Johannes V. Jensen's comments about the aesthetic merits of Dalsgaard's painting, which Jensen felt compensated for its somewhat bizarre subject matter. Both Stampe and Dalsgaard seem willing to suspend judgment on the truth of Mormonism in order to acknowledge the ways in which it contributes to the beauty and complexity of Danish culture.

In the remainder of her manuscript, which fills a large stack of blue notebooks, Stampe evaluates several Mormon teachings, including: the apostasy from Christ's original church, the restoration of Christ's church through Joseph Smith, the concept of three degrees of glory in the afterlife, the practice of proxy baptisms for the dead, and polygamy. She also discusses the general relationship between Mormon and Lutheran understandings of the Bible, baptism, repentance, and communion. Her explanations of Mormon doctrines that would have been unfamiliar to Danish Lutherans are meticulously supported by scriptural passages and other publications by LDS church leaders. She raises questions about many of them and rejects others outright, but she treats each topic if not dispassionately than without rancor. Her approach is scholarly, rather than dogmatic, which allows her to calmly lay out her objections to particular Mormon doctrines without casting aspersions on the intelligence or sincerity of those Danes who chose to believe them.

Although Stampe's ultimate conclusion is that Mormonism misinterprets certain central doctrines of Christianity and contaminates the truths it does contain with falsehoods, her determinedly open-minded approach to understanding Mormonism exemplifies the kind of religious tolerance that Grundtvig endorsed. Stampe's careful, balanced, empathetic treatment of Mormonism as an important part of Danish intellectual and spiritual life both reflects her mentor's teachings on inclusivity and anticipates the gradual development of a more tolerant approach to religious difference within Danish society. Her book on Mormonism was never published, however, and she frequently alludes to the fact that her Danish contemporaries regarded Mormonism as something ridiculous to be despised and scorned, despite the fact that so many of their countrymen had embraced it.

This disdain reveals that Danish society's self-identification as Lutheran Christian still carried enormous psychological and emotional weight more than a decade after the legal separation of religious and national identity. The eventual psychological separation of these two concepts would require much more time and more public discussion of what it meant to be Danish, what it meant to be a Danish Mormon, and what commonalities between these two groups could outweigh their differences.

Søren Kierkegaard's *Attack on Christendom*

No other text demonstrates the systemic changes that would be required to extricate Danish cultural identity from Lutheranism better than Søren Kierkegaard's series of essays, published during the final two years of his life, that are known collectively as the *Angreb på Christendommen* (*Attack on Christendom*). While both Elise Stampe's and Peter Christian Kierkegaard's views of Christianity and reactions to Mormon theology were very much in line with those of their common mentor, N. F. S. Grundtvig, Søren Kierkegaard disagreed with Grundtvig's interpretation of Christianity as a group endeavor and had a fundamentally different view of the Danish Lutheran Church. While Grundtvig focused on the confession of faith in the baptismal liturgy as evidence of an essential continuity between the church of the New Testament and his own time, Søren Kierkegaard rejected the institutional church "as a legitimate form for the historic manifestation of Christianity."[65] In fact, as Bruce Kirmmse argues, Kierkegaard "rejected 'the notion of the congregation' as such."[66] Instead, he believed religious faith was an exclusively private matter between the individual and God, and that allowing people to believe they could attain salvation simply by belonging to a national community self-designated as Christian was a cruel delusion that kept people from seeking God on their own. While Søren Kierkegaard had little to say about Mormonism directly, placing his critique of the Danish Lutheran Church alongside his brother's and Elise Stampe's views of Mormonism offers valuable insights into the way Danish Mormonism embodied certain aspects, though certainly not all, of Kierkegaard's view of New Testament Christianity.

Tremendously intelligent, well-educated, and financially independent throughout his life (as a result of his father's business successes), Søren Aabye Kierkegaard (1813–1855) belonged to Denmark's privileged cultural elite. He was generally conservative in his political views, if only in the service of dialectical critique, and was not initially a proponent of democracy or constitutional religious freedom. He detested the nationalist fever that infected his countrymen in the wake of the First Schleswig War (1848–51) and feared that the indiscriminate enfranchisement of the common man would lead to his being subsumed into the uncritical mass rather than truly empowered as an individual. At the same time, however,

FIGURE 2.4 *Søren Kierkegaard* (ca. 1840), engraving based on a pencil sketch by his nephew, Niels Christian Kierkegaard. The philosopher Søren Kierkegaard was considered eccentric by most of his Danish contemporaries, but his writings have had an impact around the globe in the century and a half since his death. Reproduced courtesy of the Danish Royal Library, Copenhagen, Department of Maps, Prints, and Photographs.

Kierkegaard was a radical thinker regarding the individual's need to take responsibility for his or her own relationship to God. Just as unfettered democracy can encourage a lackadaisical attitude toward participating in political discourse, Kierkegaard felt the Danish Lutheran Church had robbed Danes of the desire and need to work out their own salvation before God by encouraging them to believe the church was meeting all their spiritual needs.

Only a few months after his brother debated the Mormon missionaries in Haugerup in August 1854, Søren Kierkegaard launched a campaign against the Danish Lutheran establishment, producing what was to be his last work, the so-called *Attack on Christendom*. Consisting of a series of polemical articles published in the leading national-liberal newspaper, *Fædrelandet*, and in Kierkegaard's self-published journal, *Øjeblikket* (*The Moment*), in 1854–55, the *Attack* presents Kierkegaard's most sweeping indictment of contemporaneous Danish society. He critiques the unity of state and church that had been an integral part of Denmark's political structure for nearly a thousand years and calls for the "permanent, legal, and final separation of Church and state."[67] Many of the pseudonymous texts from Kierkegaard's first authorship, primarily from the 1840s, aimed veiled satirical critiques at certain facets of Danish society, while religious themes dominate his second authorship. In these final texts, however, the religious and the political come together in Kierkegaard's denouncement of the dominant and domineering position of the Danish Lutheran Church as an obstacle to true Christian belief.

The *Attack* begins as an impassioned public denouncement of Bishop Martensen's hagiographic treatment of the recently deceased Bishop J. P. Mynster as part of "the holy chain of truth-witnesses stretching back to the days of the apostles,"[68] and ends by challenging the legitimacy of the entire Danish Lutheran establishment. Kierkegaard contests Bishop Martensen's characterization of Mynster as a "truth-witness" on the grounds that Mynster did not suffer for the gospel but instead profited from the preaching of it. In Kierkegaard's opinion, *Folkekirken's* pastors responded to the potential threat to their congregations (and thus their tax base) that the introduction of religious freedom posed by continuing to emphasize the reassuring blessings of Christianity rather than its more stringent spiritual requirements. Kierkegaard objected to this "comfortable" version of Christianity, particularly the status of Danish pastors as well-paid bureaucrats whose salaries depended on lulling their parishioners into a sense of complacent self-righteousness instead of prompting deep reflection and potentially painful self-examination. For Kierkegaard, despite his reservations about the potential costs of democracy, the new constitution did not go far enough in its reforms of the Danish Lutheran Church. Rather than just making a superficial change to the church's structure and extending the rights of citizenship to non-Lutherans, Kierkegaard wanted to overthrow the established order and dissolve the institution of the state church altogether in order to free its members from the illusion of being good Christians merely by having been born in Denmark. The *Attack on Christendom* aims to call out the Danish church on its theological flaws and strip its members of their illusions of easy salvation, but in the process it challenges the political solution that preserved state sponsorship of the Danish church and thus the symbiosis of national and religious identity that had been central to Danish culture for centuries.

While the *Attack on Christendom* does not manifest the same degree of structural and philosophical complexity as many of Kierkegaard's earlier, pseudonymous texts, it is still a dense, multifaceted work that employs sophisticated rhetorical strategies and vivid metaphors from everyday life. All of the texts in the *Attack* are attributed to Kierkegaard himself, but his narrative persona bears a striking resemblance to some of his pseudonymous alter egos, particularly in the repeated protestation that the writer is not himself a Christian but simply an imperfect person striving to become a Christian. Like several of Kierkegaard's earlier texts, the second series of articles in the *Attack* are self-published, funded by the remnants of Kierkegaard's inheritance. They could conceivably be dismissed as vanity publications divorced from audience demands, but the first series appeared in a mainstream newspaper, which presupposes a certain readership size. Many of these articles engage explicitly with responses to previous ones, demonstrating that they were provoking a reaction among readers.

In his memoirs, Bishop Martensen reports that Kierkegaard's articles "created ill-will" toward the church among the common people and "contributed in no small measure to the growth and strengthening of unbelief in this country."[69] Yet Martensen himself acknowledges, however reluctantly, that religious indifference and opposition toward the church was already a common phenomenon among Danes at the time. Many Danes found legitimization for their own views in Kierkegaard's *Attack*, whether they wanted to join a different religious community than *Folkekirken* or be free from religious obligations. All of these details confirm the relevance of the *Attack* to the restructuring of traditional institutions of governmental and societal authority that is, on a macro level, a hallmark of the modernization of European societies in the nineteenth century and which, on a micro level, made possible the introduction and spread of Mormonism in Denmark.

Although firmly rooted in Danish Lutheranism and Pietism, Kierkegaard's challenge to the dominance of *Folkekirken* was just as destabilizing to the orderliness of Danish society as the clarion call of the Mormon missionaries to throw off the yoke of social oppression and gather to Zion. On one level, the *Attack* outlines Kierkegaard's particular theological position, which defines faith as inherently resistant to rational comprehension and privileges the individual's striving for a relationship with God over the community of believers' mutual support and enjoyment of the rituals of worship. On another level, however, the *Attack* is an implicitly political work, a series of short texts intended to incite the average Danish newspaper reader to rebellion against the state church and its pastors.

In the ironically titled essay "Vi er Alle Christne" ("We Are All Christians"), Kierkegaard makes it clear that true religious freedom would come at a significant cost to social order and the financial stability of *Folkekirken*'s pastors. He illustrates this with a hypothetical example, but one that would soon be within the realm of possibility in Denmark:

> If a person were to live among us, a free-thinker, who, in the boldest of language, declared all of Christendom to be a lie, *item* in the strongest language declared himself not to be Christian: it will do him no good; he is a Christian. According to the law, he can be punished, that is something else entirely, but a Christian he remains. "What nonsense," says the State. "What will it lead to? If we allow one man to declare himself not a Christian, it would surely end with everyone refusing to be Christian. No, no, *principiis obsta* [nip it in the bud] and stand by our principles. We have all of the records in order, everything is organized, everything has its place, based on the assumption that we are all Christian—*ergo* he is also a Christian; such conceit, that just wants to stand out, cannot be tolerated; he is a Christian and thus it stands [emphasis in original].[70]

In this text, Kierkegaard alleges that the state's fear of losing both the political clout and cultural cohesion provided by a national religion rests on an implicit acknowledgment that compulsory religion stunts the individual's spiritual growth.

The imaginary bureaucrat's complaint—"What will it lead to? If we allow one man to declare himself not a Christian, it would surely end with everyone refusing to be Christian"—suggests that Danish Christianity is just a façade imposed by tradition and regulation, not the expression of true religious conviction. Once granted in 1849, religious freedom and its consequences could not be undone, as the spread of Mormonism in the 1850s made plain. Nevertheless, the cultural pluralism facilitated by religious freedom, however burdensome it might be to state bureaucracy, has played a central role in the development of modern Danish society, including the inevitable secularization that Kierkegaard foresaw.

Although there is no cohesive narrative across the texts that make up the *Attack*—each essay is a self-contained unit taking an irreverently critical view of the Danish Lutheran Church and clergy—Kierkegaard does not simply lay out an array of theological quibbles with the state church that could be solved by reforms. Instead, he challenges the legitimacy of the very concept of a state church, which exists, in his view, primarily to ensure social order and earn money for itself, with little regard for the individual's adherence to Christian doctrine. In some areas his critiques overlap with individual points of Mormon doctrine—for example, regarding the benefits of a lay clergy and the problematic implications of infant baptism.

In one satirical essay, "At Præsterne ere Menneske-Ædere, og paa den Afskyeligste Maade" ("That the Pastors are Cannibals, and in the Most Abominable Way"), Kierkegaard denounces paid clergymen as "cannibals" who sustain themselves and their families by devouring authentic truth-witnesses: "He has these glorious ones in salt-meat barrels."[71] He mocks the idea that the state can certify pastors as Christians, as if a "royal certificate" were enough to shape reality[72]; chastises the state for enticing young theology students with the promise of a lucrative career path at the expense of their faith[73]; and demands the abolition of the one thousand "royal livelihoods for teachers of Christianity," since the existence of these royal appointments ensures there will always be at least one thousand people to fill them. He explains,

Among these there may be a few who perhaps have discovered a call to proclaim Christianity. But at the very moment when they should really do this in earnest by taking the responsibility of acting as teachers at their own risk and trusting only in God— then the state offers them the comfort of accepting a royal post, whereby these few are, Christianly, spoiled. The far greater number will have no call whatever to proclaim Christianity but will regard it simply as a livelihood.[74]

Kierkegaard's condemnation of state-funded pastors is related to his critiques of the state church for fostering the "spiritlessness"[75] that he believed afflicted the Danish people. The professionalization of Christian discipleship causes average church members to ignore the need to develop their own religious consciousness and fail to exercise their religious agency, having delegated that responsibility to their pastor. He describes complacent Danish Lutherans as fatted geese ready for the slaughter, unwilling to try out their wings to see if they can fly. Again and again, he critiques the automatic equation of Danishness and Christianity as repressive and stunting, preventing individuals from achieving self-knowledge in order to preserve social order.

In another essay, "Hvad Man Saadan Kalder en Christen" ("The Sort of Person Who Is Called a Christian"), he outlines his objection to infant baptism on the grounds that, though a newborn cannot possibly make such a serious commitment as baptism implies, the church performs infant baptisms for the financial reward of securing a large membership:

A silk-clad pastor gracefully sprinkles water over the sweet little baby three times, gracefully dries his hands with a towel—
—and one dares to offer this to God in the name of: Christian Baptism. Baptism; it was by this holy ceremony that the Savior of the world was consecrated to his life's task, and after him the disciples . . . promised to live as sacrificed ones in this world of lies and evil.
Yet the pastors, these holy men, do indeed understand their job, and likewise, that if it were to be, as Christianity unconditionally must require and every reasonable person, that not until one has reached maturity and the age of discretion does one receive

permission to decide what religion one will have—the pastors understand very well that then their livelihood would never really amount to much.[76]

As a result of this subordination of spirituality to profitability, the state church had become, in Kierkegaard's opinion, the greatest obstacle to the individual's ability to become a true Christian.

The early nineteenth-century Danish church over which Bishop Mynster had presided was primarily concerned with protecting social order, not fostering the individual's relationship with God. This inversion of priorities was a major cause, Kierkegaard believed, of the lack of "earnestness" among his Danish Lutheran contemporaries. In the essay "Læge-Skjønnet" ("The Medical Opinion"), Kierkegaard charges that religious conditions in Denmark are wretched and the "people are in a pitiable condition religiously," but that the proposed solutions are purely cosmetic: "one person thinks that it would help if we had a new hymnbook, another a new altar book, a third a musical worship service, etc., etc." After permitting himself this little jibe at Bishop Mynster's expense (Mynster had proposed all of those reforms), Kierkegaard proposes a more radical solution—the complete separation of the church from the state:

> This whole junk heap of a state Church, where from time immemorial there has been, in the spiritual sense, no airing out—the air confined in this old junk heap has become toxic. Therefore the religious life is sick or has expired. . . . Let this junk heap tumble down, get rid of it; close all these boutiques and booths . . . and let us once again worship God in simplicity instead of making a fool of him in magnificent buildings. Let it again become earnestness and cease to become play—because a Christianity proclaimed by royal officeholders, salaried and protected by the state, using police against the others, a Christianity such as that has as much connection with the Christianity of the New Testament as swimming with a life jacket or water wings has with swimming—it is playing. Yes, let it happen. What Christianity needs is not the suffocating protection of the state; no, it needs fresh air, persecution, and—God's protection.[77]

As long as the state dictates the terms of Christianity, Kierkegaard argues, the state's needs will take precedence over the requirements of the gospel and the individual will never learn to engage earnestly with God.

Kierkegaard believed the spiritual consequences of this state of affairs for the individual would be immense. At the end of "A Medical Opinion," he tells of a patient who is starving to death, not from a lack of food, but because he does not know what hunger is. "So it is religiously," he warns: "The most corrupting of all is to satisfy what is not yet a need. . . . Yet this is what is done in the religious sphere; people are thereby cheated out of what is the meaning of life and are assisted in wasting their lives."[78] While Kierkegaard was himself very devout, he insisted on the importance of the individual's own choice of the religious sphere; it would be less sinful, he asserted, to carouse and debauch and murder than to mock God by pretending faith without true belief. Some may choose the aesthetic sphere and others the ethical, but the important thing is that they choose for themselves.

This insistence on individual choice is one of the most strikingly modern aspects of Kierkegaard's work. As Danish historian Søren Mørch asserts, one of the hallmarks of modern Danish life is the almost infinite array of choices involved in shaping one's individual identity.[79] Religion was a fundamental aspect of Danish identity for at least one thousand years, but it was not something an individual could choose, at least not until 1849. In his 1844 *Begrebet Angest* (*The Concept of Anxiety*), Kierkegaard defines anxiety as "the dizziness of freedom," acknowledging that freedom can be daunting to exercise. The June Constitution gave Danes the freedom to choose their own religion, but Kierkegaard insisted that they needed to choose for themselves whether and how they would worship God.

It is no coincidence that Kierkegaard's outspoken critique of Danish state-sponsored religion appeared just a few years after the establishment of religious freedom in Denmark, which had already destabilized the dominance of the Danish state church and allowed individual Danes to choose their own means of worshipping God. Despite his apparent aversion to politics and his concerns about the ability of the people to govern themselves, Kierkegaard regarded the advent of religious freedom in Denmark as an opportunity to help people "differentiate between religion as an absolute and prior commitment of the individual to God *and* religion as a socially supportive institution" (emphasis in original).[80] His outspoken assertion of the individual's ability and responsibility to choose for himself, in matters both political and religious, rather than accepting the judgment of the masses, the media, or the authorities is closely linked to the modernization of Danish society over the course of the nineteenth century. It anticipates a fundamental distrust of official institutions that characterizes modern, twenty-first-century societies. His insistence on the need for individuals to make earnest but often unfashionable choices about their convictions, their identity, and their relationships to God ultimately positioned him as a seminal influence on the gradual liberalization—and, paradoxically, the secularization—of Danish society.

Indirect Communication between the Brothers Kierkegaard

Even though both Peter and Søren Kierkegaard held passionate and conflicting opinions about religious freedom, the brothers Kierkegaard did not ever publicly debate their positions, either before or after the adoption of the Danish constitution. As a result, their respective views on the subject have rarely, if ever, been juxtaposed. However, that does not mean they didn't communicate about the subject, merely that their communication was, appropriately enough, indirect. The close chronological proximity of Peter's *About and Against Mormonism* (1854–55) to Søren's *Attack on Christendom* (1854–55) offers an opportunity to explore the implicit dialogue between the brothers. Since Søren's *Attack on Christendom* commenced in December 1854 and culminated in the spring and summer of 1855, it is possible, though not documented, that Søren had read Peter's text about Mormonism while writing the *Attack*. Regardless, juxtaposing these texts will allow us to see how the brothers' opinions on religious freedom and cultural identity relate to Denmark's increasing cultural heterogeneity as represented by the spread of Mormonism.

The personal relationship between Peter and Søren Kierkegaard provides important background for this implicit dialogue. The Kierkegaard brothers shared many character traits and one passionate interest inherited from their father: religion. From a family of six children, they were the only two still alive by the time Søren was twenty-one years old and Peter was twenty-nine, which might have drawn them closer

together were it not for their very different but equally firm views on religion. Both men were influenced by the devout Pietism of their father,
Michael Pedersen Kierkegaard, but their reactions to this influence
took them on very different paths. Peter supported Grundtvig's concept of a church founded on the oral confession of faith, while Søren
insisted on a text-grounded interpretation of Christian doctrine rooted
in the New Testament.

Although Søren Kierkegaard's name and works are known across the
globe today—by scholars and intellectuals if not the general public—
while his brother has been forgotten (even in Denmark), the situation
was very different during their lifetimes. Leif Grane explains,

> If a foreigner or a Dane returning from abroad had asked, in 1850,
> who Dr. Kierkegaard was, it is most likely that he would have been
> informed about Peter Kierkegaard, who was a well-known and
> respected man in the public sphere, perhaps with the offhand
> comment that there was also another Dr. Kierkegaard, namely
> his brother Søren, who wrote strange books, with which very few
> people knew what to do. It is true, that Søren's criticism of the
> dominant theology had recently attracted attention, because of
> the publication of Hans L. Martensen's *Christian Dogmatics*, but
> most people were probably more interested in what Peter had to
> say, both about his brother and about Martensen.[81]

Peter studied theology at the University of Copenhagen, was appointed
a parish priest in Sorø, and became very prominent in Danish intellectual
and political circles, while Søren completed degrees in both theology
and philosophy but never held down a formal job. Instead, he mean-
dered conspicuously through the streets of Copenhagen and published
copiously under a range of witty pseudonyms as well as his own name.

The brothers' different views of religious freedom proved to be a hindrance to their personal relationship. Søren disagreed with Grundtvig, as
he often noted in his diary, but he did not speak out against him publicly,
perhaps out of respect for his brother. In 1845, however, when Peter was
pressured to participate in the forcible baptism of Baptist infants into the
Lutheran Church and sought Grundtvig's assistance to defy this order,
Søren wrote to his brother to express not only his sympathy for Peter's

situation but also his solidarity with the conservative Bishop Mynster, on whose insistence the Baptist ordinance had been issued. Peter's decision to publicly denounce his brother's views on religion led to a prolonged estrangement between them. In an October 1849 speech to a pastoral convention in Roskilde, Peter described Søren as "an ecstatic," in contrast to Martensen, whom he described as levelheaded.[82] Søren was furious and hurt by this incident, which he interpreted as an accusation of being insane. Even on his deathbed in November 1855, Søren refused to see his brother, but left Peter nearly all of his belongings, including his papers, journals, and manuscripts. Peter delivered his brother's eulogy at a funeral service held, at Peter's insistence, in the Church of Our Lady in Copenhagen on November 18, 1855.

This decision to allow Søren to be buried as a member of *Folkekirken* infuriated both Bishop Martensen, who raged at the "*tactlessness* shown by the family in having him buried on a *Sunday*, between two religious services, from the nation's *most important church*" (emphasis in original)[83] and Søren's favorite nephew, Henrik Lund, who protested during the funeral that the church "has laid violent hands upon him [Kierkegaard]. It has condemned itself by regarding him as 'a Christian,' i.e. as a member of the 'official Christian Church.'"[84] By holding the funeral under the auspices of *Folkekirken* and thereby implicitly asserting its claim on his brother, Peter Kierkegaard chose to uphold the status quo and disregard his brother's self-exclusion from Christendom. By contrast, Henrik Lund defiantly asserted the primacy of his uncle's own convictions, whatever the social repercussions of his choice of religious identity. This historical moment, which so uncannily echoes Kierkegaard's essay "We Are All Christians," illustrates the tension between the administrative orderliness of a state in which everyone belonged to the same religion and the disorderliness generated by the freedom to choose differing religious identities.

Unlike Peter's lengthy treatise on Mormonism, Søren never directly addressed either the existence or the beliefs of Danish Mormons in his public writings. He alludes to Mormonism only a handful of times in his voluminous diaries, and then only indirectly or peripherally. In 1854, for example, Søren Kierkegaard noted his amusement over the clergy's agitated but hypocritical opposition to the new sects that had established themselves in Denmark, of which the LDS Church was by far the largest.

Under the heading "Formentlig Hævd" ("Presumed Prescriptive Right"), he comments,

> It is quite amusing to see the shamelessness with which the official clergy, in connection with sects and the like, always know how to direct attention to the fact that it is really about money. And the congregations view this as entirely in order—because the official clergy indeed has a prescriptive right to make a profit for themselves. But if profit is reprehensible in religious matters, then the official clergy is much worse than the sectarians, inasmuch as the official clergy has guaranteed itself far more profit and, in addition, enjoys the profit of honor and esteem.[85]

Later that same year, in the entry "Bagvendt Fremskridt" ("Backwards Progress"), he comments on a book by a German professor named Jacobi about the Irvingian movement, which apparently claims that "the Mormons assume that God is not present at all places at the same time, but moves with great speed from star to star. Fantastic!"[86] He then muses about how progress usually entails intellectual movement from fanciful to more rational theories, but speculates that perhaps the development of the telegraph and the railroad prompted this retrograde explanation. That is as much direct commentary as Søren devoted to the topic of Mormonism.

Yet, despite the lack of any direct contact between Søren Kierkegaard and the Mormons, some of Søren's Danish critics saw a clear connection between his critique of Folkekirken and the growing popularity in Denmark of non-Lutheran religious groups, including the LDS Church, and blamed him for the perceived destabilization of Danish society. In May 1855, an anonymous article in Kjøbenhavns Posten (The Copenhagen Post) denounced Søren Kierkegaard for attempting to overthrow the Christian establishment in Denmark. It concludes scathingly, "The only thing he can have cause to be proud of is that he has worked on behalf of Catholics, Mormons, and other sects, and that he is praised by those who define freedom of religion as being free of all religion."[87] This article thus recalls the prophecy made five years earlier by Bishop J. P. Mynster that the introduction of religious freedom in Denmark would lead to the destruction of all religion. It also underscores the importance of Danish

Lutheranism as a source of public order rather than a vehicle for individual religious engagement, which the mass conversion and emigration of Danish Mormons threatened to destabilize.

Other critics argued that Søren's radically individualistic theology and challenge to the legitimacy of the Danish church was akin to Mormonism's claims of apostasy and restoration. In an article published in *Dansk Kirketidende* on August 25, 1855, Peter's Grundtvigian colleague, Lutheran pastor Vilhelm Birkedal, protests that endorsing Søren's unorthodox view of God is blasphemous, equivalent "to spitting in our Lord's face by making him, as the Mormons do, a gambler who has overplayed his hand and must lock his doors, because he can no longer redeem his own promise, which states that 'the gates of Hell shall never prevail over His Church.'"[88] This accusation is almost identical to Peter's charge in *About and Against Mormonism* that the Mormons' insistence on the disappearance of Christ's church from the earth undermines the divinity of Christ. The irony in Birkedal's comment, of course, is that Søren conceived of God as anything but unreliable. In his 1851 sermon "On the Unchangingness of God," Søren praises the eternal sameness of God amid the changeability of human existence:

> At every moment he holds all actuality as possibility in his omnipotent hand, at every moment has everything in readiness, changes everything in an instant, the opinions of people, judgments, human loftiness and lowliness. He changes everything—himself unchanged. . . . One complains about the changefulness of humanity, about the changefulness of everything temporal, but God is changeless; that is the consolation, sheer consolation, so says even light-mindedness. Yes, indeed God is changeless.[89]

It is in this firm belief in the unchangingness of God, in his decision *not* to change despite his unlimited power to do so, that Peter and Søren Kierkegaard might have been able to find common ground. Peter's own writings, including *About and Against Mormonism*, similarly affirm the immutability of God in relation to his church and his covenant people.

Yet where Peter felt threatened by the possibility of his parishioners choosing to change their religious affiliation in order to either draw closer to or disconnect entirely from God, Søren advocated boldness in spiritual

matters. He cautioned his readers to avoid being fattened up on compla-
cency, like geese destined for slaughter on St. Martin's Day, and encouraged them to instead try their wings and fly on the strength of their own
convictions. Where Peter saw in the Mormons' insistence upon the constitutional right of Danes to religious freedom a threat to the established
order of Danish society and the stability and harmony of his own parish,
Søren supported the expansion of that right to include the option not
to believe anything at all. In the hypothetical situation posited in "We
Are All Christians," in which the state cannot allow a free-thinking man
to proclaim he is not Christian for fear that everyone would follow his
lead and abandon the church, Søren articulates the fear implicit in Peter's
active campaigning against the Mormons: that unrestrained freedom of
religion in Denmark might lead to freedom *from* religion—from morality and social order—and to the collapse of a collective Danish identity
founded upon shared Christian faith.

It is in the semantic minefield regarding the definition of being a
Christian that both the crux of Peter's opposition to the Mormons and
Søren's attack on Christendom are located. From Søren's perspective, as
expressed in the essay "Den Religieuse Tilstand" ("The Religious Situation"), Peter's distinction—like his brother-in-law Christian Anker
Winther's—between Mormon and Christian would be irrelevant, since
the entire country of Denmark at the time was, "as it is called, a 'Christian' nation but in such a way that not a single one of us is in the character of the Christianity of the New Testament, no more than I am."[90]
Where Peter asserts the legitimacy of the claim of all Danish Lutherans
to call themselves Christian by virtue of their membership in the state
church, Søren contends that such large-scale, indiscriminate use of the
term invalidates it. He argues instead that Christian is a designation that
must be earned by the individual's "sobriety of spirit, the integrity of eter-
nity."[91] By this standard, Mormons and Muslims would have equal access
(or lack thereof) to the possibility of earning the designation Christian
alongside Lutheran Danes, dependent upon each individual's personal
commitment to a lifestyle in harmony with the values enshrined in the
New Testament.

Thus, despite the many differences between Søren's view of Christianity and Mormon doctrine and the fact that he would most certainly

have objected to the theocratic tendencies of the LDS Church in the nineteenth century, Søren's definition of Christian would encompass Danish Mormons just as easily (or not) as Danish Lutherans. While Peter Kierkegaard insists on the unbroken continuity of the transgenerational community that makes up Christ's holy catholic church (and protests the Mormons' physical and doctrinal disruption of the same), Søren Kierkegaard declares that the process of "becoming a Christian in the New Testament sense is designed to work the individual loose (as the dentist speaks of working the tooth loose from the gums) from the context to which he clings in immediate passion, and which clings in immediate passion to him."[92] In Søren's opinion, God requires this painful isolation from society and family as the price of discipleship, of becoming a Christian. If society no longer lives up to this standard, he argues, it is not because God has changed it but because the church does not teach it.

Since Mormon missionaries and their converts in Denmark believed in and lived the principles of being willing to sacrifice society, family, and friends in order to follow the will of God, they were entitled, in principle at least, to call themselves Christian according to Søren Kierkegaard's standard. Where his brother mocked the lay Mormon missionaries in Haugerup for their lack of theological training and shabby clothing, Søren advocated a return to the New Testament practice of preaching, as Mormon missionaries did, "without purse or scrip," though he was aware from his own self-financed publications that such a practice would arouse public contempt. In a diary entry in 1854, in which he rails against his brother for demanding 2,000 rigsdaler in salary as a professor of theology at the University of Copenhagen, he explains, "When someone works without pay, people regard it as madness, but on the other hand, the more he earns from his efforts, the more they respect him."[93] It is more than likely that Søren would have applauded the Mormons' endurance of mob violence and harassment in cities across Denmark as proof of the strength of their faith and devotion to Christian truth. As he declares in the essay "Præsten Ikke Blot Beviser Christendommens Sandhed, men Han Modbeviser den med det Samme" ("The Pastor Not Only Demonstrates the Truth of Christianity, but He Simultaneously Refutes It"): "That which is able to inspire the human being to sacrifice everything in this way, to risk life and blood, must be the truth."[94]

Conclusion

The disagreements between Peter and Søren Kierkegaard, Christian Anker Winther, N. F. S. Grundtvig, and Elise Stampe over the extent to which Mormons should be characterized as Christian may seem anachronistic in light of today's highly secular Danish society. However, the discussion to which each of these authors contributes implicitly revolves around questions of national belonging and cultural identity—that is, what it means to be Danish and whether one could be Danish and Mormon at the same time. While Peter Kierkegaard subscribed to Grundtvig's close identification of Danishness and Lutheran Christianity, Søren felt automatic association was antithetical to his conception of individualistic Christianity. Grundtvig himself supported the individual's right to determine his or her own religion, but he felt the best place for such explorations was within the bounds of a "free state church" that could bring people of various Lutheran denominations together. Elise Stampe surpassed her mentor in terms of her willingness to look for truth and beauty within Mormonism, despite the fact that it defined itself in opposition to, rather than as a subset of, *Folkekirken* and thus the predominant national faith community. Even Christen Dalsgaard's reading guide to his painting *Two Mormons* reveals the tensions between tradition and novelty, between conformity and risk-taking, that emerged in mid-nineteenth-century Denmark over the question of religious belief. Both paths offered unprecedented opportunities for individual self-determination as well as unforeseen dangers to the cohesion of the national community.

Each of the individuals whose works were examined in this chapter belonged by birth, education, profession, or social status to nineteenth-century Denmark's cultural elite, even though their degrees of personal affinity with that categorization varied widely according to gender, profession, and areas of personal interest. Their pronouncements and speculations about religious freedom, particularly regarding Mormonism in Denmark, can thus be viewed as representative of attempts by this cultural elite to come to terms with the effects of the new freedoms granted to the Danish people by the June Constitution. It is easy to forget that "national culture" was a relatively new concept in mid-nineteenth-century Denmark, the product of both Enlightenment ideas of the nation and, rather paradoxically, romanticism's rejection of the Enlightenment ideal of the universality of reason. The rise of romantic nationalism placed new emphasis on a shared cultural identity in place of the political-religious fellowship centered on an absolute monarch that had characterized the Danish state for two centuries. Denmark's cultural elite, from the romantic poet Adam Oehlenschläger to the gifted dramatist Johan Ludvig Heiberg, played a leading role in shaping this new Danish national culture, but that role gradually began shifting to the people themselves, as we will see in the next chapter.

The Danish high culture responses to Mormonism considered in this chapter depict it as many different things: as a source of hope for the weak and empowerment for the downtrodden, as a threat to public order and the stability of Danish social hierarchies, as a grandiose delusion and devious marketing ploy for emigration, as a misguided but poetic attempt to restore faith in the common man's access to the divine, and as a courageous but misguided attempt to live New Testament Christianity. None of the authors discussed in this chapter joined the Mormon Church, but their serious, generally critical—but also occasionally sympathetic—engagement with both Mormon doctrine and the social repercussions of Danish Mormonism reveal the extent to which Mormonism factored into public discourses about Danish cultural identity in the 1850s on every level of society. By their very existence, Danish Mormons embodied the possibility—and made evident the increasingly urgent necessity—of crafting new definitions of Danishness that could encompass a greater range of difference than the automatic equation of Danish identity with Lutheran belief.

3

"Mormons, Mormons!"

Provocative Portrayals of Mormonism in Danish Popular Culture

How did the average Dane in the late nineteenth and early twentieth centuries view his or her Mormon countrymen? How consciously did members of the Danish public reflect on their own cultural identity and consider how it was changing in tandem with and as a result of the increase in religious difference in Danish society, particularly as symbolized by the growing numbers of Danish Mormons? In the absence of eyewitness testimony from most of the roughly two million people who lived in Denmark at any given time between 1850 and 1920, Danish popular culture—particularly such genres as newspaper articles, popular music, theater, and film—offers an important access point for understanding the average Dane's view of Mormonism. Such texts also reveal how popular perceptions of Mormonism intersect with and illuminate changes in Danish cultural norms.

Nearly everyone in Denmark came into contact with Mormonism during this period in some way, either directly or indirectly. Many were visited in their homes by traveling missionaries or attended a public meeting, while others had friends, neighbors, or family members who joined the LDS Church and immigrated to Utah. While such personal encounters with church representatives were undeniably important in shaping individuals' views of Mormonism and its compatibility with Danish culture, they were often preceded and preconditioned by depictions of Mormonism in Danish popular media. The changing tone and style of such portrayals over time reflect ideological and existential shifts taking place in Danish society, revealing not only the way the public's criticism of Mormonism evolved but also how Danes viewed their own community and the Mormons' position within it.

After the first wave of boilerplate anti-Mormon articles in the 1850s, the greatest number of newspaper articles and diverse other cultural products depicting Mormonism—including caricatures, songs, and films— appeared in Danish media during the 1860s to 1880s, after the initial, alarming novelty of Mormonism had given way to familiar contempt, and then again in the 1910s, when a perceived connection between Mormonism and white slavery gave rise to a renewed wae of public interest. The songs, stories, and images about Mormons that Danes of this period read, heard, saw, and discussed with their friends and families shaped the ways in which they viewed Mormonism and treated its representatives and adherents in Denmark. Such media portrayals, regardless of their accuracy, contributed significantly to the social construction of Mormonism's public image in Denmark as something inherently foreign, even dangerous, to the Danish national character and culture. Psychologist Claude M. Steele argues that when people feel their sense of self is threatened, they are strongly motivated to reaffirm the beliefs that define their identity rather than explore the validity of the challenge.[1] In addition to reflecting negative public opinions of Mormonism, therefore, depictions of Mormonism in Danish popular culture also reveal the public's preoccupation with its own cultural identity, which was in flux due to the rapidly changing political and social parameters of Danish life around the turn of the twentieth century.

As a result, Danish popular cultural texts about Mormonism from this period tell two distinct stories. The overt, surface narrative deals with the question of how Mormonism and its distinguishing features, in particular its perceived oddities and eccentricities, differ from and challenge traditional, mainstream Danish Lutheran culture. The other, implicit narrative describes Danishness in terms of the norms and values that were regarded as foundational for Danish culture, the customs and beliefs that could be taken as self-evident, and the collective self-image upon which the depiction of Mormon "otherness" is predicated.

Although some media depictions of Mormonism were openly hostile, others that presented themselves as objective or simply humorous often concealed implicit value judgments that were shared by their readers and were thus imperceptible. In Denmark, negative attitudes toward Mormonism became "the seemingly inevitable norm based on which most discussion of the movement tended to proceed,"[2] requiring little commentary or explanation. In his study of the representation of Mormonism in the nineteenth-century Finnish press, Kim Östman notes that while print media depictions of Mormonism frequently labeled the movement as "other," the depictions themselves were not the sole source of this perception.[3] Instead, they reflect opinions and attitudes informed by disruptive societal trends, such as democratization, urbanization, and modernization. The media simply became the mouthpiece for articulating and reinforcing such perceptions.

With that in mind, it is important to note that while media depictions of Mormonism in Denmark during this period were almost universally negative, their focus and tone changed subtly but distinctly over time. This change came about as a result of both the Danish people's increasing familiarity with Mormonism as a religious and social movement as well as the rapid secularization and liberalization of Danish society around the turn of the twentieth century. During the first few years after Mormon missionaries began converting large numbers of Danish citizens, serious doctrinal condemnations of the LDS Church appeared regularly in Danish newspapers and periodicals, as well as in book form. As the numbers of both converts and emigrants peaked and began to drop off toward the end of the century, however, such scholarly treatments became quite rare. Instead, Mormonism became a popular subject for more humorous and entertainment-oriented media depictions in print, in song, on the stage, and on screen—somewhat like the Tony Award-winning Broadway musical *The Book of Mormon* (2011) that has been performed in New York and around the world in recent years.

Over the seven decades between 1850 and 1920, the mob violence and theological denouncements of Mormonism discussed in the preceding chapters gave way to parody and farce. Although there are, of course, individual exceptions, this general shift away from condemning Mormon heresies and toward laughing at Mormon idiosyncrasies draws attention to how Mormonism in Denmark functioned as a foil for defining mainstream Danish identity. While the earlier texts employ an "otherness-promoting hegemonic discourse," by which an image of Mormonism is identified as something foreign or "not us," later representations of Mormonism in Danish popular culture rely on a "counter-discourse that offers nuance and calls into question some aspects of the Mormon image of otherness," thereby promoting a view of Mormonism that is imbued with a sense of "familiarity, normalcy, something related to and more or less part of 'us.'"⁴ This type of counter-discourse becomes increasingly apparent in popular media treatments of Mormonism in the decades surrounding the turn of the twentieth century, as the specter of Mormonism—particularly regarding emigration and polygamy—is most frequently depicted as a familiar eccentricity used to critique Danish culture itself.

It is not feasible in this chapter to provide either a quantitative or comprehensive survey of references to Mormonism in Danish popular culture between 1850 and 1920, nor is it necessary, thanks to the efforts of Danish historian Jørgen W. Schmidt. In the early 1980s, Schmidt published a compendium of articles about Mormonism in Danish newspapers that appeared between 1850–1851⁵ as well as a chronological listing of Danish publications relating to Mormonism between 1837 and 1984.⁶ Instead, the following pages consider the qualitative aspects of the types of representations to which Mormonism is subjected in the Danish media of this period in order to reveal the two narrative strands discussed above. Analyzing *how* Mormonism was depicted at a particular time can illuminate the underlying societal trends in Danish society and culture informing the depictions. Although the Mormon missionaries in Denmark established their own periodical, *Skandinaviens Stjerne* (discussed in chapter 4), this chapter focuses exclusively on portrayals of Mormonism in Danish media outlets by non-Mormons. The types of media depictions discussed in this chapter date from the early 1850s through the mid-1920s and include newspaper articles, street ballads, revue songs, and silent films.

The Mormon Threat to Danish Monogamy

One of the topics that featured most prominently in Danish mass media treatments of Mormonism in the late nineteenth and early twentieth centuries century was the contemporaneous Mormon practice of polygamy (more specifically polygyny, since only men were allowed to have multiple spouses) or plural marriage, as it was often referred to within the LDS community. Although LDS Church founder Joseph Smith began practicing plural marriage in the early 1840s, claiming to have received a divine revelation that he do so, it did not become a common practice within the Mormon community until 1852, after the church had established itself in the Utah

Territory. The Mormon endorsement of polygamy as a divine commandment was not known in Denmark until 1853, when it was announced publicly
by John van Cott, president of the LDS mission in Scandinavia at the time.

Public media discussions in Denmark about Mormon polygamy
focused on four major concerns. The first was simply the alleged immorality and exploitative nature of plural marriage itself, which posed a
perceived danger to women who, as a Pastor Vahl warned in the book
Is Mormon Doctrine True or Not?, "are weighed down with sins and subject to all manner of lusts."[7] Many of the anti-Mormon publications in
newspapers from the 1850s and 1860s fixate on the problem of polygamy
and cite it as evidence of not only the inherent depravity of Mormon
theology but also a related and fundamental incompatibility between
Mormonism and Christian society in Denmark.

The second area of concern involved the question of whether Danish
converts to Mormonism had adopted the practice of polygamy, which
was illegal in Denmark. In a newspaper article published in *Dansk Kirketidende* (*Danish Church News*) in 1854, Pastor H. C. Rørdam publicly
accused the Mormon community in northern Jutland of "living in sin,"
which prompted the minister of religion to conduct a survey of *Folkekirke*
pastors in Vendsyssel, a region in northern Jutland with a high percentage of Mormons, about immoral behavior.[8] The results vindicated the
Mormons, but indicated that Danish Lutherans had moral challenges of
their own. Bishop Bindesbøll of Aalborg concluded, "After the passage
of three years [since the Mormons arrived in Aalborg], only one case of
fornication among 157 Mormons can be proven, while in the rest of the
population, 15% of children have been born out of wedlock."[9] Striking a
similar note, Pastor Hass in Hals wondered if "Dr. Rørdam has, based on
inaccurate information, confused the *Vendelboer* [residents of the Vendel
area] with the Mormons, for 'living in sin' is quite common among *Vendelboer* and can continue to affect those who have become Mormons."[10]
These responses indicate that, contrary to the perception that Danish
Mormons were more likely to live an immoral lifestyle as a result of their
new faith's peculiar doctrines, in fact the Danish Lutheran population
was already engaging in extramarital sexual activity.

A third concern related to Mormon polygamy among Danish critics
was the fear that Danish women who converted to Mormonism and
immigrated to Utah would be forced into becoming the plural wives of

older men. This scenario was a fertile source of material for the *Skill-ingsviser* (street ballads), which served a similarly voyeuristic popular entertainment function as reality television shows do today. While seri-ous anti-Mormon tracts warned women away from the Mormons by underscoring the danger of such a fate, more entertainment-oriented media depictions proffered woeful laments about girls who had already made that grievous mistake. They also made fun of Mormon polygamist families, particularly church leader Brigham Young, who was rumored to have dozens of wives.[11] Rather than warning Danish men against the practice of polygamy, however, street ballads tended to mock them for embracing it, as the song "Ole Peersen og Hans Kone Dorthes Rejse til Mormonerne" ("Ole Peersen and His Wife Dorthe's Journey to the Mormons"), discussed later in this chapter, illustrates.

The final aspect of Danish opposition to Mormon polygamy, partic-ularly in the first few decades of the twentieth century (after the LDS Church had officially renounced the practice), was the suspicion that it was merely a cover for selling women into white slavery, more specifi-cally sex slavery. By the turn of the twentieth century, concerns about the white slave trade had given rise to international collaborative efforts— such as the French organization *Les amies de la jeune fille* (Friends of Young Women) and the German *Jungfrauenverband* (Young Womens' Association)—to raise public awareness of the existence of the white slave trade, protect young women from falling victim to it, and bring its perpetrators to justice.

The Danish National Committee for Combating the White Slave Trade was established in 1898 for the express purpose, as committee chairman Axel Liljefalk declared in a 1911 report, of exposing "those monsters in human form who dishonor and debase their fellow crea-tures as completely as can be imagined out of miserable greed."[12] Lilje-falk described these efforts as a "crusade, in which Jews march alongside Christians and do their own share of the work," born from the conviction that it is the will of God that "the human race must cleanse itself of the shame, infamy, and unhappiness that the white slave trade brings upon it."[13] Although Liljefalk claimed his crusade was blind to nationality, lan-guage, or faith, he made explicit charges against the LDS Church in a 1914 report that held the Mormon missionaries in Denmark directly responsi-ble for the disappearance of more than ten thousand Danish women per year. These accusations led to a published debate with an LDS member of the Danish Parliament, F. F. Samuelsen, whose biography is discussed in chapter 4. Allegations of a connection between Mormonism and white slavery also feature prominently in several early Danish silent films discussed below.

Mormonism in Danish Print Media

As mentioned in chapter 1, print media provided one of the most influential and far-reaching venues for articulating and discussing conceptions of Danishness in the nineteenth and early twentieth centuries. The period from 1848 to 1917, which spans from the end of absolutism to World War I and encompasses the peak years of Danish Mormonism, has been described as the golden age of the Danish press.[14] In this period, processes of urbanization and industrialization caused the population of major Danish cities—notably Copenhagen, Aarhus, and Aalborg—to increase exponentially, while the development of a network of inexpensive public schools across Denmark raised literacy rates among members of the lower social classes, thereby expanding the market for newspapers, books, and other print media.

The more than four hundred newspapers (albeit many of them short-lived) that sprang up in Denmark in the wake of the June Constitution's guarantee of freedom of the press played a crucial part in mediating public discourses about Danish national and cultural identity. As a result of the massive geopolitical shifts Denmark experienced during the mid-nineteenth century, from the abolition of the absolute monarchy in 1848 to the loss of Schleswig and Holstein in 1864, the country completed its drawn-out transformation from a medieval multiethnic empire into a modern, more or less ethnically homogenous nation-state.[15] The foreign policy disaster of the Second Schleswig War in 1864 provided a powerful impetus for national introspection about the nature of Danishness and a critical (as well as humorously self-deprecating) examination of the factors, such as Mormonism and emigration, that seemed to threaten it.

Coverage of Mormonism in Danish print media during this period was, unsurprisingly, generally negative. This tendency was not unique to Denmark; in fact, it illustrates the same type of antagonistic relationship to Mormonism that was displayed by Protestant churches in the United States,[16] except that Danish society was, for all intents and purposes, exclusively Protestant, while the religious landscape in the United States was highly diverse. Based on her study of American newspaper coverage of Mormonism between 1860 and 1960, historian Jan Shipps concludes, "If the author could definitely be identified as Protestant, whether religious leader or not, the article was seven times more likely to be negative."[17] This predisposition toward a negative view of Mormonism, reinforced by the fact that many of the most outspoken Danish critics were in fact Lutheran pastors, set the tone for nearly all discussions of Mormonism in Danish newspapers. That does not mean, however, that all newspaper coverage of Mormonism was exactly the same, nor does it lessen the relevance of such texts for determining how Mormonism functioned as a foil for defining Danish identity.

Certain thematic trends emerge in the articles that were published about Mormonism in different eras. The handful of references that predate the arrival of the Mormons in Denmark are generally articles about America that include some description of Mormonism as an American novelty, either referring to the peculiarities of Mormon doctrine, the death of Joseph Smith, the conversion of Norwegian immigrants in Illinois, or the settlement of Utah. Once the Mormon missionaries had established the LDS Church in Denmark, the articles became more concerned with the relationship between Mormonism and Danish society, particularly the ways in which Mormon doctrine and the treatment of Danish Mormons reflected on Danish cultural norms. For example, several of the articles that appeared in the first year after the church's arrival in Denmark condemn the mob violence against the Mormons even as they criticize or ridicule Mormon theology for various doctrinal points, such as the belief in prophets and continuing revelation.[18]

Many of the articles published during the 1850s and 1860s explicitly aim to dissuade potential converts, either through doctrinal explication or scandalmongering. One early example that combines both strategies is the five-part article, "En Advarsel mod de Falske Profeter" ("A Warning against False Prophets"), that appeared in the *Lolland-Falsters Avis* (*Lolland-Falster Newspaper*) and *Flyveposten* from September 29–November 7, 1851.[19] However, the majority of doctrinal treatises appeared as small books and pamphlets, particularly after the 1850s. After large-scale Danish Mormon emigration began in 1852 and polygamy was officially confirmed in 1853, articles purporting to expose the miserable living conditions of the convert-immigrants in Utah, often in the form of (fictional) letters from emigrants or reports from Protestant missionaries in Utah, made up the majority of Mormon-related newspaper items.

The number of newspaper articles about Mormonism lagged significantly behind the rate of conversions to Mormonism, but they appeared with increasing frequency over the course of the 1850s and 1860s. As the missionaries held successful meetings, baptized converts, and organized congregations, the perception of Mormonism as a persistent threat to the status quo and not merely a fleeting foreign oddity grew exponentially. The only explicitly anti-Mormon newspaper article to appear in 1850 was the reprint of an excerpt of Bishop Mynster's booklet, "The Provisions of the Constitution with Regard to Religious Conditions in Denmark" (discussed in chapters 1 and 2), on the front page of the *Aalborg Amtstidende* (*Aalborg County Times*) on December 14, 1850, which provides a brief, rather derogatory history of the LDS Church. This publication was followed, in the same paper a week later, by a proposed petition to the Danish Parliament in favor of suspending religious freedom, pending a popular referendum, since, as its authors bemoan, "the Mormon sect here in town continues to grow and now boasts ca. 30 members."[20] In 1851, however, more than twenty-four articles appeared in eight different Danish newspapers, primarily in Aalborg and Copenhagen—where preexisting Baptist congregations had given the Mormon congregations a solid membership basis—as well as on the island of Bornholm, where Mormon missionaries had arrived in June 1851.

Since newspapers are, after all, in the business of selling papers, their primary concern is printing information their readers will find interesting, not necessarily promoting a particular view of morality. Mormonism was an international curiosity that many Danish papers covered for the sake of familiarizing their readers with the world outside Denmark. A characteristic example of this kind of coverage is a six-page article that appeared in Copenhagen's *Illustreret Magazin* (*Illustrated Magazine*) on September 2, 1854, under the headline "Brigham Young." Accompanied by a large engraving of Brigham Young, "the leader or president of the Mormons," the article describes him as "equipped with a rare intelligence, sensitivity, and cleverness; with a strong, energetic, and pleasant character; inherent boldness and competence; in short, with all of the qualities necessary to unify and rule over a checkered mass of people of different characters and educational levels, of different tribes and tongues."[21] Two weeks later, the magazine ran a portrait and biographical sketch of Joseph Smith.

The remainder of the Brigham Young article strikes a much more critical tone than the introductory paragraph, describing the history of the LDS church and its doctrines as "surpass[ing] everything we can recall having read or heard in arbitrariness, confusion, and contradictions."[22] Although the article mentions the activity of Mormon missionaries in many parts of the world, it does not acknowledge their presence in Denmark or refer directly to the many thousand Danes who had converted to Mormonism by this time. It does, however, reflect the Danish sense of affront resulting from the Mormons' insistence not only that they are Christians, but that "they alone are true Christians, while all other so-called Christians are thus in essence nothing but heathens."[23] The unstated implication is that Mormonism both denies the legitimacy of Danish Lutheranism and seeks to supplant it.

This dispute over Danish Christianity is crucial for understanding the function of Mormonism as an Other against which Danish cultural identity could be measured, a subtext that underlies many of the articles about Mormonism in Danish newspapers. Bishop Mynster's 1850 diatribe against religious freedom prophesied the dissolution of the state church and the danger to religion in Denmark in general if religious freedom was adopted. Such anxiety over the creeping secularization of Danish society was aggravated by the Mormon predilection for condemning Danish Lutheran pastors as "heathens" and declaring that "no Christian church exists in Denmark."[24] Such accusations outraged many Danes, although the same allegations prompted others to join the Mormons in search of the salvation they no longer believed *Folkekirken* could give them access to.

Though religion had provided an unshakable foundation for Danish national identity for centuries, it no longer sufficed to define a more diverse Danish society. The anonymous author of an article titled "En Advarsel mod Falske Profeter" ("A Warning against False Prophets") that appeared in *Flyveposten* in October 1851 speculates that the popularity of Mormonism in Denmark, as well as in England and the United States,

Illustreret Magazin

Nr. 36.   Kjøbenhavn. Løverdagen den 2den September.   1854.

Brigham Young,

Mormonernes Overhoved eller Præsident, som oprindelig var Tømmermand af Profession og som nu er omtrent 50 Aar gammel — er ligesom Sectens Stifter, Joseph Smith, født i Staten Vermont. Denne Mand var en af Mormonismens første Bekjendere. Han er udrustet med en sjelden Forstand, Omsigtighed og Klogskab, med en fast, energisk og udholdende Charakteer, indvortes Driftighed og Dygtighed, fortsagt med alle de Egenskaber, som udfordredes til at sammenholde og regjere over en broget Menneskemasse af forskjellig Charakteer og Dannelse, af forskjellige Slægter og Tungemaal; thi, som bekjendt, udsende Mormonerne Missionairer til alle Verdens Hjørner, og de have da ogsaa bragt afstillige Tilhængere fra andre Lande, selv fra andre Verdensdele (Europa) over til  Saltsøen i Nordamerika, hvor Mormonerne i den senere Tid have opstaaet deres Paulsmuer. — Men forat give Læseren et tydeligere Begreb om Sagen, meddele vi her et kort Omrids af Sectens Historie fra Begyndelsen af.

Om Mormonismens Oprindelse kan bemærkes følgende: Sectens Stifter, Joseph Smith, hans Fader og hele Familie

horte til den Slags Folk i Amerika, som kaldes „Saltgravere", det vil da egentlig sige Bedragere, der reise omkring og bilde eenfoldige og lettroende Mennesker ind, at de have fundet Guld-, Sølv- eller andre Miner, men trænge til Hjælp for at kunne benytte dem; de fortælle ogsaa, at de vide, hvor Skatte ligge skjulte i de gamle Gravhøie, hvoraf der findes en Mængde i Amerika; og paa denne Maade fraliste de Folk hvad de selv behøve.

Den unge Joseph Smith blev snart bekjendt for sin Snildhed og sit gode Hoved, Faderen gav ogsaa at forstaae, at der vilde blive Noget af den Dreng, enten General eller Præsident i Fristaterne. Men Joseph Smith blev berømt i en anden Retning, nemlig som Sectstifter eller Reformator. Hertil gave de religieuseOpvækkelser, som dengang fandt Sted i Amerika, den første udvortes Anledning. Først drog han omkring som Skattegraver og forgav at have fundet en Steen, som havde den Egenskab, at naar den laa i hans Hat, kunde han see de skjulte Skatte i Jorden. Saaledes bedrog han mange Lettroende under mangfoldige Paaskud; men Skatterne kom aldrig for Lyset. Og nu vendte han Bladet om, og begyndte at foregive, at han havde overordentlige Syner og Aabenbaringer, at Christus selv havde vist sig for ham i en skinnende Glands, og

2den Aargang.

must be connected to "the confused state of Christianity in our time, when one person teaches thus and another thus, when only few even know what Christianity is."[25] He notes that Mormon teachings challenge the validity of Lutheran infant baptism, question the divine authority of Lutheran pastors, criticize the lack of prophetic revelation to guide *Folkekirken*, and allege that the state church is corrupt.[26] Although he rejects Mormon doctrine, the author does not shy away from the disheartening conclusion that "if our baptism has been distorted and rendered invalid, then the church door has been locked and the church has vanished from among us."[27] Regardless of whether Danes embraced Mormonism, the missionaries' charge that Danish Lutheranism was corrupt resonated with philosopher Søren Kierkegaard's criticism of the state church, discussed in chapter 2, and aligned with the increasingly secular orientation of Denmark's intellectual and artistic elite, such as literary critic Georg Brandes and authors Herman Bang and J. P. Jacobsen.

Once Mormonism had become firmly established in Denmark, more sensational stories about Danish Mormons began to appear in various newspapers, emphasizing their difference from mainstream Danish culture, particularly with regard to religious belief and practice. Most such stories are jokes or mocking anecdotes, such as a parody of the Ten Commandments "as a Mormon farmer should explain them to his hired hands" that appeared in the humorous weekly paper *Krydseren* (*The Cruiser*) on April 11, 1856.[28] Structured like a Lutheran confirmation primer, each Biblical commandment is paired with an ostensibly "Mormon" explanation for how it is to be interpreted. For the first commandment, "Thou shalt have no other Gods," the article explains, "You should above all things fear, love, and rely on Joseph Smidt [*sic*] and Brigham, along with all of the other inventors of doctrine, and not concern yourself with Balle's Catechism or the like; for those books might make you more clever than the average Mormon, which would not be appropriate!"[29] The image of Mormons conveyed in these few lines is one of simple-minded, deluded, oppressed idolaters, in implicit contrast to the newspaper's implicitly educated, enlightened, Lutheran readers. The casual manner in which the article throws out references to Joseph Smith, Brigham Young, John van Cott, elders, Zion, and polygamy suggests these terms were familiar enough to the average Dane not to require explanation.

As its tone of derisive familiarity makes apparent, the article makes no pretense at offering a faithful representation of Mormon doctrine or even an earnest rebuttal of the same, but instead satirically exaggerates Mormons' veneration of their prophet and founder Joseph Smith and his successor Brigham Young. It suggests that, for Mormons, blind devotion to church leaders replaces true worship of God. Moreover, with its dismissal of "Balle's Catechism," an annotated edition of *Luther's Little Catechism* by Bishop Nicolai Balle that all Danish schoolchildren were required to study until 1856,[30] the article insinuates that Mormons did not value education, particularly religious education of the kind that contributed to the civic training of all Lutheran Danes. The newspaper's readers might have been aware that conflicts had arisen between Mormons and the Lutheran pastors who ran most Danish schools in the nineteenth century. In many cases, some of which will be discussed in more detail in chapter 4, pastors refused to accept Mormon children as pupils, Mormon students were bullied by their peers, or Mormon parents removed their children from Lutheran-run schools rather than allow them to be taught Lutheran doctrine. In a few instances, Mormon communities in Denmark opened their own schools to avoid raising children in a system that conflated secular and religious education. The first Mormon primary school in continental Europe was established in Aalborg in April 1851 in response to severe persecution of the children of Mormon converts in the area.[31]

The rest of the "commandments" elaborate on the same theme of Mormon ignorance and idolatry—alleging that Joseph Smith is regarded as the Mormons' god; that corrupt and authoritarian church leaders aimed to fleece their Danish converts and seduce their wives; that the converts themselves are deluded enough to believe that the moon is made of green cheese and the sun of clay; and that traveling to Zion will result in poverty, misery, and exploitation.

By contrast, a series of articles published by journalist Henrik Cavling (1858–1933) in the left-leaning Copenhagen daily newspaper *Politiken* in January 1889 offer a rare example of relatively unbiased coverage of Mormonism and its relationship to Danish culture in print media during the late nineteenth century. Cavling wrote his articles while visiting Utah, which allowed him to rely on firsthand impressions to inform his opinions. In doing so, he followed in the footsteps of a handful of Danish travel writers, such as Vilhelm Topsøe (1840–1881) and Robert Watt (1837–1894), both of whom visited the United States in the 1870s and devoted approximately one hundred pages each to depictions of Mormonism in Utah. Cavling, who served as editor-in-chief of *Politiken* from 1905 to 1927, later rewrote many of the articles with a much more negative spin for inclusion in his 1897 book, *Fra Amerika* (*From America*).[32] However, the original articles offer a much more objective depiction of Mormon life, particularly regarding polygamy, than other Danish print media depictions, including Topsøe's and Watt's. Jørgen Würtz Sørensen suggests that Cavling's decision to later distort his initial descriptions of Mormonism was a result of the uniformly hostile reception of his article series, which drew fire from both the Danish and Scandinavian American press for its apparently favorable treatment of Mormonism, as well as from the Scandinavian Mormon newspaper *Bikuben* (*The Beehive*), which took offense at his coquettish depiction of Mormon women.[33]

Published in 1872, Topsøe's *Fra Amerika* (*From America*) is a sober, largely factual description of the landscape and its history. His account of the Mormons is generally dispassionate, with a few disparaging comments about the unattractiveness of Mormon women and their lack of fashion sense.[34] Topsøe, who later became the editor in chief of the Danish newspaper *Dagbladet* (*The Daily Paper*), reports on conversations with a few Mormon leaders, including Apostle George Q. Cannon, and a non-Mormon newspaper editor who had apparently drunk tea with King Christian and Queen Louise in Copenhagen. He does not seem to have spoken with any average Mormons, however, whom he characterizes (on the basis of their physical appearance) as "simple or in any case common and uneducated, . . . people with limited and little-developed intelligence."[35] Topsøe seems more interested in the history of Mormon missionary work around the globe and the characteristics of each of Brigham Young's wives than in understanding or explaining the attractiveness of Mormon theology for his countrymen. His only acknowledgment of the Danish dimension of Mormonism is the comment that, although Sweden had rejected Mormon missionaries, Denmark had proven to be "one of their most fertile fields,"[36] with no further elaboration.

Although similar in many respects to Topsøe's report, Robert Watt's discussion of Mormonism in his 1874 *Religieuse Sekter* (*Religious Sects*), the third volume of his travelogue *Hinsides Atlanterhavet: Skildringer fra*

Amerika (*Beyond the Atlantic: Depictions of America*), is far more sensationalistic. Watt begins by promising to illuminate some of America's social "abnormalities . . . that could never have succeeded in the old world."[37] To this end, he visits various "bizarre religious 'families' or communes," including Mormons, Shakers, and Bible Communists.[38] He acknowledges that Mormonism has been successful in recruiting converts from Scandinavia, but prophesies that it will soon "vanish as a religious community."[39] Throughout his account, Watt rehashes old allegations, such as the allegedly fictional origins of the Book of Mormon, and eagerly reports new scandals—for example, Brigham Young's financial stake in the success of the department store ZCMI (Zion Cooperative Mercantile Institution), or the danger of being either sentenced to death by Brigham Young or murdered by his henchmen for any trivial offense.

In contrast to Topsøe, Watt seems interested in forming a first-hand impression of the kinds of people who join the LDS Church. He describes several conversations with ordinary Mormons, including one young man from Lolland who had three wives and six children, but he invariably mocks them in his report, either for their belief in the truth of Mormon doctrine in general or for their practice of polygamy. He describes attending a Mormon worship service in the Salt Lake Tabernacle, which he found "characterized by crass materialism," disrupted by conversations and laughter, and generally lacking anything "that could capture and uplift one's thoughts."[40] He also spends a chapter summarizing the Book of Mormon, a copy of which he had received from Apostle George Q. Cannon. Watt concludes, "When one visits the Mormons, there are many things that arouse admiration, despite the negative overall impression one gains as a result of the teachings they preach."[41]

In his dispatches from Salt Lake City in 1889, Cavling makes a special point of reporting about Danish Mormons, with many references to encounters with his "countrymen" and exploring the apparent affinity of Danes for Mormonism. He tells of visiting a senior Mormon apostle and former editor of the *Deseret News*, George Q. Cannon, in the prison where he was serving a sentence for unlawful cohabitation and discussing with him the Mormon missionary efforts in Scandinavia. Cavling reports that Cannon, with whom both Topsøe and Watts had spoken, had previously visited Denmark, Norway, and Sweden. According to Cavling,

Cannon attributed the astonishing success of Mormonism in the Nordic countries to the fact that Scandinavians "were descended from the tribe of Ephraim, which had been chosen by God to be saved first," an explanation that both surprised and flattered Cavling.[42]

Cavling contacted some of the Danish Mormons who had immigrated to Utah to see how they fared. On one occasion, he dined with a polygamist family, in which the second wife (of six) was a native of Copenhagen. He concludes:

> We have discovered that our countrymen in Utah [are] just as good and honorable and, as is apparent, just as content in their new homeland as our other countrymen elsewhere in the United States. What many of these good people may have suffered for their erroneous religious views is their own matter. The simple fact that they suffer for a spiritual opinion at all does not seem to us to diminish their character.[43]

Cavling's endorsement of the moral virtue and integrity of his Danish Mormon countrymen in Utah, particularly the assertion that they were just as happy as the Danish Lutherans in the Midwest, is unique in nineteenth-century Danish media coverage of Mormonism, which tends to insist on the misery that must inevitably result from adopting Mormonism and emigrating to Utah.

Throughout the series, Cavling stresses that the Danish Mormons he encountered particularly appreciated his connection to Denmark, underscoring their continued interest in and affection for the land of their birth. He reports commiserating with the Danish polygamous wife mentioned above over the death of the Danish comic actor Carl Wulff, as reported in the *Illustreret Familiejournal* (*Illustrated Family Journal*) that she was reading when he visited her home.[44] In the prison where he visited George Cannon, he also encountered a Mormon elder he had interviewed in Copenhagen a few years earlier about the Mormon emigrant ship *Cato*. On both occasions, he informs his readers, the elder exclaimed, "*Politiken* pokes its nose into everything!"[45] In his memoirs, *Journalistliv* (*The Life of a Journalist*), Cavling reports that Danish Mormons invited Cavling to give a farewell speech in the Salt Lake Tabernacle, in which he "brought them greetings from their far-off home. While I spoke, the women sat and cried."[46] Given Cavling's disinterest in Mormon theology and his critical view of their society, the Danish Mormons' affection for Cavling is clearly a result of his incarnation of Danishness.

In marked contrast to nearly all other depictions of Mormonism in the Danish press, Cavling's account treats the issue of polygamy neutrally, despite—or perhaps because of—the fact that federal prosecution of Mormon polygamists was, following the Edmunds Anti-Polygamy Act of 1882, at its peak during the years surrounding his visit to Utah. He visited the offices of *Bikuben* and chronicles with sympathy its preoccupation with reporting on the fate of Scandinavian Mormon polygamists; he allows Cannon to defend his determination to obey the laws of God rather than man, even at the cost of imprisonment; he accurately describes the reports of non-Mormon missionaries to Utah about the scandalous conditions there as false; and he characterizes the federal persecution of Mormon polygamists as an obvious attempt to "get their hands on the possessions which the Mormons have acquired through incredible exertion."[47]

Cavling does not approve of Mormon polygamy, but he is sympathetic to the Mormons' legal plight and explicitly disdains the hysteria with which the topic was generally discussed in both the American and Danish press, which he labels *"præsteløgne"* (pastors' lies).[48] Declaring his own firsthand investigative reporting more reliable than the fanciful imaginings of so many other reports, he expresses indignation at the lengths to which federal investigators go to convict polygamists, including sneaking around at night to spy into homes and subjecting small children to sexually explicit cross-examination in court, "questions which under no circumstances could be reprinted in a Danish paper!"[49] In this case, Cavling is far more critical of American coarseness than the idiosyncrasies of Mormon marriage.

Even in his more negative book chapter about Mormonism, published almost a decade later, Cavling's explanation of plural marriage is succinct and pragmatic: "The introduction of polygamy was not just a result of Joseph Smith or Brigham Young's coarse sensuality, but also the practical consideration that the more wives a man married, the more children, it could be assumed, he would provide for the Mormon church."[50] While not endorsing the practice of polygamy, Cavling offers a rational explanation for its introduction. The fact that his refusal to reproduce

well-worn myths about Mormonism or indulge in sensationalistic spec-
ulation about Mormons' private lives was unpopular with his Danish
audience demonstrates the pervasiveness in Denmark of Mormonism's
reputation as dangerously foreign. At the same time, that image was in
the process of being transformed into a source of entertainment rather
than grounds for moral education.

The View of Mormonism from the Danish Street

Since the burgeoning field of Danish newspapers catered primarily to
the educated bourgeoisie, members of Denmark's lower social classes
were far more likely to get their news and opinions from sources such as
skillingsviser (literally "penny songs" or "penny ballads"). These songs,
often called street ballads, were a popular genre and a major mass media
outlet, especially among the lower social classes who were far less likely
to read newspapers, either because of illiteracy or poverty. The lyrics were
often composed by professional poets, among them the celebrated fairy
tale author Hans Christian Andersen, but also by amateurs, and they
were set to well-known melodies so they could be sung without accompaniment. These often melodramatic songs were printed on cheap, thin
paper and sold for a penny by street sellers and door-to-door salesmen
(hence the name "street ballad"), although they could usually be bought
at bookshops in larger towns as well. The most prolific and successful
publisher of street ballads in late nineteenth-century Denmark was Julius
Strandberg, who printed between two and five hundred thousand copies
a year. A single popular ballad might sell fifty thousand copies in a year,
excluding anthologies and reprints, which is an astounding number for
a country of not quite two million inhabitants.[51]

Street ballads were often written in connection with current events,
particularly scandalous, sensationalist, or violent ones such as a notorious murder case, the death of a prominent person, or a battle. Although
they told specific stories, they also dealt with general themes of love,
melancholy, Christianity, and the Danish landscape, as well as social
trends like emigration, seafaring, and urbanization. A compilation of
street ballads from the 1860s and 1870s might contain several songs
about the disastrous war of 1864, news of Princess Dagmar's departure
for Russia in September 1866, and the death of Frederick VII's morganatic
wife Louise Rasmussen (Countess Danner) in March 1874, as well as

generic laments about such topics as earthquakes, flooding, heartbreak, and infanticide. With their emphasis on immorality, stupidity, ignorance, gullibility, greed, and desperation, street ballads have much in common with the fabliau type of folktale that Hans Christian Andersen used as a basis for some of his early fairy tales, including "What Father Does is Always Right" and "Little Claus and Big Claus."

The exact number of street ballads dealing with Mormonism is difficult to determine precisely, since archival collections of folksongs in Denmark are not organized thematically but by first line. The majority of ballads that treat Mormonism do so in the context of emigration to America, with little to say about Danish Mormons who remained in Denmark. This is most likely because there was nothing particularly sensational about Danish Mormons going about their daily lives in Copenhagen or northern Jutland, while the topic of emigration and all of its potential dangers proved to be very popular with audiences over several decades. It is also possible that ballads about Mormonism were not preserved as assiduously as others, given the relatively small number of Danish Mormons remaining in the country who would have been interested in collecting them. In any case, the total number of surviving street ballads explicitly concerned with Mormonism is quite low, perhaps as few as ten—unless one includes religious hymns written by Danish Mormons, in which case the number jumps to several dozen. In his collection of Danish ballads about America, Thomas Thomsen discusses eleven ballads about Mormonism, including two hymns that were written or translated by the prominent Danish Mormon historian Andrew Jenson while serving as a missionary in Denmark. Robert and Rochelle Wright incorporate seven ballads, including three Mormon hymns, into their collection of Danish emigrant ballads and songs. Out of a total collection of several hundred *skillingsviser*, this is a very small sample in quantitative terms, but a significant one in qualitative terms, given both the extensive circulation of such ballads—far wider than any newspaper or philosophical treatise—and the insight they provide into popular discourses about Mormonism and Danish emigration.

Both those songs written by Danish Mormons and those produced by their critics tend, with a few exceptions, to be highly propagandistic, with the goal of either encouraging or discouraging listeners from immigrating to the United States. This section will deal exclusively with anti-Mormon songs, while pro-Mormon narratives will be discussed in chapter 4. Thomsen notes that in the Mormon-themed ballads written by Danish Lutherans

> Emigration is always described *negatively* without any qualifications, because the decision must appear to be a hostile action against everything that the fatherland stood for. The converted Mormons broke with the established religious direction and they wanted to emigrate in order to stay in a foreign land, as opposed, for example, to many gold-diggers. Conditions in Utah are also described negatively, by which the myth of Eldorado is not just sought to be discredited, but reformulated into a diametrically opposite myth about a *Sodom and Gomorrah* [emphasis in original].[52]

Two fundamental concerns underlay this strategy—one was undermining the pro-America propaganda that was proving to be so attractive to the general Danish population, and the other was painting the LDS Church as morally decadent. What is unique to the anti-Mormon emigration ballads, however, is the extent to which emigration was presented as anti-Danish, in that Danish Mormon emigration was not purely economically driven (as was that of gold diggers headed to California or impoverished farmers) but ideologically motivated. This fact suggests that the convert-emigrants had transferred their loyalties to a foreign country and turned their backs on their homeland and native culture.

The earliest known Danish street ballad about Mormonism was published between 1855 and 1859. Written by H. E. Nissen and published under the pseudonym R. James, it bears the title "Langt Bort til Fjerne Strand" ("Far Away to a Distant Shore") and the subtitle "The Mormon, the rich farmer Morten Petersen, who is going to the land of Zion."[53] At the time this ballad circulated, the Mormon emigration from Denmark (which started in 1852) had begun to take on significant proportions, while general emigration from Denmark had not yet begun in earnest. Until 1870, Danish Mormon convert-emigrants accounted for approximately half of all emigration from Denmark. This state of affairs, combined with the general tone of scandal in the more serious anti-Mormon treatises that appeared with some regularity in Danish newspapers and bookstores, might account for the publisher's expectation that the general public would be interested in hearing about the motivations and fate of a Danish convert-emigrant.

The ballad begins by describing the neighbors' reactions to Morten Petersen's decision to emigrate:

> Far away to a distant shore, far away to Zion's land, now Morten Petersen wants to journey at once. He sells his house and farm, and horses, cows, and sheep—you'd think the devil himself had gotten into the man. So many people ask: What's the matter with that fellow? It's all because Morten a MORMON has become. Therefore to a foreign shore, to "Zion's lovely land," he now does depart, the stupid farmer.[54]

Thomsen points out that the ballad both presents emigration as a novelty that caused the neighbors to marvel while simultaneously showing Mormonism to be a well-known con designed to trap the stupid and gullible.[55]

Though many Danish critics of Mormonism congratulated themselves that it was only the poor and landless Danes who were susceptible to the lure of Mormonism, this ballad explicitly identifies Morten as a rich landowner. Since other ballads generally perpetuated the stereotype that Danish Mormons tended to belong to the lower classes, Thomsen speculates that this ballad was intended to appeal to a higher-class audience, though he notes that a precise depiction of reality was rarely a priority for ballad-writers.[56] While that may be true, the fact that Morten is described as a wealthy man who chose to embrace Mormonism and emigrate hints at a social and economic fear of the power of Mormonism to attract even stable, prosperous citizens. This could, in turn, be read as fairly mild class criticism, reflecting the increasing empowerment of the Danish peasantry and a corresponding lack of respect for wealthy landowners.

While "Far Away to a Distant Shore" is primarily concerned with ridiculing Morten for giving up a good life in Denmark to seek his fortune among the Mormons in Utah, other ballads are more sympathetic to the emotional cost of emigration. They tend to use pathos and a first-person narrator to dissuade audiences from considering such a radical step, much like the newspaper articles purporting to be firsthand accounts of the miseries of life in Utah. The popular, widely reprinted song "Mormonpigens Klage" ("The Mormon Girl's Lament") is representative of the sentimental genre of street ballads intended to warn virtuous Danish girls away from the Mormon missionaries' promises of paradise in America.[57] Published by C. O. Jordan in Copenhagen in the early 1870s, the song is prefaced by a brief summary of the protagonist's unhappy fate:

> Including a detailed and truthful account of a rich farmer's daughter from Fyn, who a short time ago was lured by the Mormons, so that she journeyed with them to Utah, after having sacrificed great sums of money to the priests; and about how she was forced to marry a man who already had seven wives, and about how after innumerable trials she returned impoverished to her home.[58]

Although this summary alludes to polygamy as a factor in the girl's unhappiness, it is not blamed as the primary source of her anguish. Instead, this protagonist, as in the ballad of Morten Petersen, is depicted as a wealthy person who was swindled by the Mormons out of her fortune and tricked into leaving the fertile Danish countryside for the barren wastes of Utah.

While wealthy young women were not a particularly common demographic of Danish Mormon converts, this narrative circumstance increases the pathos of the fictional protagonist's situation. At the same time, however, her emotional pain at the geographical and ideological distance from her native land overshadows her financial loss. The girl's feelings of isolation and abandonment lead her to cherish "sweet memories of childhood [that] continually appear, / And speak tenderly of Denmark, my beloved distant home." She dreams of the Danish landscape, from the forests to the "sea's calm expanse," picturing the fields ready for harvest and fertile meadows populated by sweetly singing nightingales. She sees her "home, in the mists of memory, / And over there the church stands where once I was baptized; / I hear the ones I love, I recognize their voices, / But alas! No longer do they rest in my embrace."

Estranged from both the land of her birth and the faith of her forefathers, the protagonist is weighed down by sorrow, exclaiming, "How heavy it is to walk alone far from one's home." She regrets her choice to emigrate, to believe in the promises of Zion, and in the final stanza she

Mormonpigens
Klage.

Tilligemed en nøiagtig og sandfærdig Beretning om en
rig Gaardmandsdatter fra Fyn, der for kort Tid siden
blev forlokket af Mormonerne, saa at hun drog med
disse til Utah, efterat have ofret store Pengesummer til
Præsterne; samt om, hvorledes hun blev tvungen til at
ægte en Mand, der alt havde syv Koner i Forveien,
og om, hvorledes hun efter utallige Prøvelser vendte
fattig tilbage til sit Hjem.

Faaes hos E. O. Jordan, Ny Adelgade 14
(Hjørnet af Grønnegade).

FIGURE 3.2 Street ballads were one of the most common, popular, and inexpensive forms of entertainment for the majority of Danes in the late nineteenth
century, which gave songs such as "Mormonpigens Klage" ["The Mormon
Girl's Lament"] the opportunity to reach large audiences. Reproduced courtesy
of the Danish Royal Library, Copenhagen, Department of Maps, Prints, and
Photographs.

vows to pray to God for "vigor and courage and hope" to sustain her on her journey back to Denmark, for "here I cannot live, here I cannot die!" The remedy for her emotional ills is to return to the "same dear spot" where she can "smile once more at everything I see."[59]

The song itself is primarily concerned with the protagonist's sense of displacement, but it is accompanied by a prose narrative of the Mormon girl's purported biography that reproduces familiar allegations of the Mormons' duplicity and coercive tactics in luring converts both into the waters of baptism and then to Utah. This account makes an explicit claim to truthfulness, but it provides neither details of the protagonist's identity nor evidence of her alleged experiences. Instead, the ballad tends to prioritize the sensational over the plausible in order to heighten the pathos of the girl's plight. No attempt is made to account for the protagonist's susceptibility to Mormonism; the reader is simply informed that she was persuaded by Mormon missionaries to withdraw her money from Fyn's Savings Bank and give them all of her earthly possessions in order to flee with them to Utah, "where all the splendor of the world awaited her." Once there, she is reportedly forced into a plural marriage and set to labor in the fields alongside her husband's seven other wives, while "the priest did nothing but drink liquor and sleep," despite the Mormon prohibition against drinking alcohol. She is beaten when she falls down exhausted and punished for trying repeatedly to flee.

Although this ballad significantly predates the white slave trade films of the early twentieth century (discussed later in this chapter), the pattern is the same as that outlined by Axel Liljefalk in 1911: "The white slave trade is traffic in women with immoral intent. The business consists of capturing young women, who, once they have been 'broken down' (the technical term for being seduced and brought completely under their captor's will), are doomed to constant enslavement."[60] The generic tropes of forced labor and confinement that underpin later stories of English brothels and pirate ships are simply applied to Mormon polygamy and emigration.

The alleged biographical sketch concludes with the revelation that the Mormon girl was finally successful in joining up with a group of other disaffected Danish Mormons who helped her return to Denmark, where she died soon after as a result of her suffering, "with her heart turned toward the true faith, and thanking God, who nevertheless has not abandoned her."[61]

Although the girl's death is a typical feature of a white slavery narrative, the unique elements in this ballad are her return to Denmark and to Danish Lutheranism, which are shown to be inseparable. Approximately 10 percent of Danish Mormon emigrants later re-immigrated to Denmark, which is only a slightly higher percentage than for Danes in general,[62] but the significance of the Mormon girl's return to her faith gives her homecoming additional significance in terms of her cultural identity.

While such tragic ballads were quite popular, other street ballads took a comical approach by caricaturizing Mormon polygamy. One of the most popular examples of this was a parody called "Jeg er Mormon, som Du nok Ved" ("I Am a Mormon, You Surely Know"), composed and published by Julius Strandberg in 1871, which deals with "the Mormons' High Priest Brigham Young and his 16 wives."[63] In the first verse, the speaker explains, "I am a Mormon, you surely know, and therefore I have a lovely flock of wives,—sixteen, I believe." He then acknowledges, with an implicit wink and nudge, "But one can't always stay at home, of course, and so I naturally have a little on the side; since a man ought to have two mistresses for each of his wives, I've got 32 mistresses, 64 girlfriends, and 96 acquaintances." The refrain admonishes the listener, "Don't laugh!" while each of the verses laments the difficulties of taking so many wives out for hot chocolate, giving them gifts, or taking a family outing to the forest, which requires the rental of at least seven omnibuses to transport his seventy-two children, but "when my girlfriends and my wives' friends come along, we need 16 omnibuses, and some of us have to hang on behind!" Alluding perhaps to the passage of U.S. federal laws outlawing polygamy, the song concludes that "the Americans want to chase us off our land; they say we must be content with one wife at a time." Because of this, the speaker proposes that "we all run away to Mexico," as many real-life Mormon polygamists in fact later chose to do, beginning in 1885 (although Brigham Young himself did not, as he died in 1877).

While the caricature of Brigham Young was no doubt amusing to Danish audiences if only for its over-the-top exaggerations of real-life situations, the ballad "Ole Peersen og Hans Kone Dorthes Rejse til Mormonerne" ("Ole Peersen and His Wife Dorthe's Journey to the Mormons") was far more relevant to Danes' perceptions of Mormonism and its pros and cons. Written in a Jutlandic peasant dialect by Bernhard

Kølle and published by Strandberg in 1874, the ballad includes spoken monologues between verses, which suggests that it was intended for stage performance.[64] The song implicitly acknowledges the popularity of Mormonism among the residents of northern Jutland, but makes it clear that Ole's motivation for emigration was purely venal, with no pretense of religious conviction. In the first stanza, sung to the lively polka melody "Lotte Is Dead," Ole reports,

> One day to our mother I said:
> "Listen, do you know what, my dear?
> We'll go to the Mormons,
> For there it's pleasant to be.
> There they live on roasted goose
> That's filled with parsley.
> And there you and I don't need
> To do anything at all.
> Oh there, oh there, just imagine for yourself,
> Each man can keep just as many wives as he likes.[65]

In Ole's view, the attractions of the Mormon settlement in Utah are threefold: abundant food, a life of leisure, and polygamy. In the following monologue, he notes that his wife, Dorthe, didn't like the idea of her husband taking additional wives and "started to bawl as if she'd been whipped. But when I said that the women up there had it as good as the day is long and the night too, that they never do anything except stuff themselves with all kinds of steak and drink good aged beer and then go to bed and get up again, she changed her mind."

Neither Ole and Dorthe's grossly unrealistic expectations of America nor the inevitability of their disappointment are unique to Danish Mormon emigrants. In fact, the words of Strandberg's song echo the Norwegian-American folksong "Oleanna," written by Norwegian journalist Ditmar Meidell in 1853, published by Strandberg in Denmark, and made popular in the United States in the twentieth century by folksinger Pete Seeger. "Oleanna" mocks the would-be residents of famed Norwegian fiddler Ole Bull's failed mid-nineteenth-century colony in Pennsylvania for their belief in a paradise without work. Not only is this mythical land free for the taking, but the farm takes care of itself: "The little pigs they roast themselves, / Then trot around this happy land / With knives and forks stuck in their backs / Inquiring if you'd like some ham."[66] The cows milk and churn and make cheese, calves slaughter and flay themselves, "and the sun shines so faithfully all night, so you can see in the dark like a cat."[67] Even the famous writer Hans Christian Andersen wrote a parody song, for the operetta *The Count of Kenilworth* in 1836, which promises, sarcastically, that in America, "Every chestnut's roasted; / Loving kindness all around. / The springs are of champagne! / . . . / And on field and meadows / Only money blooms."[68] The trope of the disillusioned immigrant was thus quite well worn by the time the ballad of Ole Peersen appeared, but Strandberg gave it new currency by placing it within a Mormon context.

When Ole and Dorthe get to Utah and set themselves up as pioneers, they are disappointed in every aspect of their new life. Their transatlantic voyage makes them seasick, their house is a ramshackle hut, and the man who claims to be a prophet is a "hideous ruffian" with "a belt around his stomach with four guns stuck in it." Cultivating the desert requires Ole to "toil . . . like a mule," but he can't get an alcoholic drink "for love or money." Instead of roast goose stuffed with parsley, Ole and Dorthe eat nothing but potatoes and salt pork. As for polygamy, it is not the harem of fair maidens or the private brothel that public imaginings made it out to be. Ole complains that the prophet has a flock of "young women only" with whom he has fathered around "four million children," but when Ole is assigned two additional wives, he moans, "God spare me, poor miserable wretch," for Dorthe gives him no peace: "To humor Dorthe, I had to toss out those two and be content with my own grating old lady."[69]

In the end, when their anticipated new life of ease and pleasure turns out to be illusory, Ole and Dorthe decide to return to Denmark, declaring, "The devil can keep this place. / Here I must toil like a horse, / And barely get enough food, / No, in Denmark it is best, / There you get porridge and cakes. / . . . Now I've sworn never again to leave Denmark!" Although Ole and Dorthe's motivations were always self-interested and they cannot claim to be the victims of any deceit but their own gluttony, the solution is the same as it was for the mistreated girl in the previous song: return to Denmark. In this case, however, the audience is not expected to feel pity, but rather to laugh at Ole and Dorthe's misadventures and their gullibility in believing the promises of both the Mormons in particular and America in general.

By the 1880s, mainstream Danish emigration had overtaken Mormon emigration and there was little market for the kinds of anti-emigration diatribes and parodies of Mormonism that had been popular in earlier decades. Instead, one of the last Mormon-themed street ballads to appear from Strandberg's press pushes the satirical tone that was already evident in "Ole Peersen" even further, making fun of both Mormon and anti-Mormon Danes for their venality and gullibility. This strategy is evident in a ballad Strandberg published in July 1884 under the title "Den Sidste Nye Vise om de to Kjøbenhavnske Murersvende der Solgte Deres Koner" ("The Most Recent New Song about the Two Journeymen Masons from Copenhagen Who Sold Their Wives"), with the subtitle, "For 2,000 crowns to a Mormon priest, who journeyed to Utah with them."

Like the other ballads discussed above, "Two Journeymen Masons" positions itself as a realistic account of a true event, though no evidence exists to support it and the first stanza admits the story is based on hearsay. Entertainment value trumps truth value, however, and "you can truly believe / that it's a good story,"[70] as the song itself proclaims. According to local gossip, two journeymen masons "squabbled constantly with their wives / Who wanted to journey to the Mormons, / And walk on boulevards with philanderers / And sing the sacred notes." The situation is not, in fact, implausible—the percentage of female converts to Mormonism was somewhat higher than male converts in Denmark and cases of a converted spouse emigrating alone were not unheard of, though certainly not the norm. These women are not, however, the focus of this song, whatever their beliefs. Instead, the audience's attention is directed at the two men and their relationship to their wives, religion, and homeland.

The masons seem at first to represent the home-loving, nationalistic viewpoint that was reaffirmed at the end of both "A Mormon Girl's Lament" and "Ole Peersen." In response to their wives' entreaties, they protest, "Here in Denmark it's fine. / That's as clear as day. / And why should we then / Journey away?" It is soon revealed, however, that their reasons for wanting to stay in Denmark have nothing to do with the dense forests, peaceful oceans, or Lutheran churches longed for in "A Mormon Girl's Lament." Instead, they are afraid of repeating Ole's mistake and finding themselves adrift in a dry (in more than one sense of the word) Mormon desert: "Here we're acquainted with the pavilions, / We know the ropes and kick up a row, / There's life enough in the old fellows here, / What would we do there with the Mormons?"

The idealized, romanticized Denmark that figured in "A Mormon Girl's Lament" has been replaced here by a decadent, secularized society in which Mormonism is not perceived as scandalous, but simply boring. The masons' pious wives weep, for they believe the missionaries' sermons promising "death and damnation to the masons. / . . . But those sly dogs / Were more familiar with trips to the tavern, / His nostrum had no effect."[71] In short, the Danish men prefer their pubs to any church or their wives' scolding.

The solution the masons find for their dilemma proves to be as audacious as it is illegal, foreshadowing the association of the Mormons in Denmark with the white slave trade a few decades later, despite the fact that it is the masons who take the initiative in the ballad. Tired of beating and haranguing their wives to give up their new faith, the men decide to sell their wives to the Mormon missionary: "The Mormon is taking their hearts in tow, / Well then, let's distribute the suffering, / If only he'll pay for our wives, / Then they can have the Mormons." The masons protest that their wives are so dear to them that only gold can ease their suffering, and the missionary agrees: "And the husbands got / About a thousand apiece, / And the Mormons got / The wives, by God."

By the end of the tongue-in-cheek song, everyone seems happy with the deal, especially the masons. The men see their wives off on the ship along with the Mormon elder, then head to the pub, exclaiming, "Now there's peace in our homes, / And now money will quench our sorrow and loss. / Hurrah! We'll stay in Copenhagen." This final verse alludes to a variety of socially relevant issues, such as the contentious effect of differing religious views on a marriage, the corrupting influence of money, and the carnal delights of late nineteenth-century Denmark. While the intimation that the women will come to regret their decision to convert and emigrate may lurk behind the laughter, it is the men's shallow delight at shedding an inconvenient responsibility, profiting off the sale of their wives, and carousing through the streets of Copenhagen that stays with the listener.

Taken together, the various street ballads dealing with Mormonism reflect the emergence of two tendencies toward the end of the nineteenth century. The first was to regard Mormonism as an object of ridicule rather than as a serious threat to the integrity of Danish society. The second was to make Danish society and its changing mores the actual target of satirical critique. As Danish society became increasingly secular over the course of the century, the Mormons' claims to a superior Christian authority no longer aroused the same outrage nor prompted the same level of social introspection as before, while their unique theology made them an easy target for jokes. Meanwhile, the waves of emigration that began with and then surpassed the Mormon gathering to Zion drew attention to the flaws in Danish society and brought the discussion of such issues into a popular public forum.

Mormonism on Stage: Danish Revue Songs

While newspapers catered primarily to bourgeois Danes and street ballads to the working class, both groups came together to enjoy revues, a kind of musical theatrical production that references both clichés and current events in witty sketches and satirical songs. The revue became tremendously popular in Denmark in the first few decades of the twentieth century. Although the term "revue" was not used in print until Fritz Holst's "Nytårsrevy 1872" ("New Year's Revue 1872"), the Danish revue tradition goes back at least as far as Johan Ludvig Heiberg's satirical musicals in the early nineteenth century.[72] Over the course of the nineteenth century, the revue evolved from a highbrow, largely dramatic form in the 1830s to a more popular, cabaret-style variety show made up of a hodgepodge of comic sketches and cheeky songs by the 1890s.[73] At the turn of the twentieth century, there were between twenty-five and thirty revue theaters in greater Copenhagen, with a comparable amount in the provinces.[74] Revue performances across the country—from the Scala Theater and Tivoli Gardens amusement park in Copenhagen to the Aalborg Theater in northern Jutland—were known for their impertinence and willingness to push the limits of good taste in order to get a laugh. In 1901, Minister of Justice Peter Adler Alberti ordered the censor to prohibit any mention of the royal family or the Danish government in revues, but the theaters had the last laugh when they skewered Alberti in a sketch about a dishonest businessman in the summer of 1908, a scant few weeks before Alberti was arrested for embezzling funds from the credit union he directed.[75]

The scandal-seeking nature of the Danish revue made it inevitable that Mormonism would supply fertile material for comedy, not least because of the titillation provided by Mormonism's history of polygamy. By their nature, however, revues flit from topic to topic, keeping audiences interested by offering a constant stream of novelty, so it is not surprising that Mormonism does not feature in many revue songs. The fact that it appears at all testifies to widespread familiarity with Mormonism as a concept and as an object of ridicule within Danish public discourse at the time.

A song performed as part of the summer 1911 season of the Copenhagen revue in Tivoli Gardens called "Mormoner! Mormoner!" ("Mormons, Mormons!") illustrates the humorous, self-ridiculing tenor of public discourse about Mormonism after the turn of the century. This particular song was included in a production entitled *Sommerrejsen 1911* (*Summer Voyage 1911*) that was written by Charles and Alex Kjerulf and set to music arranged by Georg Prehn. It was performed in Tivoli's Glass Hall Theater by a group of theater and silent film actors, including Jutta Lund, Oscar Stribolt, and the legendary Carl Alstrup, who was one of the most famous and beloved stars of the comedy stage despite his own preference for tragic drama.[76] Coherency and accuracy of content is decidedly secondary to sensationalism and satire in revues such as this, and most revues made no pretense at a unified theme or overarching narrative. This is evident in the case of *Summer Voyage 1911*, which features—alongside "Mormons, Mormons!"—nearly a dozen songs, including "I Think It Is Loveliest in Denmark," "Peasant Culture," "A Real Scout," "Copenhagen for Copenhageners," and "Dear God, Is He Still Alive?"[77] The revue only ran for a few months, which, along with its exclusive performance at Tivoli Gardens, limited the number of people who would have heard this particular song. However, Alstrup recorded a 78 rpm of the song with Gramophone Records in Copenhagen, while the published version of the collected songs from *Summer Voyage 1911*, with piano accompaniment, went through at least three editions. Thus, audiences who enjoyed the songs could purchase the record or the sheet music for private use, thereby endowing an ephemeral, geographically limited performance with considerably longer life and potentially a broader circulation.

Like many of the street ballads that preceded it, the song "Mormons, Mormons" pokes fun at the notorious Mormon practice of polygamy.

FIGURE 3.3 Publicity photograph of Carl Alstrup, Jutta Lund, and Oscar Stribolt in the 1911 Tivoli revue *Sommerrejsen 1911* (*Summer Voyage 1911*), which featured several of Denmark's most beloved variety-show actors. Courtesy of the Danish Royal Library, Copenhagen, Department of Maps, Prints, and Photographs.

Although polygamy was officially abandoned by the LDS Church in 1890, U.S. Senate hearings from 1903–1907 over the question of whether to admit Utah senator Reed Smoot brought the issue back into the public eye, particularly in the United States but also overseas. Although Smoot was a monogamist, the Senate wanted to ascertain whether the LDS Church was abiding by its renunciation of plural marriage and whether Smoot, as an LDS apostle, could be trusted to uphold the U.S. Constitution if his church sanctioned unlawful behavior. Speaking in favor of seating Smoot, Pennsylvania senator Boies Penrose famously announced, "I would rather have seated beside me in this chamber a polygamist who doesn't polyg than a monogamist who doesn't monag."[78] Smoot was eventually allowed to assume his Senate seat and served as a Utah senator until 1933. The influence of the subsequent wave of anti-Mormon rhetoric in the United States became evident in Denmark during the spring of 1911, when anti-Mormon lectures were held throughout the country, prompting Scandinavian mission president Andrew Jenson to debate the church's accusers in Copenhagen on June 21, 1911, followed by an extensive lecture tour throughout Denmark and Norway over the subsequent two years.[79]

The first verse of "Mormons, Mormons!" begins by striking a familiar note of caution about the Mormon threat to Danish women: "I agree with our pastors, the Mormons have to go. / They steal all of our girls, especially the pretty ones. / Many a Maren, Karen, and Jutta has bitterly regretted being lured to Utah, where she married some old sparrow, becoming number twelve in the same nest."[80] The first line of the song already reveals the tongue-in-cheek sarcasm that audiences would have expected from a revue song, with the speaker's complaint focusing on the dearth of pretty girls in Denmark because of Mormon emigration. In the next line, instead of offering an earnest, allegedly authentic, firsthand account of a Danish woman trapped in a polygamous relationship like "A Mormon Girl's Lament," this song simply acknowledges the widespread perception that Danish Mormon convert-emigrants were often young, attractive women who were exploited as polygamous wives upon arrival in Utah.

The remainder of the verse throws off the pretense of moral concern, however, with the declaration: "Mormons, Mormons! / America's help's just a burden to us. / We sophisticated playboys, we can surely manage this ourselves!" This comic twist reveals that the speaker is not actually concerned about the fate of women lured to Utah by the Mormons, but rather with the fact that this means there are fewer pretty girls around for the Danes themselves to seduce. The line "America's help's just a burden to us" hints at the gradual emergence of a mildly anti-American and somewhat stronger anti-Mormon sentiment in Denmark that would lead to laws in the 1920s restricting American—in particular Mormon—immigration to Denmark, which hampered the LDS Church's missionary efforts.

The second verse abandons the pretense of social criticism in favor of a satirical celebration of Denmark's own increasingly lenient sexual morals:

> On Sunday in his parlor,
> Jensen hosts a party with dancing.
> He's going to get together with Hansen's wife,
> while Hansen will have his.

But instead Jensen must content himself with Mrs.
  Hansen's sister,
while Mrs. Hansen openly cavorts
with her brother-in-law's brother,
who is married to Hansen's mother!

Mormons, Mormons!
Yes, they must be persecuted,
we must fight against them.
But wife-swapping, wife-swapping!
We have the right to do that here too![81]

There is no indication that the people mentioned in the verse should
be presumed to be Mormon—their names are common Danish surnames and no mention is made of Utah. The only reference to Mormonism in this verse appears in the chorus, but here the persecution
of Mormons is more of an afterthought, a habitual attitude rendered
unjustified, even ridiculous, by the increasingly liberal social mores of
Danish society.

Mormonism in Danish Silent Film

Following the invention of moving pictures at the end of the nineteenth
century, silent film became an effective and lucrative medium for "educating" the public about the dangers that lurked out in the world, in particular the white slave trade but Mormonism as well. Early Danish silent
films essentially picked up where street ballads such as "A Mormon Girl's
Lament" left off, depicting Mormonism as a dangerous foreign element
in Danish society that could ensnare the unwary, while also aiming to
entertain middle- and lower-class audiences with a compelling story that
offered more narrative coherence than a revue song. Denmark was a pioneer in the field of silent film, particularly after an entrepreneur named
Ole Olsen founded the Nordisk Film Company (hereafter referred to as
Nordisk) in 1906. In the first few decades of the twentieth century, the
Danish film industry—with Nordisk at the forefront—played a leading
role in the technological and economic development of silent film into
a popular, profitable entertainment venue.

Danish silent films became a valuable export to the European
(and, to a lesser extent, American) markets with the rise of the erotic

melodrama, a feature-length genre that was pioneered in Denmark around 1910. Rather than adapting literary or theatrical works for the screen, as would become common practice later, the earliest Danish erotic melodramas tended to specialize in sensationalist narratives concerned with private intrigues and dangers to the general public, in particular involving criminality and sexuality. The film camera's dispassionate, all-seeing eye made visible interpersonal relations and spaces previously considered private and hence invisible to outside observers, while the increased length of the new films, more than double the standard for the era, allowed for more complex plots and audience identification with the film's protagonists.

Many of the earliest and most successful erotic melodramas produced in Denmark belong to the cinematically innovative and commercially successful "white slave trade" genre. The films in this category capitalize on international public concern (discussed briefly above) about the dangers lying in wait for young women who leave home to seek employment in cities or immigrate to America. This was by no means an exclusively Danish concern, nor was it a particularly new problem, but it took center stage in the decades surrounding the turn of the twentieth century.

In his 1911 report, Axel Liljefalk, chairman of the Danish National Committee for Combating the White Slave Trade, admits that sex trafficking has taken place since the beginning of human existence, but argues that its particular incarnation in the early twentieth century is closely connected to the changing social conditions, global criminal networks, and increased physical mobility of the industrialized world. He provides a laundry list of the false promises made by agents of white slavery, who recruit women to work in restaurants, hotels, pubs, dance halls, music halls, and female orchestras, and warns against schemes by masseuses, midwives, impresarios, retail merchants, and emigration agents that force women into compromising situations and make them vulnerable to white slavery.[82] Although his report does not mention Mormons, in his discussion of unreliable emigration agents Liljefalk warns that "an offer of marriage, made at the proper moment, rarely misses its mark."[83]

The film generally credited with being the first Danish erotic melodrama is *Den Hvide Slavehandel* (*The White Slave Trade*), directed by Alfred Cohn and produced by the Aarhus-based Fotorama Studio in

April 1910. At 706 meters long (roughly 40 minutes), it was the longest film ever made in Denmark up to that time. It built on both sensationalist literature and widespread contemporary political activism directed against white slave gangs that abducted young women and sold them into prostitution. The film tells the story of an impoverished Danish girl, Anna, who answers an ad for a British lady's companion but is handed over to a London brothel instead. She manages to preserve her virginity by fighting off her first client and is rescued from further dangers in the nick of time, after a harrowing car chase, thanks to the assistance of a compassionate chambermaid and the heroic efforts of both her fiancé, Georg, and Scotland Yard. The film's suspenseful premise, fast-paced action sequences, and titillating visualizations of such forbidden spaces as a brothel and the criminal underworld made the film a box office success across Denmark.

Fotorama's white slave trade film was so successful that Nordisk decided to copy it outright, frame for frame, though the final Nordisk version is approximately one hundred meters shorter than Fotorama's original. Nordisk had released a short film on a similar theme, called *Den Hvide Slavinde* (*The White Slave Girl*) (directed by Viggo Larsen) in 1907, but it did not achieve the runaway success as Fotorama's much longer film, which allowed audiences to identify more with the characters. Nordisk's remake of *The White Slave Trade*, directed by August Blom, was released in August 1910 and ran head-to-head with the Fotorama original across Denmark, often in the same towns at the same time. In contrast to Fotorama's almost exclusive focus on the Danish market, however, Nordisk had extensive distribution networks across continental Europe and was able to export its film to a wide European audience, which brought in substantial revenue.

The White Slave Trade's success ensured that Nordisk became keenly attuned to the marketability of the titillating combination of romance, danger, and scandal. While state film censorship was becoming increasingly common across Europe in the early 1910s, white slave trade films made taboo topics admissible by virtue of their ostensible pedagogical aim of enlightening the public about the dangers awaiting young women who ventured out into the wide world. Nordisk's marketing materials for the film expostulate on the dangers lurking behind the phrase "the white slave trade—three words full of unease and horror, which cause the fearful motherly heart to tremble and brings a flush of shame and indignation to a father's cheeks; three words that impertinently strip away all of the twentieth century's civilization and progress!"[84] Although Nordisk claimed to be primarily concerned with exposing the problem of white slavery, these two films rely heavily on the disheveled immodesty of young women in compromising situations for their appeal. Domestic and international box office receipts for *The White Slave Trade* prove the profitability of this type of sensationalist film about criminal activity, liberally laced with sexual danger and violence.

Both Nordisk and Fotorama also made films that offered audiences unprecedented access to another social space considered to be both mysterious and dangerous—namely, Mormonism.[85] Fotorama's 1911 film, *Mormonbyens Blomst* (*The Flower of the Mormon City*) (director unknown), depicts the travails of a Danish Mormon girl in Utah who narrowly escapes a forced marriage with a Mormon polygamist. This film does not conform to the conventions of the white slave trade genre in several regards, however. The protagonist Kristine Olsen's predicament is not the result of her own decision, but comes about because of her father's decision to immigrate to the Mormon settlement in Utah and subsequent failure to conform to the expectations of his new religion, which antagonizes the leaders of the isolated Mormon frontier community. Kristine's forced marriage has no financial benefit for her abductors, but is intended as punishment for her father's transgressions. Kristine ultimately escapes her fate with the assistance of her father and a non-Mormon American cowboy, Tom Carter, who eventually brings her back to Denmark. There they purchase her father's abandoned smithy and integrate themselves into rural Danish society. No prints of this film exist today, but distribution records suggest it enjoyed only modest success at the box office.

By contrast, Nordisk's far more successful film, *Mormonens Offer* (*A Victim of the Mormons*) (directed by August Blom, 1911), conforms to the paradigm of white slave trade films in nearly all respects, but with Mormons as the villains. Running an unprecedented 1,080 meters (3,200 feet), *A Victim of the Mormons* carries the subtitle "A Drama of Love and Sectarian Fanaticism" and stars Valdemar Psilander, the popular Danish actor. Psilander plays a Mormon priest named Andrew Larsson (spelled "Larson" in the English-language market release) who persuades a young woman named Nina Gram (Florence Grange, in the English release) to flee with him to Utah.

Produced in the Nordisk studios in Valby, Denmark, *A Victim of the Mormons* was intended for both domestic and international consumption. It premiered in Copenhagen at the Panoptikon Theater on October 2, 1911, and was released in London soon after, on October 11, 1911, and in the United States on February 5, 1912. *A Victim of the Mormons* was only Psilander's third film, but he was already one of the highest-paid actors in Denmark and had acquired a reputation as a heartthrob and the nickname "the whole world's Valdemar."[86] His costar, playing the hapless Nina, was Clara Wieth, who had previously starred in *Den Hvide Slavehandels Sidste Offer* (*The White Slave Trade's Final Victim*) (directed by August Blom), which premiered in Denmark on January 23, 1911, and was released in Britain and the United States the following year under the title *In the Hands of Imposters*.

The Mormon elder Andrew Larsson's behavior in the film follows the pattern laid out in Liljefalk's report, namely "seeking out the necessary prey, catching it in his net, developing a relationship that inspires trust, and then delivering the victim to the transportation agents,"[87] with the sole deviation that Larsson accompanies Nina overseas. When Nina changes her mind shortly before boarding the ship, Larsson resorts to violence to keep her captive and smuggles her on board. Nina's desperate brother Olaf (or George, in the English version) and her fiancé, Sven Berg (also called Leslie) pursue her all the way to Utah, where they finally succeed in rescuing her—again, after a harrowing car chase—with the assistance of the police and a compassionate housekeeper.

While the story of the film's reception abroad is an interesting one in its own right (which Jacob Olmstead has analyzed[88]), *A Victim of the Mormons* offers intriguing insights into the ways in which the changing reception of Mormonism in the early twentieth century intersected with the modernization of Danish society. Unlike the other films discussed in this chapter, a great deal of advertising for this film survives, which explains why Danish studios were motivated to make the world's first anti-Mormon films. The short answer is to make money. The commercial success of the previous films about the white slave trade had conclusively demonstrated the public's appetite for scandalous tales of sex, crime, and violence. The savvy businessman Ole Olsen at Nordisk recognized that he could continue his winning streak by adapting folklore about Mormon elders luring young girls to Utah for the screen.

Anecdotal evidence from the British and American trade press confirms the acuity of Olsen's perception. An ad in *Moving Picture World* promised the profitability of this latest installment of the white slave trade series, proclaiming, in all caps, that it "HAS NO EQUAL AS A MONEY-MAKER."[89] Similarly, the English trade paper *Bioscope* declared, "This Great Winner Creates a Record Booking," while broadside ads announced that the picture had been "obtained at enormous cost."[90] A telegram from the Feature Film Company of America in Rochester, New York, to the film's U.S. distributor, Great Northern Special Feature Film Company, dated March 18, 1912, attests to the film's financial success, reporting that it "smashes all previous records in receipts" and calling it "without doubt [the] greatest box office attraction in moving pictures ever presented in this city."[91]

A Victim of the Mormons is not terribly concerned with verisimilitude, either in terms of the plausibility of the plot, character development, or setting, let alone providing a historically or theologically accurate depiction of an obscure American religion. At the same time, however, the film presupposes a certain basic level of familiarity with the missionary representatives of the LDS Church, who had become ubiquitous in Denmark in the second half of the nineteenth century, and does not diverge notably from prevalent views of Mormonism. This measured approach suggests that demonization of Mormonism per se was not a central aim of the film, leaving open the question of what function this depiction of a Mormon threat to Danish women was intended to serve.

In keeping with Nordisk's export-marketing strategy in this period of deliberately rendering Danish films "placeless" and therefore universal, the urban setting of *A Victim of the Mormons* is supposed to represent an indeterminate metropolis. This would likely have seemed plausible to international viewers, but Copenhagen audiences would have had a harder time suspending their disbelief due to the familiarity of the exterior sets. Danish film historian Marguerite Engberg points out, for example, that the seaside shots are unmistakably filmed along the northeastern coast of Zealand, looking out at the Øresund.[92] The dock at which the characters embark for their transatlantic journey is far too small to service ocean-faring steamships and, indeed, the journey from Copenhagen to Salt Lake City is accomplished in a few minutes aboard a small ferry in Copenhagen harbor.

Given the specificity of the Mormon theme, the director had no choice but to attempt to depict a place purporting to be Utah, but even this representation of a specific, real place is rendered in broad, vague strokes. The film makes no attempt to depict the journey from New York or Boston across thousands of miles of American territory to reach Utah, and the Salt Lake City Temple is represented by one of the classical-style buildings in the Zoological Gardens in Copenhagen. Most of the scenes set in Salt Lake City are interior shots, which are suitably generic, but some crucial scenes are shot outdoors. For example, the obligatory car chase in the film crosses a bridge, which ostensibly exists somewhere in Salt Lake City, and ends at the Great Salt Lake. However, the dense cityscape behind the bridge is distinctively European and there is no sign of either the mountains or desert that surround the actual Salt Lake City and Great Salt Lake.

While such discrepancies may be jarring to modern viewers who have either firsthand or secondhand familiarity with both landscapes, contemporary audiences likely would not have been alarmed by or even aware of them. American film scholar Mark Sandberg suggests that the decision to employ geographic shortcuts for the exterior shots set in Utah relied on the presumption that few, if any, of the film's intended European viewers would have been familiar with the scenery of the Utah Territory. He explains, "For the original audience, however, the license taken would likely have been perfectly plausible, since the look of Salt Lake City was probably visually unverifiable for most viewers in the European audiences Nordisk was targeting. For most viewers, the idea of 'Salt Lake City' was simply not part of their mental geography."[93] Moreover, since Nordisk consciously oriented its productions in this period more toward a broad European market than a domestic Danish one, the producers may well have calculated that most of those viewers would not recognize the Copenhagen cityscape either.

The film's depiction of the Mormon elder, Andrew Larsson, is also fraught with inconsistencies. Andrew is first introduced as Olaf Gram's schoolmate, an association that lends him social legitimacy and presumed respectability. He is clearly admissible to Danish social circles, despite his unusual religious affiliation, which is explicitly stated in the intertitle (e.g., he raises no eyebrows among the group of Danes whom he joins for breakfast in the first scene). It is only the English spelling of his given name and the Swedish-style spelling of his surname that suggest, however obliquely, that he is an outsider in Denmark. His physical attractiveness and good manners are also emphasized, supporting the presumption of acceptability.

Throughout the portion of the film set in Denmark, Andrew appears, according to the program notes, as "thoughtfulness personified and attends on her [Nina's] slightest wish in order to fulfill it straightaway." Even in the note he leaves for Nina to coordinate their elopement, he addresses her formally with "Miss." The notes describe Andrew as "a young man—a straight-backed and handsome figure, in whose face a pair of fanatical eyes burn." This combination of respectability with a hint of the forbidden is central to Nina's fascination with him. Viewers are informed that she deliberately seeks out Andrew's company, in part because her fiancé Sven Berg is too preoccupied with sports to pay proper attention to her, but also because he represents "the mystical, the unknown."[94]

It is unclear whether the flaws in the film's depiction of Andrew's behavior, particularly regarding his adherence to the Mormon health code known as the Word of Wisdom, are simply errors or whether they were inserted intentionally, either to show how unfaithful Andrew is to the precepts of his own religion or as a means of camouflaging his identity to avoid discovery. Although the Word of Wisdom forbids both smoking and drinking alcohol, Andrew repeatedly indulges in both pursuits (which, it must be noted, was not entirely unheard of among actual Mormons of the period). During the purported Atlantic crossing, for example, after Andrew sedates his reluctant bride-to-be and locks her in the cabin, he goes out on deck for a smoke to calm his nerves. He is also wearing a false mustache that later comes unglued, causing the ship's telegraph operator to become suspicious. Later, in Salt Lake City, when Nina continues to protest her captivity and he is forced to lock her in the basement, he pours himself a whiskey in his living room.

Andrew Larsson's characterization as an unfaithful Mormon in the film bears a striking similarity to the depiction of a deceitful Mormon missionary, Mr. Evanston, in Danish Nobel Prize-winner Johannes V. Jensen's novels *Madame D'Ora* (1904) and *Hjulet* (*The Wheel*) (1905). The first novel begins onboard a ship to America, where Madame D'Ora meets Mr. Evanston. Although he has been explicitly identified to the reader as a Mormon, Evanston smokes a cigar and drinks whisky with a British policeman.[95] Later, when Madame D'Ora is giving a concert in Salt Lake City, she learns Evanston is regarded as "one of their [the Mormons'] best agents, who constantly travels around and gathers proselytes. I was given to understand, with great respect, that Evanston was the son of one of the very first Mormons . . . who had not come to America because he had 'done something'. . . but had emigrated from Europe because of a vague sense of having a spiritual call far from home."[96] Despite the respect he enjoys among his fellow Mormons, however, Evanston turns out to be a swindler, who runs a revivalist megachurch in New York City, dabbles in spiritualism, and attempts to trick Madame D'Ora's scientist husband with skillfully managed séances. Just as Evanston's anachronistic behavior on the ship foreshadows his unreliability and dishonesty in the rest of the book, Andrew Larsson's consumption of alcohol and tobacco on the ship reveal him, however subtly, to be an unreliable representative of Mormonism.

Other unlikely details in *A Victim of the Mormons* have less narrative significance, but are merely obvious devices for advancing the plot. When Olaf and Sven reach Utah, they have no trouble finding Andrew's home and obtaining unstinting assistance from his housekeeper (or first wife, as she is described in some English-language reviews), despite the fact that she has never seen them before and most likely speaks a different language. When they storm into the house and confront Andrew, he naturally protests his innocence, but Nina is able to push a button in her basement prison that triggers a secret trapdoor in the middle of his living room floor, causing Andrew to plunge into the basement and revealing Nina's prison. The Danish men tear the curtains from the windows and attempt to hoist Nina up, but Andrew, despite the injuries he sustained in the fall, manages to foil them by shooting the curtains to shreds. When Olaf and Sven finally discover the secret panel concealing the basement stairway, they crash through the door only to find that Andrew has died of an accidentally self-inflicted gunshot wound.

Despite these somewhat distracting details, however, the foregrounding of Mormonism as a central element of the film and the implicit association between Mormonism and the white slave trade it alleges make this film a particularly fascinating testament to the relationship between Danish and Mormon cultural identity at the time. By 1911, both Danish conversions and Mormon emigration were at a fairly stable, relatively low level. The mass emigration of Danish Mormon converts and public riots against Mormonism had become a distant memory, while the increasingly secular character of Danish society meant that religion itself could be treated as a source of entertainment.

The claim of public advocacy that defined and justified the white slave trade films required that *A Victim of the Mormons* situate itself in opposition to a clear and present moral danger facing Danish society. In addition to rehashing boilerplate anti-Mormon propaganda—including accusations that Joseph Smith was a fortune-teller, that the witnesses to the golden plates were a band of felons, and that the Book of Mormon is identical to a lost novel written by an obscure American named Solomon Spalding, to name just a few examples—the program notes for *A Victim of the Mormons* exaggerate the threat posed by Mormonism to Danes, both in terms of heretical doctrine and Mormon enticements to emigration:

> In the same manner as the great film dramas exposed the evil deeds of which the so-called "White Slave Trade" has made itself guilty and thereby performed a valuable public service by warning young girls against the traps laid for them by the representatives of this shady business,—in the same way this art film ought to be well-suited to opening people's eyes and directing their attention to the agitation promoted by the spokesmen of Mormonism in order to lure young men and especially women over to Salt Lake City. Anyone who has seen this film and read these notes has been warned against Mormonism's deception. May this warning bear fruit![97]

The audience is then promised the opportunity, by means of "the powerful imagery of the silent theater," to witness firsthand the "unhappiness, the infectious disease that erupts in a harmonious family circle by association with a heartless representative of modern Mormonism."

Despite these inflammatory claims, the depiction of Mormon religious services in the film is fairly neutral and realistic, although it emphasizes the LDS Church's American origins. One of the longest scenes in the film depicts Nina's attendance at a Mormon worship service in Copenhagen, which is unique among portrayals of Mormonism in Danish popular media. The meeting is held in a nondescript storefront, as was common for Mormon services in late nineteenth-century Denmark before permanent meetinghouses were built in the early 1900s. Signs in the windows and sandwich boards on the sidewalk out front announce, in English, "MEETINGS" and "WELCOME." The camera documents several groups of people entering the building before Nina arrives, dressed in sumptuous black satin and an ostentatious hat that sets her apart from the rest of the attendees, most of whom are quite plainly attired. Nina's clothing suggests she belongs to a more privileged social class. Upon entering the building, Nina passes a board outlining the meeting schedule, again in English: Sunday School, Relief Society, Mutual, and Service. The room is decorated with festive garlands. Andrew is the primary speaker. Nina sits in the front row and looks rather ill at ease during the meeting, but there is nothing overtly inflammatory or disrespectful about the scene.

The representation of Mormon practices in Utah is slightly more sensationalized, with considerably less theological accuracy, but still without apparent ridicule. Shortly after his return to Utah, Andrew participates in what the intertitle describes as "A Mormon Baptism in the Temple," though the generic pillared façade bears little resemblance to any existing Mormon temple, let alone the distinctive Salt Lake Temple with its six towers. The scene ostensibly takes place in the temple baptistry, where a large font rests on the backs of three pairs of kneeling golden oxen, with a large pipe organ behind it. Men and women dressed in black are seated in the foreground, while a row of young women in flowing white robes and long, loose dark hair take turns entering the font to be immersed.

Contrary to actual Mormon baptismal practice, which requires the person being baptized to grasp the forearm of the person performing the baptism, in *A Victim of the Mormons* the man in the font pushes down on the women's heads to immerse them. After this unceremonious dunking, the women exit the font, line up in a row, and point in unison across their bodies out of the frame, a completely anachronistic but highly dramatic gesture. Somewhat incongruously, neither the

FIGURE 3.4 Still from the popular silent film, *Mormonens Offer* (*A Victim of the Mormons*, 1911). In this scene a young, upper-class Danish woman, Nina Gram, played by Clara Wieth, attends an LDS sacrament meeting in Copenhagen. Reproduced courtesy of Nordisk Film and the Danish Film Institute, Copenhagen.

women's hair or robes, nor the robes of the man in the font, appear at all wet. Aside from the inherently voyeuristic nature of a sequence set inside a space sacred to Mormon believers and inaccessible to non-believers, however, the scene does not succumb to the temptation to depict Mormon ordinances as immoral or obscene like many American films do later in the century.

On a metaphorical level, the film's association of Mormonism with the white slave trade serves to position the LDS Church as a threat to the safety of Danish women that can only be defeated by the aggressive intervention of male protectors. This strategy reflects broader cultural discourses about gender roles and modernity in early twentieth-century Denmark. At a time when women's emancipation movements were

FIGURE 3.5 Another still from *Mormonens Offer* depicting a proxy baptismal
service in an LDS temple. After abducting Nina and taking her to Utah, Mormon
elder Andrew Larsson, played by Danish heartthrob Valdemar Psilander, participates in the proxy baptism while Nina remains locked in his house. Reproduced
courtesy of Nordisk Film and the Danish Film Institute, Copenhagen.

gaining momentum across Scandinavia and America, these allusions to
the Mormon practice of polygamy triggered righteous Lutheran indignation that any man should think himself entitled to more than one wife.
They also indicate a lack of confidence in women's mental and physical
abilities to make the best choices for either themselves as individuals
or society as a whole. When Nina chooses to run away with Andrew
to Utah, her susceptibility to making such a choice is attributed to her
irrational, emotional reactions to her fiancé's boorish behavior and her
seducer's aura of mysticism. When she changes her mind, her physical weakness and timidity prevent her from being able to escape successfully, even when Andrew's housekeeper helps her flee through her
open, unbarred window.

A final passage from the program notes for *A Victim of the Mormons* illustrates the way in which the film implicitly conflates the existential threat posed to Danes by Mormonism with the dangers of modernity:

> Is it not a source of shame for civilized humanity, that—in precisely the same century that the cause of enlightenment and liberalism has made such giant strides forward everywhere that the white race builds and dwells—America and then the rest of the world have witnessed the rise and spread of such a cancer as Mormonism, thanks to thousands and thousands of men and women, of whom one would have expected greater acuity and less gullibility, welcoming this false and fraudulent doctrine and praising this new "gospel" as an authentic revelation![98]

By highlighting the importance of the fact that the dawning twentieth century seemed to be such a liberal and enlightened age, as evidenced (ironically, to the modern reader's eyes, but not, presumably, to its intended audience) by the spread of European colonialism and imperialism, the author of the notes intends to prove the anachronistic and therefore suspect nature of Mormonism.

In the process of maligning Mormonism, the author casts doubt on the rationality and maturity of his fellow Danes, the "thousands and thousands of men and women, of whom one would have expected greater acuity and less gullibility." Citizens of such an enlightened world should apparently have been better able to resist the lure of smooth-talking, good-looking, well-mannered Mormon missionaries than Nina Gram was, but they were not. By implication, what other false ideologies might such innocents be susceptible to? By 1911, the alleged dangers of Mormonism were old news in Denmark, but their dramatic defeat in *A Victim of the Mormons* may have been intended to warn viewers that many kinds of "false and fraudulent doctrines," including ones that could be particularly dangerous to women, lurked behind the alluring freedoms of the new century and changing customs of modern life.

Two final examples provide a humorous contrast to the melodramatic depiction of Mormonism in *A Victim of the Mormons*. Both are short comedies directed by Lau Lauritzen: *Min Svigerinde fra Amerika* (*My Sister-in-Law from America*) (1917) and *Han er Mormon* (*He's* a Mormon) (1922), which also had the alternate title *Nalles Forlovelse* (*Nalle's Engagement*). Both films are only seven minutes long (about 350 meters) and were intended to be shown between the newsreel and the feature film—therefore, there is little room for nuance in the stories they tell. Their primary function is to make people laugh. Accordingly, in the program notes, *My Sister-in-Law from America* is labeled a "farce" and marketed with the tagline, "A sure comedic success!"[99] Neither film actually includes a Mormon character. Instead, Mormonism is used in both films simply as a shorthand explanation for polygamous relationships. The alleged polygamists in question are, however, bourgeois Danish men who have no apparent affiliation with the LDS Church.

My Sister-in-Law from America features a philandering middle-aged husband, Mr. Particulier Balle, played by the comedic actor Frederik Buch (1875–1925). Balle decides to entertain his young mistress, Anni, in his elegant home while his wife visits her mother, but is thrown into a panic when his wife returns home unexpectedly and interrupts their intimate tête-à-tête. In desperation he introduces Anni as his sister-in-law from America. Since he does in fact have a brother in America, Mrs. Balle believes his story and welcomes her warmly. Unfortunately, Mr. Balle then receives a letter from his brother, who signs himself with the informal Americanized nickname "Tommy," announcing that he and his wife Käthe are on their way to Denmark to pay him a visit. The film cuts to Tommy and his wife, both plump and prosperous looking, promenading on deck as their ship enters Copenhagen harbor.

The film pokes fun at the American identity of the returning Danish emigrant and his wife, who are, we learn from Tommy's letter, returning to Denmark for the first time. Tommy looks like a caricature of Uncle Sam, with vertically striped trousers, a skinny tie, a pointed grey goatee, comically bushy eyebrows, and a top hat ringed with a band of stars. Tommy and Käthe are separated at the dock by the crush of people disembarking, but rather than trying to find his wife, Tommy takes a taxi to his brother's house on his own. Alone in a foreign land, Käthe sits on her suitcase and tries in vain to find a passerby who speaks English. Unlike modern Danes, most of whom speak English as well as native speakers, the people Tommy's wife approaches for directions simply shake their heads in incomprehension—a group of Danish sailors even laugh and joke that they didn't learn Pig Latin in school.

Meanwhile, the adulterous farce plays itself out in the Balles' apartment. When Tommy arrives, Mr. Balle persuades him to pretend that Anni is his wife in order to save "my life and my honor and the skin of my back!" When Käthe finally arrives, the game seems to be up, until Mr. Balle explains to his wife that Tommy is, in fact, a Mormon, "the lucky beast!" By diverting attention to Tommy's alleged polygamy, Mr. Balle thus manages to prevent his wife's discovery of his own infidelity and thus preserve his domestic harmony.

Aside from momentary surprise, Mrs. Balle is apparently unfazed by this revelation, although she is concerned that "if any more show up, it'll be a tight fit." She directs both ladies to the guest room, where they immediately come to blows. Mr. Balle comes to the rescue, whispering his secret in a mix of Danish and broken English to Käthe and promising, "Now shall jeg exportere den overflødige lady out of Lokalerne" ("Now I shall export the excess lady from the premises"). While Tommy Balle is certainly a comic figure, who encourages Käthe and Anni to duke it out in a mix of Danish and English, crying "Go on, mine Damer!" ("Go on, my ladies!"), the film is more concerned with depicting the embarrassing consequences of Mr. Particulier Balle's infidelity than condemning outdated Mormon marital practices.

This film, which is entirely in character with the more than two hundred short farces and comedies Lauritzen directed for Nordisk between 1914 and 1919, highlights the immorality of Danish society, using both Mormon polygamy and Danish emigration as narrative devices to make its point. Emigration in this film functions quite differently from the way it appeared in the street ballads published a few decades earlier, reflecting the difference in emigration discourse and practice in Denmark. Most noticeable is that this film does not deal with people leaving Denmark, but rather with former emigrants returning to Denmark, either as tourists or permanently. Even among first-generation Danish Americans, heritage tourism was quite popular, as it allowed emigrants to revisit their native land, refresh their language skills, reconnect with friends and family, and show off the fruits of their new life. American newspapers from this period often contain ads encouraging Danish Americans to spend Christmas in Denmark, for example. Levels of return migration to Denmark increased markedly in the early twentieth century, facilitated by: improvements in the comfort, safety, and speed of transcontinental and

FIGURE 3.6 Still from Lau Lauritzen's 1917 short comedy, *Min Svigerinde fra Amerika* (*My Sister-in-Law from America*), which uses the excuse of Mormon polygamy to rescue a philandering Danish husband from his wife's anger. Reproduced courtesy of Nordisk Film and the Danish Film Institute, Copenhagen.

transatlantic transportation; a corresponding decrease in cost; improving economic prospects in Denmark; and the rise of nativist sentiments in the United States that peaked during and immediately after World War I.

As the caricatured figure of Tommy Balle exemplifies, however, returning Danish Americans occupied an ambiguous cultural position in their native land. On the one hand, they were sometimes ridiculed by Danes for their loss of fluency in Danish and their strange new habits and beliefs, exemplified by the explanation that Tommy is a polygamous Mormon. This half-indulgent, half-mocking view is illustrated by Danish composer Carl Nielsen's undated poem "Da Dansk-Amerikanerne Omsider Rejste Hjem" ("When the Danish-Americans Finally Went Home"), which blends bits of Danish and English together to convey that Danish-American visitors are primarily interested in Danish food, alcohol, and pretty girls, but also to illustrate the intimate connections between both peoples. The first strophe reads:

> Afskedstime, Brotherhood.
> Very sorry. Det er Slut.
> Sorg i Danmark. Sorg ombord.
> Fem Orkestre. Afskedskor.
> Flere Tusind. Fyldt paa Kaj'n.
> Hils Chicago. Very fine.
>
> [Hour of parting, Brotherhood.
> Very sorry. It's all over.
> Sorrow in Denmark. Sorrow on board.
> Five Orchestras. Farewell Choir.
> Several thousand. Fill the quay.
> Greet Chicago. Very fine.]

On the other hand, Danish Americans often returned to their homeland, particularly after the turn of the twentieth century, with greater wealth or status than they would likely have had if they had stayed. In many German and Danish silent films from this period, returning emigrants play the role of the economic rescuer, a wealthy relative who saves the day with an inheritance or other financial assistance.

The second short film by Lau Lauritzen, *He's a Mormon* (1922), is subtler about its allusions to Mormonism. Although no prints of the film have survived, the screenplay reveals that the story involves two friends, Nalle and Erik, who are vying for the love of the same girl, Lise. When her father refuses to allow Lise to marry before her disagreeable older sister Sofie, Nalle decides to sacrifice his own aspirations in order to help Eric marry Lise. He proposes to Sofie, but he also orchestrates a way out of his engagement once Eric and Lise have become engaged. While Nalle and Sofie take a romantic walk through the city park, several women from a sewing shop near Nalle's apartment intrude and berate him for betraying them with another woman, implying that he is a polygamist in search of an additional wife—or at the very least an adulterer. Their tirade eventually prompts Sofie to break off her

FIGURE 3.7 Still from *Nalles Forlovelse/Han er Mormon* (1922), another Lau Lauritzen comedy, in which the protagonist pretends to be a polygamist in order to get out of marrying a shrewish wife. Reproduced courtesy of Nordisk Film and the Danish Film Institute, Copenhagen.

engagement in a huff, paving the way for the happy ending in which Eric marries Lise and names Nalle as godfather to his children, as we see in the film's final frame.

Mormonism is not explicitly mentioned in the film's intertitles, nor anywhere in the screenplay, but the decision to title the film *He's a Mormon* reveals the subtext of religious belief as the motivation for Nalle's purported involvement with multiple women at the same time. In both this film and *My Sister-in-Law from America*, the viewer is aware that the association with Mormonism is unfounded, but this knowledge merely heightens the comic tension of the situation. The allusions to Mormon polygamy are only a narrative tool employed to extricate the main character from the consequences of his own ethically and morally questionable actions. Nevertheless, it is striking that no characters in the film react to the allegation of Mormonism with any degree or alarm or concern, which suggests that although Mormonism was still associated with polygamy in the public mind, the concept of Danish Mormons, even polygamous ones, no longer elicited automatic disapproval. After more than half a century, Danish Mormons had been accepted as a part, however idiosyncratic, of Danish society.

Conclusion

In closing, let us return to the question of what these varied depictions of Mormonism in Danish popular culture reveal about the changing values and preoccupations of Danish society between 1850 and the early 1900s. Initially, newspaper coverage of Mormonism in Denmark tended to present theological arguments, historical scandals, or emigrants' tales of woe in order to demonstrate how foreign and dangerous Mormonism was to Danish culture and society at a time when the possible repercussions of the separation between Danish national identity and Lutheran Christianity were still unknown. Although some of the first street ballads about Mormonism strike a similar tone, particularly as Danish emigration gained momentum, the tendency among later popular cultural productions to poke fun at Mormonism, Danish Mormons, and Danes in general rather than inciting fear of the possibility of social change reflects a steadily increasing acceptance of religious and cultural difference within Danish society. Thematic correspondences between these popular depictions of Mormonism in Denmark and the economic, social, and historical conditions that inspired them justify their consideration as an important thread in a complex web of contemporary Danish cultural identity constructions.

On a very basic level, the matter-of-fact treatment of Mormonism in so many different popular culture and media venues over more than six decades reveals that Danes had become familiar enough with the religion by the mid-1860s to associate certain traits and consequences with it, notably polygamy and emigration. The almost uniformly negative depictions of Mormonism in Danish mass media confirm that the Danish public retained at least some measure of distrust toward or discomfort with Mormonism well into the early twentieth century, even though it no longer drove them into the streets to protest.

Looking beyond the texts themselves, however, it is apparent that the issues at stake in these depictions of Mormonism go beyond theology, however unusual certain aspects of Mormon belief might have appeared to Danes at the time. The close association between Mormonism and emigration in many of these texts reveals the Danish public's anxieties about such large-scale emigration—not only did emigration destabilize socioeconomic conditions at home and carry an air of rejection, it also posed a significant risk to the emigrant's safety, sanity, and sense of cultural belonging. Similarly, the preoccupation of so many texts with polygamy and the white slave trade reflects social ambivalence about the competence of women to make responsible, respectable life choices.

4

The Price of Conversion

Cultural Identity Negotiations among Early Danish Mormons

How did nineteenth-century Danish Mormons experience the changes in their relationship to their native culture as a result of conversion? What price did they have to pay for this new identity? As the examples of denunciations and mockery of Mormonism discussed in the preceding chapters reveal, the decoupling of Danish citizenship from Lutheranism and the subsequent exercise of religious freedom by individuals adopting new, unfamiliar faiths was a contentious issue in Danish society. It was also an emotionally tumultuous experience, both for those Danes who chose to abandon the Lutheran Church and for those whose neighbors and friends made that choice. For nineteenth-century Danes, the decision to join the Church of Jesus Christ of Latter-day Saints was a momentous one with far-reaching consequences, ranging from suffering verbal and physical abuse to a vastly increased likelihood of emigrating. In many cases, conversion led to estrangement from family and friends, loss of employment, exclusion from parish schools, and uncertainty about such previously self-evident questions as how and where to be married and buried.

Yet despite the many obstacles and voices raised in opposition to Mormonism in the second half of the nineteenth century, tens of thousands of Danes were converted during this period, although a significant percentage of them became disillusioned and left the church within a few months or years. The composition of the early Danish Mormon community was quite fluid, with converts at many stages of commitment to their new religion, ranging from enthusiastic proselytizers to tentative investigators. This chapter aims to illuminate how these early Danish Mormons viewed their own cultural identity in the light of their conversion and, in many cases, emigration. Since many of those who left the LDS Church became hostile toward it, their accounts—often written for publication with the goal of dissuading potential converts—are of less use in describing the self-perception of Danish Mormons in this period than private documents written by converts who remained faithful, which are the focus of this chapter.

What all of these early Danish Mormons had in common, even those who later disassociated themselves from the LDS Church, was their willingness to investigate an alternative religious identity than the Lutheranism with which they had been raised. Although their reasons for conversion were diverse, identifying common characteristics of converts is helpful in understanding their shared identity. In general, Danish converts to Mormonism tended to be inclined toward religion already—thus, residents of areas where the "godly awakenings" of the early nineteenth century had flourished tended to be particularly receptive to the teachings of the Mormon missionaries, as were members of Baptist congregations. In addition to their sincere interest in discovering spiritual truth, these population subsets had already demonstrated a willingness to challenge prevailing notions of Danishness in the pursuit of that truth. On a more subjective level, as historian Margit Egdal documents in *Miraklet på Fyn* (*The Miracle on Funen*), many Danes who embraced Mormonism were in an emotionally sensitive state, having either lost a loved one or witnessed a miraculous healing performed by the Mormon missionaries.[1] Other recurring, though by no means definitive, traits of many Danish Mormon converts in the late nineteenth century include living in an isolated or rural area, belonging to an economically disadvantaged social class, and having a family member who converted. The decision to leave *Folkekirken* was, however, just the first step in a much longer process of transformation that changed not only the course of these converts' lives but also their sense of social belonging and cultural identity.

Not all converts were willing to submit to such a comprehensive reorientation of their lives. The challenges, disadvantages, and demanding requirements of being a Danish Mormon in this era—not to mention pressure from family, friends, and Lutheran ministers—induced many converts to regret their decision and seek to be received back into

Folkekirken. Others questioned the truth of Mormon doctrine or were excommunicated for such transgressions as adultery, dishonesty, or lack of commitment. The LDS Church's emphasis on "gathering to Zion" by emigrating after conversion exacerbated the tension between Danish Mormons and their Lutheran countrymen and served to brand Mormonism as an "American" element within Danish society, despite the fact that nearly all of the converts, local church leaders, and Mormon missionaries in Denmark were native Danes. The willingness of Danish Mormons to emigrate, especially at a time when few of their countrymen had yet taken the same step, appeared to demonstrate the convert's willingness to adopt, along with a new religion, a new cultural and national identity, even while still living in Denmark.

Despite the numerical significance and high profile of the Mormon movement in late nineteenth-century Denmark, Danish Mormons' own assessments of the effects of their conversion on their cultural identity have received little attention in Danish history, primarily because the majority of Danish converts in this period emigrated. The number of Danes who joined the LDS Church in the second half of the nineteenth century and remained committed to it for the rest of their lives is nearly fourteen thousand.[2] Of this number, more than half—approximately 12,700—chose to leave their homeland between 1850 and 1920 and gather to Zion, which was located, according to Mormon theology, in the Utah Territory.

Prior to the organized emigration of Danish Mormons, there had been very little emigration from Denmark, although its neighbors Norway, Sweden, and Germany had been sending floods of immigrants over to the United States for decades. The mass immigration of Danish Mormons contributed significantly to the success of the Utah Territory and, in most cases, to the improvement of the immigrant's own socioeconomic situation, but it also weakened the Mormon presence in Denmark. As historian Richard Jensen notes, "From a high of 3,450 members in 101 branches in 1861 (organized into nine 'conferences' or districts), by 1892 Denmark had 1,085 members in fourteen branches in three conferences."[3] It was not until after the turn of the twentieth century, when the LDS Church began encouraging converts to remain in their native countries and build up the church there, that the first permanent LDS church buildings were erected in Denmark, signaling the intention of integrating the church into Danish society, a process that Jesper Stenholm Paulsen has documented in detail in *De Danske Mormoners Historie* (*The History of the Danish Mormons*).[4]

During the nineteenth century, Danes who joined the LDS Church were forced to negotiate new cultural identities in response to the ideological, geographic, and linguistic changes that resulted from their conversion. This chapter aims to sketch a picture of what those identity negotiations entailed for individual converts. Fictional accounts offer one route to understanding the choices these Danes made and their consequences, both mental and physical. Utah-born novelist Virginia Sorensen, herself a descendant of Danish Mormon convert-emigrants, attempted to capture the subjective Danish Mormon immigrant experience in her novel, *Kingdom Come* (1960), which tells the story of a young Danish farmhand named Svend Madsen, who encounters Mormonism while serving in the Danish army at the end of the First Schleswig War in 1851, then emigrates together with Hanne Dalsgaard, the daughter of his prosperous employer.[5] The structure of Sorensen's novel, which was originally intended to be part of a trilogy, resembles other Scandinavian American immigrant trilogies, such as Ole Rølvaag's *Verdens Grøde* (*Giants in the Earth*) (1927) and Vilhelm Moberg's *Utvandrarna* (*The Emigrants*) (1949). Like Sorensen, Moberg's first volume describes conditions in the home country that led to emigration, while subsequent volumes focus on the immigrant experience in America.

Sorensen incorporates a great deal of historical context into *Kingdom Come*, but her primary focus is on the internal development of the characters and their motivations for conversion and emigration. She emphasizes the conflicts between Svend and the local pastor, who clash over the question of authority to preach the word of God, and between Hanne and her parents, whose goals for their daughter include an elaborate wedding and a comfortable, middle-class life rather than the danger and drudgery of pioneer life in a faraway land. The omniscient narrator reveals Svend's sense of empowerment as he accepts Mormon baptism and a calling to preach the gospel to his countrymen, despite being occasionally arrested or attacked by unfriendly crowds, and highlights his efforts to maintain a relationship with his brother, who is not interested in the Mormons' teachings. Hanne's story is more concerned with the class differences between her and Svend that make him an unacceptable marriage partner in her parents' eyes. When

Svend rejects an offer from Hanne's relatives to pay for his education and training as a Lutheran pastor, she is forced to choose between the bourgeois life she has always taken for granted and the unknown path presented by embracing a foreign religion and immigrating to Utah alongside peasants and factory workers. At the end of the novel, as Svend and Hanne stand on the ship that will take them from Copenhagen to Liverpool, Hanne is holding a kitchen book her mother gave her, something "no Danish housekeeper could ever do without," and getting emotional at the memory of her mother teaching her how to cook and keep house the Danish way. An old sea captain, "who had lived on the island of Falster all his life until he heard the Mormon gospel," tells her, "Well, there goes Denmark. . . . She's a lovely land, that's the truth. But on a voyage, it's a strange thing. . . . Soon you begin to look for land the other way."[6] Sorensen never completed her second volume in the planned trilogy, which intended to follow the Madsens' journey to Utah and the fate of their descendants there, so the question remains as to how much of their Danish identity Svend and Hanne might have retained after settling in Utah.

In addition to literature, another valuable source for reconstructing how conversion to Mormonism shaped individual Danes' relationship to their native culture is personal histories, letters, diaries, memoirs, and conversion narratives. Despite the fact that these documents are often preoccupied with the details of everyday life and fail to explicitly address the question of cultural identity, they reveal how the author's sense of self changes in response to his or her surroundings. The group of Danes who accepted Mormonism between 1850 and 1915 is far too large and diverse to cover in a single chapter, or even an entire book, but discussing a range of individual Danish Mormons' life stories and private writings can provide a kind of "core sample" of the ways in which they negotiated their shifting sense of cultural identity. These personal narratives serve to flesh out and enliven public statements and statistical evidence regarding Danish Mormon convert-emigrants. As Mary Jo Maynes, Jennifer L. Pierce, and Barbara Laslett contend, personal narratives, precisely because of their subjective character, "open up space for new understandings of the relationship between the individual and the social. . . . Some explore in depth a particular *social, categorical or positional location* and thus address critical dimensions of social action that are otherwise opaque" (emphasis in original).[7] Whereas the predominantly antagonistic treatment of

Mormonism in Danish media during the late nineteenth century pays little attention to the actual, subjective experiences of Danish converts to Mormonism, this chapter provides a counterbalance to the preceding ones by documenting how several Danes articulated their own experience of adopting a new cultural identity as Mormons, revealing their own sense of their shifting social, categorical, and positional locations.

Cultural identity is not a zero-sum equation in which some degree of affinity with one culture must be sacrificed in order to make room for a new cultural affiliation; instead, it involves constant renegotiation within the parameters of a given situation. An object or behavior that seems acceptable or desirable in one context might feel inappropriate or embarrassing in another. Thus, individuals must choose which aspects of their cultural identity to foreground or de-emphasize according to the situation and their surroundings. This process is intensified and complicated by both conversion and migration. As the personal narratives discussed in this chapter reveal, becoming a Danish Mormon was not simply a cut-and-dried matter of joining the LDS Church, moving to Utah, severing all ties to Denmark, and abandoning all explicit markers of Danish cultural identity. Instead, it was a complex, nuanced process that often encompassed dualities and paradoxes, such as the willingness to endure financial and physical hardship in order to gather to Zion paired with resistance to the practice of plural marriage or insistence on continued consumption of coffee and beer despite the church's prohibition of alcohol, coffee, tea, and tobacco. Each convert's initial decision to embrace Mormonism became the catalyst for a host of changes and individual decisions, such as: what and how to believe; with whom to worship and in which language; whether to remain in Denmark or emigrate; whom to marry; whether to farm or work on the railroad; whether to celebrate the Danish Constitution Day or Mormon Pioneer Day, or both.

There is no set formula for the subjective transformation of individual identity, and neither the perceptions of outsiders nor statistical evidence—such as the numbers of Danish converts to and apostates from the LDS Church in a given year, or the rate at which Danish Mormons learned English and acquired American citizenship—can paint a complete picture of the emotional and psychological negotiations involved in this process. Personal narratives provide unique insights into how the individuals behind the numbers felt about becoming Danish Mormons and how this conversion affected their sense of cultural identity. Defining *ethnicity* as the "condition of cultural difference that results from migration," Jennifer Attebery uses the terms *explicit* and *implicit* to describe the different ways in which migrant populations express their cultural identity once they have been "displaced from familiar surroundings in which cultural practice is relatively homogenous to unfamiliar surroundings in which the dominant culture is dramatically different."[8] While each individual had to find his or her own way of balancing the competing claims of two homelands and two cultural-religious traditions, these personal narratives suggest that while Danish Mormons did not regard themselves as having abandoned their Danish identity by converting to Mormonism, they tended to explicitly prioritize their new religious affiliation over their cultural heritage, particularly after emigration, while still maintaining implicit elements of their Danish identity.

Self-representations of Danish Mormons in the late nineteenth century tend to fall into two general categories. The first contains published texts and print media, which the early Danish Mormon communities in Denmark and Utah used enthusiastically and effectively, producing a variety of newspapers—notably *Skandinaviens Stjerne* (*Scandinavia's Star*), *Morgenstjernen* (*The Morning Star*), and *Bikuben* (*The Beehive*)— as well as dozens of pamphlets and theological treatises. The guarantee of freedom of the press by the June Constitution proved to be crucial to the proselytizing efforts of the Danish LDS missionaries as well as to the development of a unique Danish Mormon cultural identity. Just as most of the opposition to the spread of Mormonism took the form of published texts, the LDS Church in Denmark used newspapers to spread their message and educate new converts in the history, theology, and cultural identity of their new religion. Many converts also published poems, songs, letters, and life histories that express their cultural identity for public consumption. These publications offer a sense of how Danish Mormons, as a group, were encouraged to view themselves.

The second category, which consists of private documents such as diaries, daybooks, letters, and unpublished memoirs, deals with individuals' personal narratives. Such texts rarely address cultural identity explicitly, but often demonstrate both the implicit maintenance of a sense of Danishness and the emergence of hybrid identities through gradual, often conscious, adaptation to new cultural norms. While documents from the first group reveal the public construction of a cohesive Danish Mormon identity, documents from the second group illustrate how individual Danish Mormons crafted hybrid cultural identities that often deviated from this official norm.

Thanks to relatively high levels of literacy among nineteenth-century Danes and the LDS Church's emphasis on family history, several hundred personal narratives of Danish Mormons have survived to illuminate the ways in which joining the LDS Church shaped their lives. Documents relating to some of these individuals, particularly those who served in administrative positions within the LDS Church in Utah—such as Apostle Anthon H. Lund and Assistant Church Historian Andrew Jenson—encompass thousands of pages. Jenson, for example, wrote twenty-seven books, two thousand newspaper articles, and fifteen volumes of diaries, in addition to taking part in many other historical preservation projects.[9] Given limitations of time and space, this chapter considers the personal narratives of just a few Danish Mormons who must serve as representatives of the whole, having converted and emigrated to Utah at different stages in their lives and at different points in the history of the LDS Church in Denmark. However, these Danes were never so prominent in either the LDS Church or Utah society as to tip the balance of their personal cultural calculus definitively in favor of an American Mormon identity.

The subjects of this chapter consist of three family groups: pioneer couple Hans Jørgensen and Wilhelmine Bolvig, who emigrated as unmarried young adults in the 1860s before meeting and marrying in Utah; the well-to-do farmer Mads Nielsen, his son David Madsen, and daughter-in-law Mette Marie, who emigrated as married adults in the 1880s, although Mads's wife never followed him as she had promised; and finally the Danish Parliament member Frederik Ferdinand (F. F.) Samuelsen and his family, who emigrated toward the end of Samuelsen's life, in the late 1910s. All of these individuals converted to the LDS Church while living in Denmark and eventually settled permanently in Utah, a process that required them to define their cultural identity in both contexts. While both Mads Nielsen and F. F. Samuelsen spent most of their adult lives in Denmark, Hans Jørgensen's missionary service in Denmark on two three-year missions (1865–1867 and 1881–1883), gave him the chance to reflect on his relationship to his native land and culture from the position of having already established a new identity for himself in the United States. Although none of these people explicitly address the topic of cultural identity, their life histories, personal letters, and diaries contain clues to the ways in which their decision to embrace Mormonism affected their sense and expressions of Danishness.

<h2 align="center">"God's Chosen People":
The Group Identity of Early Danish Mormons</h2>

Before turning to the personal narratives of individual Danish Mormons, it is important to establish the Danish Mormon community's collective identity in relation to which individual Danish Mormons defined their cultural identity. Published texts by and about the Church of Jesus Christ of Latter-day Saints in nineteenth-century Denmark played a central role in crafting and disseminating the self-image of the Danish Mormon community as "God's chosen people," a select group with exclusive access to the ordinances and authority of true Christianity and thereby salvation from imminent apocalypse.

Aside from the Book of Mormon itself and tracts such as *En Sandheds Røst* (*A Voice of Truth*) and *En Advarsel til Folket* (*A Warning to the People*), the major publication organ for the LDS Church in Denmark was *Skandinaviens Stjerne (Scandinavia's Star),* a semi-monthly paper published in Denmark from 1851 until 1956. The inaugural issue appeared in Copenhagen on October 1, 1851, with new issues appearing on the first of each month during the first year and subsequently on the first and fifteenth of the month. The first editor, who oversaw the selection, translation, and/or composition of each issue and thus set the tone for the self-presentation of the Mormon community in Denmark, was Erastus Snow, who later became known as the "Scandinavian apostle." Snow was followed by a succession of missionaries, primarily Danish Mormons who had previously emigrated, including such prominent men as Anthon Lund and Andrew Jenson, as well as the farmer Hans Jørgensen, whose personal narrative is examined later in this chapter.

Skandinaviens Stjerne aimed to shape and disseminate the group identity of Danish Mormons in two distinct ways. First and foremost, it instructed converts in the history and doctrine of their new faith, with articles on topics ranging from the need to prepare for the second coming of Jesus Christ to a biography of Joseph Smith to the practice of temple marriage. The newspaper also published direct communications from the leadership of the church in Salt Lake City. Since the LDS Church, then and now, depends on a lay ministry and volunteer missionaries, new converts in Denmark needed the education and training provided by the newspaper in order to be able to contribute to staffing local congregations and carrying out missionary work.

Second, the newspaper strove to counteract anti-Mormon publications in the Danish media, not primarily—as declared in the article "Et Gran af Sandhed i et Pund Løgn" ("A Grain of Truth in a Pound of Lies) that appeared in the second issue—by wasting "time, energy, and means on disproving these false reports" [10] (although the remainder of the article does precisely that), but rather by questioning the validity of the sources of criticism and proclaiming the wickedness of both the media and the so-called Christians who deny the truth of the restoration of Jesus Christ's church on earth. Thus, in addition to providing explicitly doctrinal content, *Skandinaviens Stjerne* challenged the authenticity of Danish Lutheranism and identified the implicit character and identity of Mormonism as American by printing descriptions of Utah, emigrant letters, convert poems, and songs about Zion; providing general news about Utah and the converts who had settled there; and giving instructions for future emigrants. As they read and identified with these personal narratives from fellow converts, new Danish Mormons could begin to imagine themselves as part of the community of Latter-day Saints in Utah.

An excellent example of how *Skandinaviens Stjerne* fulfilled this dual function of theological and cultural instruction is found in the first issue, which features a Danish translation of an article about the organization of the Church of Jesus Christ of Latter-day Saints. The article was written by John Taylor, an Englishman who converted from Methodism in 1836, was ordained an apostle in 1838, and would later serve as the third president of the LDS Church. In keeping with the goal of educating both new members and the general public, Taylor describes the lay leadership structure of the church, with the current prophet serving as president, supported by twelve apostles who preside over thirty-three quorums of seventy men called to preach the gospel throughout the world. He explains the church also includes a general class of "elders" whose task is to preach the gospel wherever they happen to be. Taylor lays out the various responsibilities

of each church office, emphasizing that this organization has been established and is maintained by revelation, and outlines the relationship
between the LDS Church and the American government. Near the end
of the article, Taylor recounts an experience in which he personally heard
the founder of the church, Joseph Smith, answer a question put to him by
an American legislator about how he rules over the people of his church.
According to Taylor, Smith replied, "I teach the people correct principles
and they govern themselves."[11] Taylor follows up this anecdote with the
assurance that he has witnessed this emancipatory principle in action in
Mormon congregations across Europe and the United States.

     Although church leaders in Utah were regularly accused of dictatorial
behavior by the American press during the late nineteenth century, the
participatory structure of the LDS Church in Denmark in the same period
bore out Taylor's assertions of shared governance. The early church had
neither the manpower nor the desire to send out enough representatives
from Utah to staff the rapidly increasing number of congregations in
Denmark. Instead, new Danish Mormons were given basic instruction in
the doctrine and practices of the church, organized into congregations,
and left to govern themselves, with guidance from a constantly shifting
procession of missionaries. The initial group of four missionaries that had
arrived in 1850 grew into a revolving pool of several dozen missionaries at
any given time, most of whom were either recent converts or returning
immigrants from Utah. In his *History of the Scandinavian Mission*, Andrew
Jenson provides a statistical overview of the membership and leadership
of the LDS Church in Denmark from 1850 to 1926. Jenson reveals that
there were never more than fifteen LDS missionaries in Denmark each
year from 1850 to 1879, the peak years of Mormon conversion and emigration. In 1861, for example, when church membership in Denmark
topped 3,469, including 1,297 new converts and 328 emigrants, there
were eleven missionaries serving in Denmark.[12] Under the nominal
oversight of the missionaries, therefore, who were thinly spread across
the country and spent the majority of their time proselytizing, the bulk
of the work of running each congregation and training new leaders fell
to the members themselves.

     As mentioned in chapter 2, this lay ministry model did not require
the lengthy and expensive training that *Folkekirken* pastors received, but

rather endowed its own members, however uneducated or socially insignificant they might have been, with priesthood authority and responsibility for each congregation's well-being. In a denunciation of Mormonism written by *Folkekirke* minister Carl Fog in 1851, Fog complains of precisely this dangerously empowering phenomenon: "Neither must we forget that it flatters the common man that he can become a pastor and council member without any particular education or knowledge and thus not just possess spiritual authority, but also a measure of temporal prestige, since the council decides all quarrels and conflicts within the Mormon community."[13] The fact that any common Dane who converted to Mormonism could find himself suddenly elevated to the spiritual and temporal status of a formally trained minister offended *Folkekirke* pastors like Fog, for whom the hierarchical status quo of Danish society was reassuring rather than restrictive. A career in the church had long been a way for ambitious men from humble circumstances to achieve social mobility, as was the case with Bishop Monrad, whose life is discussed in chapter 1. However, it was a highly selective path, not one that was available to all and sundry like the Mormon priesthood was. Mormonism's threat to social order was one of the factors that motivated Denmark's Lutheran pastors to advocate violent opposition to the spread of the LDS Church in Denmark, despite the protections promised by the June Constitution.

Bolstered by their newfound confidence, however, Danish Mormon citizens were determined to take advantage of the freedoms guaranteed in the constitution and not infrequently sought governmental assistance against their tormentors. One example of this is a petition submitted to the Danish Parliament on March 15, 1852, bearing by 850 signatures. In this letter, a committee representing the Danish Mormon community, whose members describe themselves as "Denmark's faithful subjects" and express gratitude to King Frederick VII, "the dear father of our country," for granting them religious freedom, request parliamentary assistance in ensuring their exercise of that same freedom by protecting them from the mob violence that had disrupted so many of their meetings in the preceding months.[14] Invoking the protection of paragraphs eighty and eighty-one of the June constitution, they declare their innocence of any transgression of the law and their intention of "honoring God and upholding the king's government and good laws." That the Danish Parliament

chose not to respond to the petition reveals the government's ambivalence toward this controversial group of its subjects and may well have
contributed to Danish Mormons' sense of mistreatment by and alienation from the Danish state.

Conversion to Mormonism in nineteenth-century Denmark was
thus both a theologically and a socially radical choice that resonated
with those Danes for whom the status quo offered few chances of economic advancement or social validation. The founding narrative of the
Church of Jesus Christ of Latter-day Saints rests on a divine visitation
granted to a poor, uneducated peasant boy, Joseph Smith, Jr., and his
subsequent elevation to prophet and president of the Lord's "only true
and living church upon the face of the earth."[15] Smith's experiences and
his claim to have restored the original church of Jesus Christ contributed
to a universal doctrine of chosenness that applied to all Mormons by
virtue of their belief in Smith's divine calling and their membership in
the restored church. This chosenness referred not only to the promise
of salvation after death, though that is a major feature of Mormon theology, but also to a more immediate emancipation from the tyranny of
social hierarchies and economic inequality. William Mulder points out
that many nineteenth-century Mormon hymns "promised a day of justice—the defeat of the clerics, the redemption of the poor."[16] For many
Danish Mormons, the way to achieve this day of justice was to separate
themselves from the institutions that dominated the Danish state (i.e.,
Folkekirken) and eventually emigrate.

The empowering message and democratic practice of Mormonism,
coupled with the fact that a large percentage of Danish Mormons were
drawn from the lower classes of tenant farmers, craftsmen, and day laborers, had a disruptive effect on Denmark's society and economy. Joining
the LDS Church seemed to validate the individual importance of many
of the least valued members of Danish society and provide them with a
way to escape their limited socioeconomic circumstances through organized, often subsidized, emigration. The late eighteenth-century land
reforms in Denmark that gave rise to a robust landowning rural middle
class—and thereby played a leading role in the shift to a constitutional
monarchy and the eventual enfranchisement of a large portion of the
Danish peasantry—had also brought about a massive expansion of the

class of landless farm workers and tenant farmers, on whose cheap labor the Danish landowning famers relied, but whose quality of life and social standing were minimal.

Many converts to Mormonism who had previously been submissive to the counsel of the local minister and aware of their subordinate position in society became much more assertive and confrontational after their baptism. They argued with their ministers about theology, questioned social norms, and demonstrated a new self-confidence rooted in the assurance of their own salvation while their neighbors were condemned to damnation. Egdal recounts the history of the smallholder Christian Nielsen from Lunge (on the island of Funen), who not only resisted his minister's exhortations to recant, but also baptized his eleven-year-old daughter Karen Marie in the spring of 1854, withdrew her from the local school to protect her from the evils of the world, repeatedly refused to pay fines for her absence, and appealed his case all the way to the Ministry of Education before emigrating in April 1857.[17] Although her father eventually relented and allowed her reenroll in school for two years prior to the family's emigration, Karen Marie later recalled her school days as painful because of the bullying she experienced from fellow students, which caused her to eagerly anticipate their emigration and devote herself all the more fervently to her new faith.[18]

As Christian Nielsen's reluctance to allow his daughter to attend the parish school for fear of moral corruption illustrates, one of the central tenets of Mormon theology in late nineteenth-century Denmark was the wickedness of "Babylon" and the need to gather to Utah to escape the destruction that would accompany the imminent return of Jesus Christ to the earth. This apocalyptic message rested upon the accusation that members of the Danish Lutheran Church were not faithful or righteous enough to warrant salvation without conversion. While many of the opponents of the Church of Jesus Christ of Latter-day Saints have often charged Mormonism with not being a Christian religion, Danish Mormons implied (and sometimes explicitly preached) that Lutheran Danes who rejected the Mormon message of Christian restoration were not themselves Christian enough to be saved. Naturally, preaching that their non-Mormon neighbors were wicked and doomed to destruction did not earn the Mormons many friends among their Lutheran countrymen, but it did persuade many

Danish Mormons to exchange their homeland for the perils of an Atlantic Ocean crossing and a trek across the American prairie.

The Paradox of Danish American Mormon Culture

Aside from such contentious doctrinal issues as adult baptism, ongoing revelation, and plural marriage, one of the primary reasons that Mormonism attracted so much attention, both positive and negative, in nineteenth-century Denmark was because of its close association with the promise of America. Mulder explains,

> Hardly a family in Denmark . . . had not read Mormon tracts by 1885, and most knew, or knew of, someone who had gone to Utah. The missionary might finger the word "Zion" in a huge scrawl across the smoky ceiling of some lowly cottage. For the wonderstruck villagers, the moment materialized and joined two myths—the Mormons and the American West. What had been rumor became an advent filling the dwelling, immediate and immense. The coming of the Mormons turned the fabulous into a fact and a disturbing personal force.[19]

Although the primary motivation for the Mormon migration was theological, the socioeconomic factors that drove the vast majority of emigration from Scandinavia in this period also applied to Danish Mormons, particularly those of lower social classes. Jørgen Würtz Sørensen identifies the Danish Mormon emigration as "a real or apparent social protest, a protest directed not just at *Folkekirken*, but toward the entire bourgeois social order as such."[20] Minister Harald Jensen Kent, who served from 1906 to 1912 as the head of the Danish Lutheran Utah Mission, which exerted itself to reclaim Danish Mormons for the faith of their fathers, published a 1913 treatise intended to combat the efforts of Mormon missionaries and their publications in Denmark. Kent attempts to account for the otherwise inexplicable fact that Danes made up the largest proportion of Mormons in Utah after English-speakers by explaining the church's emphasis on the doctrine of "gathering the Saints from Babylon to Zion," but argues that the implication of this doctrine is that "over there in Utah 'the poor' are surely to become rich." [21] Mulder agrees that Mormonism, "as native to America as Indian corn, was in fact a dynamic and very special version of the country's romantic prospects, its optimistic gospel of a promised land."[22]

Although Mormons, both those of American origin and Danish converts, were identified as "American" in Danish society, Mormonism itself was often regarded as "foreign" by Americans, mainly because of the large numbers of European immigrants that made up the early LDS Church. In adopting Mormonism and immigrating to Utah, Danish converts thus assumed a new "American" identity, but their own immigration simultaneously contributed to the perception of the Mormon Church in America as dangerously foreign. Reverend A. S. Bailey, addressing all the denominational workers in the Utah Territory, declared that a traveler visiting Utah would find not simply "more that is European than American," but also "a spirit foreign to the spirit of Americans, . . . a system indigenous indeed, but hostile to American ideas."[23] After arriving in Utah, Danish Mormons thus found themselves both physically and psychologically isolated from other Americans, including other Danish Americans. This tendency to regard Danish Mormons as simultaneously less invested in the American experience and less connected to their Danish roots because of their faith persists in historical studies of Scandinavian heritage in the United States.

With the notable exception of William Mulder's comprehensive survey of Scandinavian Mormon immigration, English-language chroniclers of Danish immigration to the United States have generally focused on the communities of Danish Lutherans who settled in places like Chicago, Illinois; Racine, Wisconsin; Elkhorn, Iowa; Blair, Nebraska; and Solvang, California, leaving the story of Danish Mormons in Utah largely untold. However, not only were the earliest Danish communities in western Iowa and eastern Nebraska founded by disaffected Mormon converts who either failed to complete the journey to Utah or backtracked at a later date, but the large numbers of Danish Mormons that settled in Utah made it possible for them to establish several heavily Danish and Scandinavian settlements throughout the state—from Elsinore in Sevier County (near the middle of the state) to Ephraim and Manti in Sanpete County to enclaves in Pleasant Grove and Salt Lake City to Cache County (in the northern part of the state).

Danish Mormon immigration began with fairly small groups but quickly scaled up to a mass movement. The first group of twenty-eight emigrants left Copenhagen in early 1852, less than two years after the arrival of the first Mormon missionaries in Denmark. Accompanied by Erastus Snow, who had been involved in many of their conversions, they crossed the plains in ox-drawn covered wagons and arrived in Salt Lake City, Utah, on October 16, 1852. *Skandinaviens Stjerne* reported of the emigrants, "They are all alive and well satisfied and they urge their friends to follow them."[24]

Though this report was intended to dispel fears about the hazards of the journey and conditions in Salt Lake, it also illustrates how Danish Mormons began to carve out a cultural space for themselves within the Mormon settlements. Mulder notes that many of the immigrants settled in Salt Lake City's Second Ward, which soon became known as "Little Denmark."[25] They were joined a year later by a second group of Danish converts, led by another of the first missionaries to Denmark, John Forsgren. Many members of Forsgren's company went south to the high country of Sanpete County, where they established the communities of Spring Town (known as "New Denmark"), Manti, and Ephraim. As the land filled up with settlers, additional Scandinavian communities emerged, such as Elsinore (in Sevier County) and Logan (in Cache County).

Although many Scandinavian communities in the United States, like these towns in Utah, marketed themselves as "Little Denmark" or "New Sweden" in order to make potential settlers feel a sense of belonging, one of the unique aspects of the Mormon migration from Scandinavia was—as Mulder's book title *Homeward to Zion* indicates—the way in which the move to Utah was pitched as a spiritual homecoming that preempted the convert-immigrants' ethnic solidarity. Harald Jensen Kent notes that messages from the LDS Church to Danish converts, published in *Skandinaviens Stjerne*, invite them to "come home" to Zion. "It is important to remember," Kent cautions, "that this 'come *home*' means that these people, who have never before left their fatherland, should call Utah, which is entirely foreign to them, their 'home' and hurry there" (emphasis in original).[26] By way of illustration, one Danish Mormon hymn, "O Du Zion i Vest" ("O Thou Zion in the West"), taught new converts to dream of "my valley home, my mountain home." In this way, Danish Mormons were conditioned to form an emotional bond with their new home that would ease their transition from Denmark and strengthen their sense of belonging to their new culture and society.

Another unique aspect of the Danish Mormon migration was its multidirectionality. Rather than just consisting of a flood of Danish Mormons coming to Utah, the migration also included a relatively consistent stream of Danish Mormons returning to Denmark. Though some returned as disaffected apostates, the majority returned to their homeland to serve as missionaries for the LDS Church for one- to three-year stints, often several times. With their native knowledge of Danish culture and their firsthand familiarity with conditions in Utah, these returning emigrants were particularly effective as missionaries and advocates of emigration. They also had the experience—which was fairly unique among Danish immigrants to the United States, most of whom did not return to Denmark for extended periods of time after their emigration—of attempting to temporarily reintegrate into their native culture after having adopted an additional national identity.

Despite differences in motivation and a more structured organization, the Danish Mormon migration functioned according to the pattern that was common among Lutheran Norwegian and Swedish immigrants to the Midwest in the same period. Mulder notes that the success of the first two Danish immigrant companies to reach and settle in Utah "was worth a pound of propaganda in Scandinavia, and a hundred companies confidently followed in their wake, their adventures continually renewing the twice-told tale of the first voyagers and pioneers."[27] This phenomenon is called *chain migration*, in which the emigration of one family member or resident of a particular area leads to the subsequent emigration of others from the same family or area. John and Leatrice McDonald define chain, or serial, migration as a "movement in which prospective migrants learn of opportunities, are provided with transportation, and have initial accommodation and employment arranged by means of primary social relationships with previous migrants."[28] Expanding on this definition, Douglas Massey, Jorge Durand, and Nolan J. Malone argue that "each act of migration creates social capital among people to whom the migrant is related, thereby raising the odds of their migration."[29] This increased social capital was the deciding factor for many of the emigrants who came after the initial wave of pioneers.

The reported experiences of the initial emigrants changed the decision-making framework for friends, neighbors, and relatives back home, making it more likely that they too would consider emigrating—and easier for them to do so. Unlike mainstream Scandinavian immigration to the United States, however, the waves of Danish Mormon immigrants were not as determined by economic conditions in either their homeland or their new land. As Mulder explains, "The Danes, proverbially reluctant to sail out farther than they could row back and traditionally considered poor pioneers, nevertheless, as Mormons, left their homeland in years of actual prosperity to become hardy grass-roots settlers well beyond the frontier of Scandinavian occupation in the United States."[30]

Not only did many prosperous Danes choose to emigrate in order to join with their fellow Mormons in Utah, the communal orientation of the church (which encouraged well-off emigrants to sponsor poorer ones), as well as loans available from the church's Perpetual Emigration Fund, made it possible for people to emigrate who would not have had the financial resources to do so on their own. The theological dimension of Danish Mormon immigration thus overrode both the economic and cultural considerations that shaped most other Danish immigration to the United States. At the same time, however, Danish Mormon immigrants faced many of the same challenges as other Danish Americans, including language preservation, intermarriage, and maintenance of cultural traditions, from traditional songs to sweet soup recipes.

As a result, the question of cultural identity maintenance and/or transformation is a complicated one with regard to the Danish Mormon community. Those accounts of Utah history that do mention the many thousands of Danish immigrants to Utah take it for granted that the converts abandoned their Danish heritage in favor of their new identity as Mormons and Americans. The initial decision to join the LDS Church and adopt its belief system already represented a major shift in the subject's cultural identity, both in terms of self-perception and perception by outsiders, as the preceding chapters have shown. By immigrating to Utah, converts added an additional layer of cultural identity by adopting American customs, language, and citizenship, but this new national identity often competed with the immigrant's identity as a Mormon—for example, when the U.S. government outlawed the Mormon practice of polygamy. When Pastor H. C. Rørdam accused the Mormon community in Vendsyssel (in northern Jutland) of practicing polygamy in 1854, an editorial in *Skandinaviens Stjerne* responded with a vehement denial, noting that "it would be a violation of the

FIGURE 4.1 Photograph of the First Presidency of the Church of Jesus Christ of Latter-day Saints in 1905, with Rex Winder (left), Joseph F. Smith (middle), and Anthon H. Lund (right). Danish Mormon Anthon H. Lund joined the LDS Church as a young boy in Aalborg, Denmark, and went on to become the first Scandinavian-born apostle and member of the First Presidency. Reproduced courtesy of the LDS Church History Library, Salt Lake City, Utah.

law of this land."[31] However, although most Danish Mormons prided themselves on being law-abiding citizens, both in the old country and the new, the percentage of Scandinavian Mormons in Utah who served jail time for violating the Edmunds-Tucker Anti-Polygamy Act of 1887 was even higher than the percentage of Scandinavians actually involved in plural marriages. It was regarded as an honor to be imprisoned for the sake of one's beliefs.[32] In the struggle between obeying the law of the land and the law of God (as revealed through the church), Danish Mormons tended to choose the latter.

While it is true that LDS church leaders expected and strongly encouraged assimilation in order to create a cohesive community out of immigrants from the eastern United States, Great Britain, Germany, Scandinavia, and many other countries, Danish Mormons were able to assert and maintain their cultural specificity in many ways, from holding church services in their native language to celebrating Danish national holidays, such as Constitution Day on June 5 (although this particular holiday, which had originated among upper- and middle-class Danes, took some time to gain traction among farmers and peasants). Although many Danish Mormons assimilated rapidly into English-speaking settlements in Utah, large numbers of Danish Mormon immigrants chose to settle in predominantly Scandinavian communities, where they could continue to speak Danish in the course of their everyday lives, intermarry with other Scandinavians, and express their Danish cultural identity in both explicit and implicit ways. Several Danish-language newspapers, such as *Bikuben* and *Utah Posten*, facilitated communication between the far-flung Danish communities in Utah, while pan-Scandinavian organizations commemorated important events. For example, the fiftieth anniversary of the arrival of the first LDS missionaries in Denmark was celebrated with a four-day jubilee featuring distinguished Scandinavian Mormon speakers (including Apostle Anthon H. Lund and the painter C. C. A. Christensen), a commemorative volume of reminiscences and illustrations, an evening concert, an outdoor carnival, and a group outing to the Great Salt Lake bathing resort Saltair.[33] The numerical superiority of Danish Mormons among Scandinavian settlers in Utah made them such an important constituency that a group of Swedish Mormons, led by Otto Rydman, protested in 1904 that the Danish Mormons received preferential treatment from the LDS Church.

The close-knit Scandinavian Mormon communities in Utah made it easier in some ways for Danish Mormons to preserve aspects of their Danish cultural identity than for other Danish Americans, who were spread more thinly across the American Midwest, though the considerations that factored into such decisions were unique to their situation. In contrast to Danish Lutherans who settled in predominantly Protestant or secular American communities, Danish Mormons' efforts to blend elements of their Danish cultural identity with a new American one had to take the norms of Mormon culture and the expectations of the LDS Church into account. These negotiations contributed to certain accommodations that other Danish Americans did not have to even consider, such as risking imprisonment in order to defend the doctrine of polygamy or giving their children Mormon-inflected names such as Erastus and Nephi.

These accommodations did not, however, require the complete abandonment of Danish values or traditions, even when those traditions came into conflict with LDS norms. Jennifer Eastman Attebery has documented the presence of such cultural identity markers among Danish Mormons in forms as diverse as self-descriptions in America letters and the celebration of Scandinavian holidays in Utah.[34] Similarly, Rachel Gianni Abbott has shown how the material culture legacy of Scandinavian Mormons, which encompasses both objects brought from the old country and objects produced in America, confirms their efforts to maintain their cultural heritage despite some inevitable modifications and adaptations.[35]

By way of example, folkloric accounts emphasize how Danish Mormon immigrants modified certain aspects of Mormon culture to accommodate their Danish habits and preferences, particularly regarding the Mormon health code known as the Word of Wisdom, which forbids the use of alcohol, tobacco, and coffee. This was not unique to Scandinavians, to be sure, but Danes in the heavily Scandinavian community of Elsinore, for example, prided themselves on their home-brewed beer and regarded coffee as a necessity of civilized life. Anthon H. Lund's bride Sarah Peterson, whose father had been among the Norwegian converts to Mormonism in the Fox River Valley (Illinois) in the 1840s, made Lund promise before their wedding that he would allow her to continue "indulging her Scandinavian fondness for coffee and tea" and would never take a second wife.[36] Although there was—and still is—a strong coffee culture in Scandinavia, the attribution of noncompliance with the Word of Wisdom to a perceived Scandinavian cultural norm may well have been little more than a convenient excuse for those convert-immigrants who found it a difficult requirement to accept.

In addition to maintaining their own Danish traits, one could even argue that Danish Mormon settlers in Utah helped shape the character of the state itself and thereby perpetuated aspects of Danish culture in their new homeland. The communal nature of many aspects of pioneer society in Utah bears a strong resemblance to such Danish traditions as cooperative economic enterprises and communal settlements. Abbott's research shows that "Mormons were indeed communal in many more aspects than other Americans; though they were pioneers in moving westward into unsettled territory, they created a rather insular

community."[37] Likewise, Davis Bitton contends that Mormon collectiv-
ism conflicted with the laissez-faire economic practices of the United
States in the late nineteenth century.[38] Instead, Mormon village settlement patterns resembled traditional (pre-land reform) Scandinavian villages, with homes clustered together and farms outside the village, rather
than individual homesteads on separate farms. It may be impossible to
determine whether such features of Utah pioneer life were inspired by
Danish Mormons, either directly or indirectly, but their presence suggests that Danish Mormons may have found certain customs and values
in their new homeland to be familiar from their old one.

Personal Narratives of Danish Mormons

While some aspects of the immigrant experience, such as those discussed
above, were likely common to the majority of Danish Mormons, others
were unique to each individual and can thus offer insights into the subjective experience of negotiating a new, hybrid cultural identity. The following personal narratives of a few nineteenth-century Danish Mormons
illuminate how both these commonalities and unique traits affected the
subject's sense of his or her own cultural identity.

Despite the large number of Danish Mormons who settled in Utah,
most of them were not well known or particularly visible in Utah public
life, with such notable exceptions as the beloved chronicler of pioneer
life, painter C. C. A. Christensen; Anthon H. Lund, who was Erastus
Snow's successor as the "Scandinavian apostle"; and the remarkably prolific historian Andrew Jenson. Most Danish Mormons in Utah lived their
lives in quiet obscurity, tending to their farms, raising their families, and
striving for happiness and salvation. Their experiences are represented
by the letters of the pioneer couple Hans and Wilhelmine Jørgensen and
the family group consisting of Mads Nielsen, his son David Madsen, and
daughter-in-law Mette Marie Madsen, all of whom devoted themselves to
building up the LDS Church and developing the Utah Territory at the cost
of their connection to their homeland and family members in Denmark.

At the same time, however, while their experiences may be somewhat
more atypical, the prominence of a few Danish Mormons in Denmark
spotlighted their approaches to adapting their Danish cultural heritage to
their newer Mormon identity. In Denmark around the turn of the twentieth century, the most prominent Danish Mormon was arguably F. F.

FIGURE 4.2 After Hans Jørgensen immigrated to Utah and settled down as a farmer in a Danish community in Pleasant Grove, he was called back to Denmark as a missionary for two and a half years, leaving his wife and four children behind. Photograph (1881) reproduced courtesy of Mary Lambert.

Samuelsen, a machinist, union representative, and member of the Danish Parliament representing the city of Aarhus. By looking at each of these individuals in turn, we can get a sense of the range of experiences and personal transformations involved in becoming and remaining a faithful nineteenth-century Danish Mormon.

The Pioneer Couple: Hans and Wilhelmine Jørgensen

The extensive correspondence between two young Danish immigrant converts to Mormonism, Hans and Wilhelmine (Mine) Jørgensen, in the

FIGURE 4.3 Wilhelmine Marie Jacobsen Bolvig Jørgensen (1881). While her husband Hans was serving as a missionary in Denmark, Mine Jørgensen struggled to provide for her family, support her husband, and live up to the expectations of her community. Photograph reproduced courtesy of Mary Lambert.

early 1880s—while Hans was serving as a missionary in Denmark and Mine ran their farm in Utah—reveals their emerging identity as Danish American Mormons. Although both Hans and Mine had immigrated to Utah at relatively young ages more than a decade earlier, their joint personal narrative shows how they preserved certain linguistic and cultural elements of their Danish heritage while incorporating the economic, social, and theological ideals that permeated their American surroundings. Most importantly, their letters reveal that their cultural identity was largely derived from factors unrelated to political or rhetorical conceptions of national identity.

Hans Jørgensen's personal history intersects with the socioeconomic history of nineteenth-century Denmark at many points, most significantly the plight of the disenfranchised cottager class in the wake of late eighteenth-century peasant reforms. Hans was born to Jørgen Hansen and Maren Nielsen in Kappendrup, on the island of Funen, on September 25,

1845. Jørgen was a cottager, part of the landless peasant class, which had been marginalized and largely disenfranchised by the peasant reforms that had enabled well-to-do copyholder tenant farmers to buy their own farms at the expense of their less fortunate neighbors, who were subjected to heavier labor dues and unfavorable, short-term tenancy contracts.

Hans's father Jørgen was drafted as a soldier during the First Schleswig War in 1848 (better known in Danish history as *Treårskrigen*, the three-year war), serving under Major Saint de Aubain during the defense of Fredericia. He was badly wounded in the battle of Isted Hede on July 24–25, 1850, and was awarded the Order of the Dannebrog in recognition of his valiant service. Although this distinction brought about little immediate improvement in his circumstances, Jørgen proudly bore the title of "Dannebrogs Mand" all of his life. By the late nineteenth century, as technological advancements alleviated the need for the cheap labor provided by cottagers in Denmark, Jørgen was able to purchase land and move up into the class of independent farmers.

When Hans was born, however, his parents were servants and did not have the economic stability to marry or maintain a permanent home. They were forced to foster him out to a neighbor, Anders Hansen and his wife Abelone, in nearby Hjadstrup, where Hans attended school from 1852–1858. During the summers, Hans worked as a farmhand for another neighbor, Knud Larsen, for which he was paid two rigsdaler and some clothing. In the fall of 1858, Hans moved fifty kilometers south to Espe Skovgaard, near Faaborg, to attend school, from which he was discharged after a year with good recommendations from the local parish priest. In keeping with local custom and by his own choice, Hans was confirmed in the Lutheran Church in Espe Skovgaard in October 1859, at age fifteen. Hans began hiring out as a day laborer at the age of seventeen, an occupation that provided little opportunity for social mobility or economic improvement.

Although the LDS missionaries had been quite successful in the Kappendrup area, Hans apparently did not encounter Mormonism until he was working on C. Hall's farm in northern Jutland, another area where the missionaries had found a receptive population. Elder Peter Nielsen baptized Hans into the LDS Church on January 21, 1863. His decision to become a Mormon incurred his master's disapproval. As punishment, Mr. Hall arranged for Hans (who was still a minor) to be transferred to the employ of Mr. Lyberg Petersen on Liverslet, whom Hans described as a "regular tyrant" and who denied him contact with the LDS Church for a year. In 1864, having attained his majority and returned to northern Jutland, Hans was ordained an elder and called to serve as a local missionary in Denmark from 1864 to 1867. He then emigrated on June 20, 1868, on the packet ship *Emerald Isle* out of Liverpool. Led by Elder Hans Jensen Hals, the company consisted of 876 Latter-day Saints, of whom 627 were Scandinavians. The crossing was unpleasant, due to harsh treatment by the crew, an outbreak of measles, and a lack of fresh water, which contributed to a death toll of 37 passengers.[39] After nearly eight weeks at sea, Hans arrived at Castle Garden in New York on August 14. He then crossed the plains by rail and ox-drawn wagon, arriving in Salt Lake City in September 1868. Much of the work he was able to find involved tending livestock and helping local farmers with their harvests. On one occasion, he built irrigation ditches; on two others, he hired on with the Union Pacific Railway but had to quit because of illness.

Sometime during his first few years in Utah, Hans met another Danish Mormon immigrant, Wilhelmine (Mine) Marie Jacobsen Bolvig. The details of her early life are not as well-documented, but she was born in Astrup parish, in the county of Hjørring, on September 19, 1849, just a few months after the adoption of the Danish constitution. She joined the LDS Church on November 17, 1861, at the age of twelve. She immigrated to Utah in 1862 along with her mother, one sister, and two brothers—her father remained behind in Denmark. Mine became engaged to Hans on April 5, 1871, and they were married on March 4, 1872, in Salt Lake City by Apostle Daniel H. Wells. Over the next seven years, they welcomed five children into their family while struggling to establish themselves as farmers, Mormons, and Americans.

Hard work and financial difficulties were an integral part of the Jørgensens' lives, as they were for most Danish immigrants, Mormon or Lutheran. After living with Mine's family for more than a year after their wedding, the young couple settled on a homestead farm in Pleasant Grove, among many other Danish immigrants, in a two-room house Hans built. Life on the farm, though more rewarding than the near-serfdom Hans had left behind in Denmark, was difficult and cash money hard to come by. When Hans's mother died, he received an inheritance of $181.57. He used the money to buy two oxen, an old wagon, and a plow in order to be in a position to work for himself.

Frontier farming was difficult and unpredictable, however, and a few years of bad weather set the young couple back in their hopes of prosperity. After losing both of his oxen in 1875, Hans found it impossible to support his family by farming his own land. For the next three years, Hans supported his family by hiring out to other farmers, for which he was paid largely in crops, as well as working for the railroad during the winters. The Jørgensens strove diligently to realize the immigrant's American dream of land ownership and self-sufficiency, but it remained just out of reach.

At this juncture in Hans's and Mine's lives, their economic priorities came into conflict with the theological demands of their faith. In March 1881, just when the Jørgensens had finally managed to regain their financial footing and replace their team of oxen, Hans was called to return to Denmark as a missionary. Despite concerns over money and the family's survival during his absence, Hans accepted the call and spent nearly three years, from April 1881 until November 1883, back in the land of his birth, thousands of miles away from his wife, children, and farm. During his mission, he and Mine wrote to each other at least once a month.

Their lengthy correspondence, which fills hundreds of pages, provides rare and candid insight into how the cultural identity of this young couple was gradually transformed, but by no means erased, by their relationship to their new religion and homeland. Significantly, Hans and Mine's letters convey little consciousness of any national identity, whether Danish, American, or Danish American. Instead, they provide both implicit and explicit evidence that the Jørgensens' sense of identity was rooted primarily in family, religion, and socioeconomic status.

Hans and Mine's correspondence challenges the thesis that Danish Mormon immigrants assimilated immediately and completely into a multiethnic LDS theocracy that suppressed the use of foreign languages. On the whole, Hans and Mine supported each other in their faith and Mormon identity, but they also made deliberate efforts to maintain aspects—both explicit and implicit—of their Danish cultural identity. Although Hans spoke English well and kept his mission diary in English, all of the letters between Hans and his wife are written in Danish, with the exception of a handful of letters written by Hans to his sons in English. Even after nearly two decades in Utah, Hans and Mine's primary language of communication with each other, their neighbors, and their fellow Latter-day

Saints was Danish. The fact that Hans's letters to his sons were written in English demonstrates the importance he and Mine placed on having their children acquire the fluency necessary to integrate fully into American society, a priority shared by many other Scandinavian immigrant families across the United States. With fewer opportunities and less need to interact with English speakers, Mine never learned to speak or write English comfortably, but she was also ill at ease writing in Danish, as she mentions in several letters, which suggests she had even less formal education than Hans. When Hans returned to Denmark in 1881, he reported no difficulty reintegrating into the linguistic community of Danes, in large part because he had continued to use Danish in his everyday life in Pleasant Grove, which was well known for its large Danish population. In 1880, the year before Hans left on his mission, the federal census documented 238 Danish-born individuals—as well as 83 Swedes and 11 Norwegians—among Pleasant Grove's total population of around 1,600 people.[40]

Conveniently located on the main road between Salt Lake City and Provo, with good grazing and farmlands, Pleasant Grove attracted so many immigrant Scandinavians between 1870 and 1890 that Scandinavians made up one-third of the town's population by the end of the century, numbering more than 110 families out of 351 total. Scandinavian immigrants tended to settle in the neighborhoods known as "Little Denmark" and "Danish Bench."[41] Scandinavians formed a sizable subcommunity within Pleasant Grove, hosting frequent private gatherings and public holiday celebrations. Assistant Church Historian Andrew Jenson, a fellow Danish resident of Pleasant Grove for many years, recalled attending frequent private parties with other Scandinavians: "Usually, a splendid meal was served after which the little company would engage in dancing and playing until midnight, when a light luncheon would be served prior to breaking up."[42] Scandinavian Christmas Day programs were held annually in the local schoolhouse from 1876 to 1916, Scandinavian New Year's Eve and Midsummer festivities were a highlight of community life, and the grand Scandinavian balls held in Orpheus Hall became so popular in the 1910s that they attracted non-Scandinavians as well and helped to integrate both communities.[43] The Scandinavian community in Pleasant Grove remained close-knit through the 1930s, when the last of the Scandinavian-born settlers passed on.

Although the Anglo American character of the LDS Church and the ethnic diversity of the Utah Territory are commonly cited as primary causes for the rapid integration of Danish American Mormons, the cohesiveness of Scandinavian identity in Pleasant Grove existed within the religious as well as the private sphere. In keeping with official church policy of the period, which allowed foreign-speaking saints to "hold religious services in their own language until they acquire a sufficient knowledge of English language to keep pace with the rest of the Saints,"[44] Scandinavian-language church meetings were held in Pleasant Grove on a regular basis over several decades. In the winter, Scandinavian-language worship services were held every Wednesday night, meeting simultaneously in three separate homes around the town in order to accommodate the large number of Scandinavian Mormons who preferred to attend services in their native language, or at least an approximation of it. In the summers, they assembled in a large hall on Sunday afternoons. A Scandinavian choir organized in 1875 performed Danish hymns at Sunday meetings and festivals until the mid-1930s.[45] Consequently, Hans and Mine's experience of the Mormon religion, even in Utah, was primarily a Danish—or at least a Scandinavian—one.

Given the intensive and sustained efforts to preserve and celebrate Scandinavian heritage and language among Danish Americans in Pleasant Grove, one might be justified in expecting Hans Jørgensen to be pleased with the chance to return as a missionary to his native land, albeit tempered by the hardship of separation from his family. However, one of the most striking, recurring themes in Hans's letters to Mine is his sense of alienation from Danish society, which demonstrates that his cultural identity was linked to but by no means identical with his linguistic practice. Despite their continued use of Danish and observation of Danish holidays and traditions, Hans and Mine Jørgensen no longer seemed to regard themselves as Danes. In their letters, Hans and Mine refer to Denmark as "the land of your [Hans'] birth" or "my native land," but they never employ terms such as "homeland," or "fatherland." "Home" is reserved for references to Pleasant Grove and Hans and Mine's family there. In one of his first letters to Mine, dated May 17, 1881, Hans writes,

I cannot say that I am happy that I have returned to the land of my birth, for my thoughts are mostly on the other side of the

Atlantic Ocean. If only I might live and be reunited with you once again in our little home, for I must truly say that I do not rejoice in this part of the world. It is as if something whispers in my ear, you are a stranger here. The green fields and the beautiful beech forests have no impact on me, nor does Copenhagen with all of its delights succeed in attracting my attention to the degree that I should desire to any degree to remain here or rejoice here.[46]

This passage makes it clear that Hans's interests and affections are more invested in his wife and family than in the land and culture of his birth and heritage. His expressed inability to appreciate the iconic attractions of the Danish landscape and the Copenhagen cityscape can be attributed both to a desire to convince his wife that he truly does miss her and to the fact that his identity is not based in nationalistic or patriotic sentiment, but rather in the private, domestic sphere.

More than just illustrating his homesickness for his family, Hans's description of feeling like a stranger in Copenhagen reflects his lack of connection to an "imagined community" of Denmark as a nation, to use Benedict Anderson's well-known concept. Instead, Hans's Danish identity was tied to the particular regions of Denmark in which he lived and to the people he knew there, both as a child and later as a missionary. In addition, Hans had spent his entire life, both in Denmark and in America, in rural surroundings, with little exposure to or appreciation for urban environments. On May 20, just a few days after his first letter, he explains to Mine, "Copenhagen is a little too much for me. . . . I cannot tell you anything about the glories of Copenhagen, for I have seen nothing, nor do I care very much about doing so."[47] After celebrating Danish Constitution Day on June 5 in the Deer Park north of Copenhagen, he writes, "I cannot say that I amused myself with anything other than the beauty of nature. Even that seemed foreign to me and there is always something missing."[48] Now accustomed to the more arid landscape of his adopted home, Hans no longer felt at home in the lushness of a Danish park, although he appreciated its beauty.

Hans's reluctance to take advantage of the "glories of Copenhagen" is connected to his dual sense of religious identity as both a Mormon and a product of the Danish Lutheran Church. This hybrid spiritual-cultural identity permeates his letters in the form of both the formulaic Lutheran phrases from his youth, such as his frequent expressions of gratitude to God for the gift of health,[49] and specifically Mormon references, such as when he urges Mine to ensure that their oldest son accepts baptism. He regards many of the Danes he encounters as sinful and oppressed, which opinion is both a cause and a consequence of his conversion to Mormonism and his calling as a missionary. On June 6, he observes, "People in this city [Copenhagen] have sunk deep into all sorts of sins. Only a few care about the life after this one."[50] He expresses deep concern over the pride and vanity of those peasants who had benefited most from the improving economic situation in Denmark in the latter half of the nineteenth century, noting:

> The peasants here in Denmark now dress so well that it is hard to keep up with them. They ride in spring carts and if someone should dare to ask to ride with them, one is regarded with the deepest contempt. Their gardens are laid out in the most sophisticated manner, their sitting rooms are papered, and they hardly recognize themselves, let alone the time of their visitation, for it is hidden from their eyes now what will come shortly.[51]

Such widespread indifference, to religion in general and the Mormon gospel in particular, frustrated Hans, whose own sense of self was deeply rooted in his religious convictions and solidarity with other Danish American Mormons in Utah. He frequently mentions the letters and money he receives from their neighbors, and he often tells Mine how determined he is to do his duty to God by completing his mission honorably, despite his longing for home: "I wish with all of my heart that I can complete this task without causing any shame, that I will never do anything that would cause dishonor to us in the future, but I am sure that it can be done if one earnestly seeks the help of the Lord in this cause."[52] He worries that any weakness on his part will reflect badly on his family and hurt his reputation in the Danish community back home. Rather than identifying with an imagined community of Danes in Denmark, Hans perceived himself as belonging to a geographically limited, ethnically homogenous, theologically unified community of Danish Mormons in Utah, whose opinion of him carried much greater weight than that of his countrymen in Denmark.

Hans's dissatisfaction with social conditions in Denmark was one of the factors that had prompted him to embrace the Mormon faith as a young man, and now, with the benefit of his experiences in Utah, where life was hard but rewarding and the promises of capitalism and Christianity often went hand in hand, he saw his objections confirmed. On June 1, 1881, he writes,

> I am happy to be able to say that the brethren here who are from Utah truly seek to preserve the spirit of God and to direct their calling to his honor. I see no reason to say anything else about them. The Saints, although poor, also do their duty as best they are able. It is a mystery how these poor people live on the trifling day wages they receive for their work, but they manage to sustain life and the hope that they will see better days someday gives them the courage to remain on the path upon which they have embarked.[53]

Both economic and doctrinal factors contributed to the runaway success of the Mormon missionaries in Denmark during this period. This passage expresses Hans's conviction that LDS doctrine combined with American opportunity created the path to success and happiness for Danish peasants, particularly those who had both the least to lose by leaving *Folkekirken* and the most to gain by immigrating to America.

Hans, who had once occupied the position of struggling Danish convert, now speaks from the vantage point of the confident, successful American missionary, particularly through his work as the editor of *Skandinaviens Stjerne*, which he took over from Andrew Jenson immediately upon arrival in Denmark. From his letters and daybook, it is clear that Hans empathized with the impoverished Danish Mormons he met and, over the next three years, helped to emigrate—though his main goal was to spread the gospel to his countrymen. In his June 14 letter to Mine, he reports:

> Since I came here I have visited many of the Saints together with Br. A. Jensen. They always receive us with joy, but you would be amazed at how high you have to climb toward the clouds to reach the lodgings of the poor. The higher one gets, the cheaper the

rents become, so they are forced to live there and their children never get to go out to play in their parents' gardens like our children, therefore if you feel that we are poor and miserable, do not entertain this feeling too much, for we have a good home when compared with the conditions of people here. They would be deeply pleased if they could possess as much as we have. How unequally the goods of this world are divided among its inhabitants. Some are incredibly poor and others excessively rich, yet the one is created in the image of God just as truly as the other. Most people had a hard time last winter, because they were forced to sell all of their clothing to be able to live because of unemployment and now they lack clothing. It is so difficult to be poor and live in such a manner.[54]

Hans identifies with the poor Danes, who remind him of the hardships he experienced as a child, but he is also critical of the political system in Denmark, which allows "those who have the power . . . [to] mercilessly oppress the impoverished ones."[55] Upon returning to Denmark as an adult, with firsthand experience in trying to support a growing family, Hans attributes his improved circumstances in life to his membership in the LDS Church and his emigration. He writes, "Since I have learned properly to understand the conditions that prevail in the old world, I have for the first time learned properly to appreciate and value our little home far in the West, where we have enjoyed together so many delights and rejoiced in the good gifts that God has given us."[56] A few months later, he continues, "I thank the Lord often that my home, although not one of the most beautiful, is not here in Denmark, for I cannot understand where people can find joy in this country, for from my perspective, it seems that there are few blessings in the things they possess and I find their manner of living their everyday lives nothing short of wretched."[57] Hopeful that his children will build on his prosperity and surpass his own achievements, Hans urges Mine to ensure their older sons attend school so they will not grow up to be ashamed of themselves or resentful of their parents.

Hans's strained relationship with his own parents is, in many ways, emblematic of his ambivalent relationship with Denmark as a whole. Fostered out as a child, he grew up away from his parents, who were never married. His mother died a few years after Hans's emigration, leaving his younger brother Niels alone in the world. His father married someone else and founded a new family, with three children who knew nothing of their half-brother Hans until he showed up at their door in July 1881 after being assigned to labor on the island of Funen. Given the lack of contact between them, as well as his position as a Mormon missionary, Hans was uncertain of how they would treat him, as he notes on July 18, 1881:

> I do not expect to be so exceptionally well received by them when they hear that I have come for the sake of Mormonism, for they are most likely fairly well acquainted with it, and therefore I may not be as welcome as if I came for the sake of the world. I have adopted the motto since I came here to this country to be faithful to my religion and community and then prepare myself for the worst, for if things turn out better, so much the better.[58]

As it turned out, Hans was pleasantly surprised by the warm reception he received from his father, stepmother, and half-siblings, but he did not waver in his determination to be "faithful to my religion and community," even when his references to Mormonism caused his father to fall silent or change the subject. The bonds of blood between Hans and his father were strained by his allegiance to the determiners of identity that Hans had chosen for himself (i.e., Mormonism and immigration to America). However, these bonds were not completely severed, although none of his family members ever joined the LDS Church or immigrated to Utah.

While Hans's letters home demonstrate how he came to identify more closely with his adopted homeland than with the land of his birth, Mine's letters to her husband reveal another side to their story, particularly regarding their determination to define their own cultural identity. In embracing Mormonism and immigrating to Utah, the Jørgensens chose to prioritize the expectations of Mormon culture over those of Danish Lutheran culture, but they still retained the right to pick and choose from both traditions. Mine's letters keep Hans informed of marriages and deaths among the other Danish Mormons in Pleasant Grove, but she also expresses concern that being back in Denmark might tempt

Hans to waver in his commitment to Mormonism. Noting that many neighbors have commended her on how honest and good her husband is, she writes, "Many a good man has fallen when he has gone back, but do not let that be your fate. I pray to God to prevent it!"[59] Such comments reveal that Hans and Mine were acutely aware of the fluidity of cultural identity and the need to balance the attractions and demands of multiple cultural norms.

One area where it becomes apparent that Hans and Mine were unwilling to subscribe to every tenet of Mormonism is the doctrine of polygamy. Although the LDS Church was reviled in both the United States and Denmark for its practice of plural marriage in the late nineteenth century, many converts to Mormonism believed fervently that it was a divine commandment from God. Some Danish Mormon men married additional wives, usually Danish or Scandinavian women, but many others resisted pressure to do so, despite the widespread perception that practicing plural marriage was a prerequisite for holding high offices in the LDS Church (though monogamous men were more likely to be sent off on missions).[60] As the exception that proves the rule, when Anthon H. Lund was called to the Quorum of the Twelve Apostles in 1889, one year before the church discontinued plural marriage, he was the only monogamist in the group. In her second letter to Hans, written four weeks after he left home (the same day he arrived in Denmark), Mine pleads with her husband to resist the temptation to find himself a second wife from among the Danish Mormon converts. She writes:

I have heard that the young sisters there cling to a man from Zion like grapevines cling to an apple tree, even though they know that he has a wife in Zion who is sitting and waiting for the day when her husband will return again and be her joy and comfort. I think that if such a one were to entice my husband to promise her marriage upon his return, then I could never forgive her, no matter who she is, even though I know that we are all weak and imperfect and often make mistakes and ought to forgive each other, but such a day would come so close to my heart that I cry at the thought of it. Now, good Jørgensen, don't be angry at this. I hope you are man enough to resist such chains and come home as a faithful servant of the Lord.[61]

While Mine never criticizes either the church or any of her polygamist neighbors for their adherence to this doctrine, her own unwillingness to allow her husband to do so is unmistakable. Hans replies, a little huffily, that he is not "out courting," but the fact that he never took a second wife—instead returning home to Mine and having three more children with her—confirms that he either shared or at least respected her aversion to the idea.

A House Divided: Mads Nielsen, David Madsen, and Mette Marie Madsen

In contrast to Hans and Mine, who converted and emigrated as single young people but spent their entire adult lives in Utah, the particularities and peculiarities of the established adult Danish Mormon convert-immigrant experience are evident in the personal narrative of the farmer Mads Nielsen (1822–1901). This account is recorded in fifty letters between Mads and his wife and children between 1878 and 1901 that were transcribed and published by Danish historian Margit Egdal at the request of his Danish descendants, the Damsted family organization (which has roughly one thousand members).[62] Mads became a member of the Church of Jesus Christ of Latter-day Saints in 1877, at the age of fifty-five, and emigrated in 1883, leaving behind his Lutheran wife and six of his seven sons, the youngest of whom was only twelve at the time.

Mads Nielsen's identity as a Danish Lutheran was firmly established by the time he converted. Born in Daugstrup, Denmark (near Otterup in the northern part of the island of Funen), to the farmer Niels Jørgensen and his wife Gertrud Madsdatter, Mads was confirmed in the Lutheran church in Østrup on April 10, 1836. He was called up to serve in the Danish army during the First Schleswig War in 1848, but his widowed mother claimed the right to exempt him from service so he could take care of her farm.[63] In contrast to the commonly held notion that all nineteenth-century Danish Mormon converts were poor tenant farmers and day laborers, Nielsen was a prosperous landowner and gardener. He inherited the farm upon his mother's death in May 1850 and married twenty-two-year-old Gjertrud Kathrine Davidsdatter, the daughter of his affluent neighbors, in November of the same year. They had eight children together, born between 1851 and 1869, though their only daughter died at four years old. In 1857, Mads Nielsen purchased the leasehold on his farm

FIGURE 4.4 Mads Nielsen left a prosperous farm, his wife Gjertrud Kathrine Davidsdatter, and all but one of his children to follow the Mormon missionaries' call to gather to Zion. Photograph (ca. 1883) reproduced courtesy of Margit Egdal and Slægtsforening Damsted.

for 1,825 rigsdaler, becoming one of the first self-owning farmers on
northern Funen. As Egdal points out, Mads Nielsen's decision to emigrate required him to give up "his fatherland, his wife, and his children,
relatives, and friends, as well as his beautiful family farm. In addition,
he had a prominent position in the parish and is often referred to as a
parish leader, since he was a member of the parish council for many
years."[64] Given the enormity of those sacrifices, Mads Nielsen's decision
to become a Mormon was clearly a serious choice that shaped not only
the rest of his life but also his identity as a husband, father, and Dane.

The story of Mads Nielsen's conversion shows how the idea of Mormonism and emigration spread virally within families and communities in Denmark and how baptism redefined the convert's relationship
to his or her homeland and family. Two of Nielsen's sisters joined the
LDS Church in the 1850s and emigrated, one in 1853 and the other in
1859, but both died before reaching Utah due to the hardships of the
journey on foot across the Great Plains. Always a spiritual person, Nielsen was initially skeptical of the Mormon faith but became a believer
by as early as 1870, although he waited to be baptized until 1877—on his
fifty-fifth birthday—in hopes that his wife and children would choose
to follow suit.

In 1878, Nielsen received a letter from his former brother-in-law
Anders C. Hansen, a widower after the death of Nielsen's younger sister
Maren Kirstine, who had converted and emigrated in 1853. Writing from
Ephraim, Utah, Anders said he had heard from a missionary named Brun
that he had baptized someone named Mads on Funen and he wondered
if it might have been Mads Nielsen. As it turns out, Brun was referring to a different Mads, but Egdal suggests the letter verifies both the
activity of Mormon missionaries in the area and the close connection
between Mormonism and emigration in this period of Danish history.[65]
As Hansen states in his letter, "If you have been baptized, then I know
it is your desire to come here."[66] Nielsen struggled for six years to convince his wife to accept Mormonism, but finally decided to emigrate
on his own in 1883, hoping she and the children would join him later.
Their parting was painful, especially since his grieving wife would not
leave the kitchen to say goodbye, though she had promised to follow
him the next year.

FIGURE 4.5 David and Mette Marie Madsen. As the only one of his father's children to join the LDS Church, David Madsen and his wife Mette Marie set an example for Mads Nielsen by immigrating to Utah in 1881. Photograph (ca. 1881) by Fotografisk Atelier Edv. Schiellerup & Co., Odense, Denmark. Reproduced courtesy of Margit Egdal and Slægtsforening Damsted.

In Utah, Nielsen was reunited with his second son David and daughter-in-law Mette Marie, who had already settled in the heavily Scandinavian community of Elsinore, Utah, in Sevier County. David and Mette Marie Madsen had emigrated in early 1881, six months after their wedding and just one month after being baptized into the LDS Church. They found a pleasant new home in Elsinore as valued members of a community full of like-minded countrymen who appreciated David's musical talents. Founded in 1874 by nine Danish Mormons (including two sets of brothers), the town of Elsinore, Utah, was 92 percent Danish in 1880.[67] Chain migration played a central role in ensuring the town's Danish character, as a large percentage of the inhabitants were family or close friends of the town's founders.[68] As a result, the town's residents spoke Danish together and worshipped in Danish until as late as 1915, which made some non-Scandinavians who attempted to settle in Elsinore feel unwelcome.

Other cultural maintenance efforts were at once more subtle and more tangible. For example, the town was known for its dairy industry, which produced six hundred pounds of cheese per day as well as milk and ice cream.[69] Ken Cregg Hansen explains that the settlers in Elsinore deliberately established the town as a center for Scandinavian culture, contrary to official LDS Church policy that immigrants should assimilate as quickly as possible. Nevertheless, the Danish-inflected name of the town was proposed by local LDS stake president Joseph Young (a non-Scandinavian), allegedly because the view of the town site in the bend of the river reminded him of the approach to Denmark by sea through the Kattegat into the Øresund.[70]

Mads Nielsen and his children's life in Elsinore contradicts the assumption that Danish American Mormons traded their cultural heritage for their new religious beliefs. Instead, they seem to have integrated their new religion into a way of life that preserved as many aspects of their Danish cultural identity as possible, from language to food. Surrounded by Danish-speaking neighbors, Mette Marie Madsen never learned to speak English well and spoke only Danish at home. Her mother-in-law sent reading materials from Denmark that she would read aloud to her children, and her own parents sent her seeds to grow Danish fruits and vegetables. Her father-in-law, who had been an avid gardener in Denmark, planted five acres of currants, a common Danish berry, around his farm and made the harvest available to the entire town. He also planted potatoes, gooseberries, a peach tree, and various types of apple trees.[71] Mette Marie Madsen consistently prepared Danish food, despite the fact that "everything is so dry and tasteless here. Nothing tastes like it does in Denmark," as she told her son Leon Torvel Madsen.[72] She made all kinds of sausages, including the quintessential Danish *rullepølse* (rolled sausage), as well as festive dishes for Danish holidays, such as "*arme riddere* [fried bread, much like French toast], doughnuts, layer cakes with a thick layer of whipped cream, ... and delicious Danish *klejnere* [a type of cookie]."[73] As her father-in-law planned his journey to Utah, she and David asked him to bring an *æbleskive* (Danish spherical pancake) pan, as well as powdered sugar, butter, pepper, and dried cherries. Each year, they would cut down a large tree in the woods to serve as their Christmas tree, which they decorated in the Danish fashion with homemade candles, popcorn, apples, and other treats.

The fact that the residents of Elsinore, including Mads Nielsen and the Madsens, cherished and strove to maintain their Danish cultural identity did not diminish their desire to adopt American customs and integrate themselves into their new nation. In a letter from January 1882, David Madsen describes the pleasure he derived from celebrating Boxing Day with a group of five other musicians, who went from house to house in Elsinore playing music in exchange for cake and beer. He compares the experience to celebrating *Fastelavn* (Shrovetide) in Denmark, but notes that in Utah the four horses that pulled their wagon were crowned with American flags, while a larger flag flew from the wagon itself. After summarizing this account, Egdal notes, rather disapprovingly, "[The Danish flag] Dannebrog is the most beautiful thing in the world for Danes. Nothing else is as symbolically important as the flag. David rode around waving the American flag and calling it 'magnificent!'"[74]

Although Mads Nielsen and the Madsens' primary motivation for gathering to Zion was theological, driven by the conviction that the second coming of Jesus Christ was near at hand and could only be survived by those faithful saints who sought shelter in the mountains of Utah, the physical conditions and economic possibilities of their new home played a significant role in keeping them there. Many of the convert-emigrants who became disaffected cited dissatisfaction with their farmland and economic prospects as a reason for backtracking to the central United States, but that was not Mads Nielsen's experience.

Anders Hansen's letter to Mads Nielsen in 1878 highlights the practical, economic incentives for emigration that were attractive to most Danes, regardless of religion. He explains, "We have a good home here, we have enough food and clothing that we do not lack the good things of life. . . . Our land gives a good return on seed, we cultivate excellent wheat in particular, as well as barley and oats and peas, but we can't cultivate corn here unless we water the land, for it almost never rains here in the summer."[75] Ken Cregg Hansen notes that the mean annual precipitation in Denmark was twenty-five inches, whereas the Sevier Valley only received thirteen.[76] Although the desert landscape of south-central Utah made agricultural endeavors challenging and often precarious, large-scale

water development projects, especially irrigation canals, allowed the settlers to fulfill their prophetic mandate to "make the desert bloom like the
rose."[77] For Mads Nielsen, this effort paid off, for, as his son David wrote
to his mother in March 1887, "He will soon be one of the richest men here
in town. I think that you must be fooling yourselves to keep going over
there in Denmark."[78]

Like Anders Hansen's letter, David Madsen's early letters to his parents in Denmark are, in general, full of praise for conditions in Utah.
Writing on October 11, 1881, on the occasion of the birth of his and Mette
Marie's first child, a son they named David after his father (according to
local custom rather than Mads after his grandfather, as would have been
the norm in Denmark), David praises the mild, warm climate and the
abundance of geese and rabbits. He also boasts about the productivity
of his land: "We have now bought 5 acres of the best land that exists. It is
just outside of town and half of it is planted with alfalfa and the other half
with oats, which was included with the purchase. When it was threshed,
it came to 70 bushels. I now have far more grain than we can use in a year;
I earn from 1 to 4 bushels a day.[79] Within a year, David acquired an additional twenty-one acres and enjoyed a bountiful harvest, despite losses
caused by grasshoppers. David and Mette Marie eventually had seven
healthy children: five sons and two daughters, for whom they envisioned
a bright and prosperous future in Utah. On November 18, 1881, after a
description of his infant son's blessing in church, David Madsen writes
home, "We are very happy that we have come here to Zion, for it is a good
place to be. Every man is free and belongs to no one, and there are no
slaves and we can do God's will here without being mocked by anyone,
and here we do not need to slave away, such as one must in Denmark."[80]
Statements like these suggest that their experiences in Utah taught them
to value the social mobility made possible by the democratic ideology of
the United States, whatever its failings in practice.

However, although economic and practical matters make up a large
part of the communications between these Danish Mormon emigrants
and their family in Denmark, their letters are also consistently and
urgently concerned with the spiritual welfare and salvation of their loved
ones back home. Their belief in the imminent return of Jesus Christ to the
earth and the necessity of gathering the saints together to greet him was
a powerful motivating force to cross the ocean and more than half of the

FIGURE 4.6 David Madsen and his wife Mette Marie established themselves in Elsinore, Utah, in this humble cabin (ca. 1882), but were eventually prosperous enough to build a larger home. Reproduced courtesy of Eris M. Black, Margit Egdal, and Slægtsforening Damsted.

American continent, despite the emotional hardship of separation from family, friends, fatherland, and native culture. On October 11, 1881, David commiserates with his father that he is "alone in the covenant" and urges both his mother and his "unhappy brothers" to accept the doctrines and authority of the LDS Church so they can be baptized for the remission of sins and receive the blessing of light and knowledge.

In an addendum to the same letter, Mette Marie admonishes her "dear friends, please come while there is yet time, for we can see in the scriptures that some will come too late. When the Saints have been gathered and the plagues begin, they will run from coast to coast and desire to be baptized, but there will be no one to baptize them. I don't want to think that you will be among them, for that will be a terrible state."[81] Similarly, Mads Nielsen's letters after his emigration are full of passionate entreaties to his wife and sons to join him in Utah. He explains that he left them because he loves them and hopes to help them avoid a terrible fate:

> I have committed no sin [in leaving] except for doing the word of the Lord and I would have done that long before if I had not loved my family. I am so loath to lose you, I thought that you might come to recognize the truth and be saved together with me, but it could not be done. Thereafter I thought that I might

be able to draw you after me, but I have not yet seen grounds to hope. I have done what I could to save you from the fate of an ungodly and corrupted world. I have warned you both in word and by my flight that peace has been taken from the world and the time is near that the Lord will chasten those who reject his saving message which he has restored to the earth, for the gospel is the light of life for those who accept it, but the light of death for those who reject it. I admonish all of you to repent in haste while there is yet time.[82]

The letter writers' frequent equation of Denmark with the wickedness of "Babylon," as motivation for both their own emigration and their entreaties to their family members to embrace Mormonism and emigrate, indicates that their identification with Mormonism and belief in its apocalyptic message preempted their loyalty to Denmark to a significant degree.

Another controversial aspect of nineteenth-century Mormon doctrine that directly affected the evolution of Mads Nielsen's cultural identity was the practice of polygamy. This doctrine gave Mormonism international notoriety and led to extensive federal persecution in the late nineteenth century, despite the fact that it was by no means the norm, involving only about 25 percent of all families in Utah on average in the 1880s.[83] Statistically speaking, relatively few Danish Mormons entered into polygamous marriages,[84] but the immorality of polygamy was an issue that appeared repeatedly in anti-Mormon literature in Denmark. However, the anecdotal experiences of those Danes who were in polygamous relationships offer little support for either titillating tales of universal licentiousness or lurid accounts of women being forced into harems. David Madsen's son, Leon Torvel Madsen, recalls two Danish men in Elsinore who had two wives each, Søren Petersen and the local bishop Jens Iver Jensen, while another resident, Søren Sørensen, "tried to get one more wife, but she wouldn't have him!"[85] In contrast to Hans and Mine Jørgensen's resistance to polygamy, Mads Nielsen found that it presented a solution to several problems he faced as a result of his wife's disinterest in conversion and emigration: his need for assistance with household labor, his desire for companionship, and his access to exaltation after death through the Mormon covenant of eternal marriage.

Despite the fact that his family and friends in Denmark undoubtedly would disapprove, Mads Nielsen's decision to enter into a plural marriage is more poignant than provocative. It illustrates his desire to conform to the doctrines of his faith and his reluctant acceptance of his new identity as an aging "grass widower" in need of a wife. He had left his family behind with great reluctance and felt torn between his two homes for many years, which kept him in emotional limbo and practical distress. In letter after letter to his wife, Nielsen complains of her absence, but adds the postscript, "If you plan never to come to me, then tell me directly and don't be ashamed."[86] In August 1887, after five years in Elsinore and many unsuccessful attempts to persuade Gjertrud to join him in Utah, Nielsen asks his wife for permission to take a second wife: "I have been slow to write this time; I delayed a little because you haven't answered my questions to you. I wrote to you to fulfill your promise and come to live with me or give me permission to take another, for I must be sealed to a wife in this life, for in the next life, there will neither be given nor taken in marriage, but we must be like the angels."[87] He requests a reply within two months as to whether or not he should continue waiting for her, but since Gjertrud's letters have unfortunately not survived, it is impossible to know if or how she responded.

In the end, tired of caring and cooking for himself, lonely, and claiming justification from the fact that his faith allowed him to take a second wife even though his first wife was still alive, Nielsen married another Danish Mormon, sixty-three-year old Ane Rasmussen, in the Manti Temple in July 1888, just two years before LDS church president Wilford Woodruff issued a manifesto discontinuing the practice of Mormon polygamy. The federal Edmunds-Tucker Act outlawing polygamy—already in effect at the time of Nielsen's second marriage—and liberal divorce laws in Utah would have permitted him to divorce Gjertrud in order to enter into an church-sanctioned eternal marriage,[88] but his letters home make it clear that Mads still loved his first wife and chose not to pursue this option. After Gjertrud's death in 1891 and the death of his second wife Ane Rasmussen in 1893, he had proxy ordinances performed on Gjertrud's behalf in the Manti Temple so they could be together after his death, according to LDS doctrine. He then married a third time, a middle-aged widow named Caroline Iversen Snow, who cared for him during his declining years and inherited his property for her maintenance until her death, with the remainder going to his grandchildren in Utah.

FIGURE 4.7 David and Mette Marie's Madsen's son, Erastus Madsen, who was
named after one of the first Mormon missionaries in Denmark, returned to his
family's homeland as a missionary in 1913. Photograph by Anna Rasmussen,
Aarhus, Denmark. Reproduced courtesy of Margit Egdal and Slægtsforening
Damsted.

Although the correspondence between the families in Daugstrup and
Elsinore ceased not long after the death of the original emigrants, their
legacy both as Danes and as Mormons continued to shape their family's
cultural identity. After nearly two decades in Utah, David Madsen died
of typhus in 1899, leaving his six sons and two daughters to run his prosperous farm with their mother; his father died a few years later, in 1901.
David's daughter Gerda married a Danish-born Mormon, John Bodtcher,
while David's second oldest son, Erastus (named after Erastus Snow),

FIGURE 4.8 Frederik Ferdinand Samuelsen, shown here with his family in Aarhus, Denmark (ca. 1905), was the first LDS member of a national parliament outside the United States. A socialist, he combined his advocacy for Danish workers with his love of the LDS gospel until finally immigrating to Utah after World War I. Reproduced courtesy of the LDS Church History Library, Salt Lake City, Utah.

went back to Denmark in 1913 as a missionary. He wrote home to his mother, Mette Marie, "You can be sure that I feel quite at home here on Funen, it truly is Denmark's garden."[89] Erastus's sense of homecoming contrasts with Hans Jørgensen's sense of alienation upon returning to Denmark and suggests that Erastus, as a third-generation Danish American Mormon, may have been more comfortable with his dual identity than Jørgensen had been.

This pattern illustrates the theory known as Hansen's law, derived from Professor Marcus L. Hansen's assertion in 1938 that "what the son wishes to forget the grandson wishes to remember."[90] In an interesting twist, two of Mads Nielsen's Danish grandsons by his third son, Gjøde, joined the LDS Church in Denmark in the early twentieth century: Johannes Valdemar Damsted, who later immigrated to Utah, and Mads Christian Damsted, who remained in Denmark throughout his life and was ordained to the priesthood in Odense in 1950.[91]

The Statesman: Frederik Ferdinand Samuelsen, *Folketingsmand*

While neither the Jørgensen family nor the Mads Nielsen family were politically engaged or publically prominent, either before or after their conversion, one of the best known Danish Mormons in Denmark in the early twentieth century was Frederik Ferdinand (F. F.) Samuelsen (1865–1929), who gained public visibility in Denmark as the first LDS member of the Danish Parliament (and, in fact, the first LDS member of any national parliament outside the United States, where Senator Reed Smoot from Utah was serving, albeit while under special investigation for his affiliation with the LDS Church). Samuelsen served in the *Folketing* from 1906 to 1917, having run unopposed in a special election in 1906, and was reelected in 1913 with an impressive 54 percent of the popular vote. He was also a member of several civic organizations, an avid patron of the theater, a devoted father and husband, and a beloved leader in the LDS Church in Denmark. Samuelsen's involvement in Danish public life as both a progressive politician and a defender of the LDS Church demonstrates how he created a hybrid identity for himself as a Danish Mormon. Although he did ultimately emigrate and settle in Utah near the end of his life, Samuelsen set an example for the thousands of Danes who would join the church in the twentieth century but remain permanently in Denmark by modeling the near complete integration of LDS Church members into Danish society that is the norm today.

Like Mads Nielsen, Samuelsen spent the majority of his adult life in Denmark and only emigrated to Utah after retiring from politics at the age of fifty-two. Born into a lower-middle-class home in Copenhagen in April 1865, Samuelsen lost his father at age nine and had to work in a match factory to help support his family.[92] As a teenager, Samuelsen apprenticed as a locksmith and mechanic, which enabled him to find work as a machinist in a sewing machine factory in Aarhus in 1889 and later with the Danish national railway in 1897. He married his first cousin, Marie Florentine Jensen, in Roskilde in 1890. They both joined the LDS Church in Aarhus in December 1892, a few months after his wife's sister Vilhelmine was introduced to Mormonism by her fiancé, the printer Peter S. Christiansen, who had joined the church the preceding year.

Though never a full-time proselyting missionary, Samuelsen served in the church in Aarhus for more than twenty years and was eager to share his beliefs with his neighbors. He held many different callings in the local and regional church administration and volunteered as an informal missionary. For example, when the Aarhus congregation set a goal of distributing ten thousand tracts in 1894, Samuelsen distributed 1,895 in one month on his own.[93] He encouraged members of the congregation to proselytize in the countryside outside the city and occasionally spent an entire Sunday doing what he advocated. His diary is full of church meetings—including weekly sacrament, priesthood, young men's, and young women's meetings—as well as branch and regional conferences. The night of his initial election to the *Folketing* in October 1906, he told his life story to the youth of the Aarhus congregation rather than celebrating with his supporters.[94]

Although he had been raised, confirmed, and married in the Lutheran Church before his conversion and was well aware of the social significance of many of *Folkekirken*'s rituals, Samuelsen was occasionally critical of fellow Mormons, who, as historian Richard Jensen puts it, "tried to turn back to Lutheranism for special occasions, letting their infants be baptized in the Lutheran Church and asking Lutheran clergy to conduct family funerals. Samuelsen condemned such halfway measures as hypocrisy and called upon the members of his local congregation to cease."[95] At the same time, however, Samuelsen's diary documents that he made judicious compromises himself—for example, regarding the Word of Wisdom.[96] Particularly at social functions, he would occasionally drink coffee, beer, wine, and champagne, as well as the odd medicinal cognac or hot port wine toddy, though he earned praise from a local abstinence activist for his restraint regarding the consumption of alcohol and often opted for hot chocolate or boiled water instead of coffee.[97]

As a craftsman, Samuelsen belonged to the same working class as the majority of Danish converts to Mormonism, but he was distinctive because of his political activism. He was well traveled in Europe and had a charismatic public presence that served him well in his political campaigns. Having worked in a factory from an early age, he was well acquainted with the burgeoning labor movement in Denmark and was elected vice president of the Blacksmiths' and Machinists' Union in Aarhus in 1891. As a union member, he was subject to a two-month preemptive lockout by his employer in 1895. During this lockout (and another in 1897), Samuelsen helped solicit funds to support the families of fellow locked-out workers. He was involved in recruiting union members and negotiating with employers for more favorable wages and working conditions. He served as both union vice-chairman and chairman in the late 1890s and was a delegate to a series of meetings in Copenhagen in January 1898, at which the various Danish labor unions joined forces to create a national organization. In his diary on January 5, 1898, Samuelsen notes, "A great work had been completed and a mighty organization formed. Denmark now stood as number 1 in the whole world, in that all organized workers were now joined together in one great federation."[98]

Samuelsen's identity as a Dane and as a Mormon was thus closely connected to his deep involvement with Danish labor unions, which he viewed as integral to improving the living and working conditions of ordinary Danes, the demographic to which most Danish converts to Mormonism belonged. On at least one occasion in 1899, Samuelsen took a visiting American missionary to task for denigrating the union effort during a nationwide one-hundred-day lockout, explaining that the labor movement in Denmark was important for the working class.[99] That lockout ended in a settlement that, according to Jensen, "established the legitimacy of Danish labor unions as an agent for collective bargaining," which, in turn, led to the passage of laws in 1910 that still constitute the

Danish labor market today. This success boosted the popularity of the reform-oriented Social Democratic Party, which would play a central role in establishing the Danish welfare state in the 1920s and 30s.

Samuelsen's leadership in his union made him an ideal candidate for political office on the Social Democratic ticket, first to the Aarhus City Council in 1900—to which he was reelected in January 1906 with the largest popular vote of any city councilman in the country outside of Copenhagen—and later, in October 1906, to the *Folketing*, the lower house of the Danish Parliament. The Social Democrats increased the number of seats they controlled in the legislature from two in 1884 to fourteen in 1901, demonstrating their increasing centrality to Danish politics, and nominated Samuelsen for a seat during a special election in the fall of 1906. Samuelsen's election to the *Folketing*, with strong support from laborers, underscores the pervasiveness of the *Systemskifte* (system change) of 1901 that completed Denmark's transition to a parliamentary system, which had been inaugurated half a century before with the June Constitution.

Samuelsen's election, twice to the city council and then to the Danish parliament, also illustrates the gradual alteration in public perceptions of Mormonism in Denmark by the turn of the century. This change was in part a result of both the growing belief among Danes that religion should be a private matter and the decision by the LDS Church in 1890 to officially discontinue the practice of polygamy. Samuelsen was quite aware of this ideological shift, as well as of the growing divide it represented between the administration of *Folkekirken* and its membership. While reflecting on his election to the *Folketing* in his diary, which he described as "the most significant moment in my life, in a worldly sense,"[100] Samuelsen recalls how, after local clergymen had campaigned successfully to remove him from the Aarhus school board, his overwhelming reelection to the city council proved "the judgment of the people was different than that of the clergy."[101] During his parliamentary campaign, a few newspaper articles poked fun at Samuelsen's unusual religious affiliation, in particular an attack by Pastor H. O. Frimodt-Møller, who, as a representative of both the conservative Home Mission faction of *Folkekirken* in Aarhus and *Folkekirken*'s clergy in general, "insisted that it was a national shame that a 'Mormon' should sit in the country's highest organization."[102] These attacks did not seem to have a negative effect on either Samuelsen's popularity with voters or his credibility with party officials and local organizers. In fact, Samuelsen comments in his diary with noticeable satisfaction that "voters across the board laughed at this fanatical position. No one could say anything against my daily life or lifestyle."[103]

As his clarification about the voters' response reveals, Samuelsen's electoral success did not mean Mormonism was considered socially acceptable at the time, but merely that it could be tolerated as an eccentricity in an otherwise respectable person. Samuelsen wrote about a conversation he had over coffee (just boiled water for Samuelsen, he noted in his diary) with a Grundtvigian pastor, Jørgen Teilmann, who hosted a voters meeting in Bering, a small town south of Aarhus, on October 26, 1906:

> Pastor Teilmann asked if it was correct that I was a Mormon. I answered, 'Yes, I have been for almost 14 years.' He could not understand that—such an enlightened person as I, and by the way it was the only unfavorable thing he had heard about me. I didn't think that should make me a lesser person. Harald Jensen [the Social Democratic representative from Aarhus in the *Landsting*, the upper house of the national legislature] felt that we should consider religion to be a private matter, with which the Pastor agreed. At this meeting I had expected opposition from the priest, but that didn't happen.[104]

Although not a member of the Social Democratic party, Teilmann was an advocate for workers' rights, women's rights, and political and religious freedom in general, and he felt Samuelsen's political credentials outweighed the unorthodoxy of his religious beliefs.

Journalist Lars Larsen-Ledet, who was put forward as an opposition candidate to Samuelsen by the *Radikale Venstre* (Radical Left) Party in 1913 (and who later uncovered the minor political scandal that forced Samuelsen to resign in 1917), seemed to agree with Teilmann. Writing nearly forty years later, he described his erstwhile opponent as

> a good, pleasant man without other raw edges than that he was a Mormon, but on the contrary lived a nice, happy family life in monogamy, there was no one who minded his religion—with the

exception of his predecessor, Harald Jensen, who found that it was something strange and admonished him to stop it. The religious feeling was obviously genuine in his case, and his personal conduct was above reproach.[105]

It is worth noting, however, that Teilmann's and Ledet's tolerant approach to Samuelsen's beliefs, even when tinged with consternation or condescension, stand in sharp contrast to the outspoken anti-Mormonism of Pastor Frimodt-Møller, who explicitly identified Samuelsen's membership in the LDS Church as grounds for his unsuitability for government service.

As a de facto representative of the LDS Church in the *Folketing*, Samuelsen was not only the target of anti-Mormon rhetoric but was also able to intervene on occasion when the LDS community in Denmark was unfairly treated. For example, when an archdeacon in Aarhus refused to allow a Mormon graveside service at a local cemetery, despite a 1907 law permitting it, Samuelsen obtained confirmation from the *Kultusminister* (minister of culture and religion) that conducting a "civil burial" did not even require consultation with the local Lutheran minister.[106] In October 1912, Samuelsen spoke out in the *Folketing* against *Kultusminister* Appel's alleged support for a proposal to expel LDS missionaries from Denmark, asking if the minister intended to "take part in the restriction of the already very limited freedom of religion of the non-recognized religious societies."[107] Pointing out that there were 1,100 *Folkekirken* ministers and only 50 Mormon missionaries in Denmark at the time, Samuelsen suggested that the honorable minister allow the pastors to defend Lutheranism and avoid introducing governmental restrictions on freedom of religion, "whereby Denmark would sink into the second rank of civilized countries."

Samuelsen's arguments validate Denmark's pride in its own significant progress toward democratization and modernization over the preceding half century, and they celebrate the kind of courageous, empowered Mormon peasant that had proved such a plague to *Folkekirken*'s pastors during that same period:

The pastors of the state church have a position of very great power. 22 of them stand opposite each one of these missionaries. . . .

> The 22 pastors are educated men, who have sacrificed years of their time on the study of theology. The one missionary is a man who has left a factory, a workshop, a warehouse, a shop, and who has not spent time studying theology. . . . I have belonged to this church for about 20 years. I know these men and I know that they are honorable, honest, and sincere men."[108]

Samuelsen's public defense of the character of Danish Mormons, as well as his characterization of them as simple, earnest blue-collar workers whose only offense was daring to challenge the institutionally supported forces of Danish Lutheranism, served to counteract the popular portrayal of Mormon missionaries as criminal agents of a secret cult.

During his tenure in the *Folketing*, Samuelsen played a central role in challenging allegations that Mormon missionaries aimed to lure young women into harems in Utah or sell them into the white slave trade, as illustrated by the silent film *A Victim of the Mormons* (1911) discussed in chapter 3. In November 1913, the state-funded Danish National Committee for Combating the White Slave Trade issued a report for the year 1912, which alleged that "it has been proven that several hundred Danish women, particularly from Jutland, have been kidnapped by Mormons and taken to America" and recommended that the state "prevent the spreading Mormon agitation, which can so easily be used to conceal traffic in women."[109] In a series of letters that were later published in *Skandinaviens Stjerne*, Samuelsen challenged committee chairman Colonel Axel Liljefalk to produce his proof of these charges. Although unable to provide any evidence, Liljefalk claimed the report was merely an attempt to warn women against the perils of Mormonism, for "there is no doubt here at home and abroad that the Mormon teaching of polygamy etc. contains a moral danger, or at least is in stark opposition to common Christian moral teachings."[110]

Liljefalk's condemnation of polygamy, decades after it was discontinued by the LDS Church, was intended to demonstrate the inherent incompatibility of Danish Christianity and Mormon identity. However, Samuelsen took him sharply and decisively to task for his irresponsible reporting and for blindly perpetuating the persecution of Mormons in Denmark on the basis of false accusations of immorality, in contrast to the verifiable statistical evidence that 25–30 percent of all children born between 1906 and 1910 in Copenhagen, presumably to Danish Lutherans, were illegitimate.[111]

As his lifelong efforts on behalf of both Danish workers and Danish Mormons illustrate, Samuelsen was proudly and passionately invested in the welfare of his church and his country. He was a strong supporter of the new Danish constitution that was adopted in 1915, writing in his diary, "This is the greatest red-letter day I have experienced. Denmark now has the freest constitution in all Europe, with equal and universal suffrage for all. The earl has no more right to vote than his day laborer or his servant."[112] Another high point in his life came that same year, when he and Marie celebrated their twenty-fifth wedding anniversary. Thorvald Stauning, national chairman of the Social Democratic Party and later Danish prime minister, brought them his congratulations in person, and the event was mentioned in several Copenhagen newspapers as well as in *Skandinaviens Stjerne* on September 1, 1915.

Despite his love of Denmark, Samuelsen ultimately made the decision to emigrate after his political career came to an abrupt and unfortunate end. In the fall of 1917, he sent an anonymous postcard to a newspaper, leaking insignificant information about a Social Democratic Party meeting, as a way of getting even with a rival. When this scandal was revealed by journalist Lars Larsen-Ledet, the local Social Democratic Party asked for Samuelsen's resignation. Samuelsen confessed in his diary, "I must admit that I have fought against going to Zion,"[113] but he chose to regard his political disgrace as a prompting from God to go at long last to Utah in order to attend the LDS temple in Salt Lake City, where he could perform proxy ordinances of baptism and confirmation in behalf of his deceased parents. The death of his mother-in-law on April 2, 1919 gave the family an additional reason to make the journey and likely made it emotionally easier to do so.[114]

In contrast to the expectations of economic opportunity that motivated so many impoverished nineteenth-century Danish Mormons, Samuelsen's decision to emigrate was not motivated by the desire for a better life, nor was it easy to arrange. As he notes in his diary, it entailed "a very big sacrifice economically," a considerable loss of social status, a wrenching separation from his beloved homeland, and the disheartening prospect of becoming "just another middle-aged Danish emigrant who spoke English with difficulty and with a pronounced accent."[115]

Complications caused by American involvement in World War I and nativist sentiment in the United States delayed matters for a year or two, but with the help of Utah senator Reed Smoot—whose own legislative service in the United States had been considerably complicated by his affiliation with the LDS Church and whose mother was a Norwegian Mormon immigrant[116]—Samuelsen, his wife, and their two sons Wilford and Kaj were permitted to immigrate to Utah in early May 1919. They arrived in Salt Lake City on May 17, where they joined Samuelsen's two daughters Julie and Ella and his brother- and sister-in-law, the Christiansens, who had emigrated earlier in the decade.

Although the LDS Church had begun discouraging the immigration of foreign converts some years earlier, dozens of Samuelsen's friends had left for Utah, he had seen dozens of missionaries come and go, and he had long felt personal and theological pressure to gather to Zion. His two daughters had already emigrated and, at the time, the only LDS temples where proxy ordinances could be performed for deceased family members were located in Utah (although the first temple outside the continental United States was being built in Hawaii at the time and was dedicated shortly after Samuelsen's arrival in Utah, as he noted with great enthusiasm in his calendar). A temple would not be built in Copenhagen until nearly a century later, though the first LDS temple in Europe was dedicated in Switzerland in 1955. Given that attending the temple was a central motivating factor in their decision to emigrate, it is not surprising that Samuelsen, his wife, and their son Wilford received their temple endowments in the Salt Lake Temple in October 1919 and performed proxy ordinances for Marie's parents a month later. The entire Samuelsen family became frequent visitors to the temple, often attending three or four times a week.

Although the Samuelsen family was welcomed with open arms by friends, family, and the church in Utah, F. F. Samuelsen never became involved in American society to the extent he had been in Denmark, nor did he ever relinquish his Danish cultural identity. Samuelsen and his family settled in Salt Lake City, where he presided over the Scandinavian-language worship services that were held in the assembly hall on Temple Square four times a year, attended the theater, and worked in the Salt Lake Temple. Despite having taken periodic English classes back in Denmark, he never became fully fluent in English, and associated primarily with other Danish Mormons. He had a rich social life with his many Danish friends and neighbors, who understood the customs and traditions of home. In late November 1919, a few months after his emigration and immediately after the American Thanksgiving celebration, Samuelsen invited his daughter Ella and her family, along with a few other friends, for a traditional Danish holiday meal of roast pork, red cabbage, and caramelized potatoes.[117] Several years later, he celebrated his sixtieth birthday by inviting fifty guests to an elaborate Danish *smørrebrød* (open-face sandwich) feast.[118] Ten years after his emigration, F. F. Samuelsen died on May 9, 1929, at the age of sixty-four. His longtime friend Andrew Jenson spoke at the funeral, but notes in his autobiography that the "general opinion was that he [Samuelsen] died broken-hearted as the quiet life he had been forced to lead in Utah was such a contrast to his public activities in his native country."[119]

While it is entirely possible that Samuelsen regarded his final years in Utah as a professional disappointment, his legacy as a Danish Mormon bore fruit on both sides of the Atlantic. Andrew Jenson notes that Samuelsen "obtained for the Latter-day Saints in Denmark many privileges which had not previously been accorded them."[120] Samuelsen's great-grandson Steven Wilford Harris frames the impressive accomplishments of Samuelsen's life as a latter-day fairy tale:

> Who would have imagined that a stoop-shouldered child laborer in a matchstick factory in Copenhagen, Denmark would . . . rise through the leaderships ranks of the unions; be baptized in the icy waters of Aarhus Bay as a member of the true church of Christ; be elected to the Danish parliament as the *only* non-North American Mormon politician at that time and then humbly leave his wealth and positions of power to emigrate to Utah to become a diligent temple worker in the Salt Lake Temple [emphasis in original].[121]

Unlike the many Danish Mormons who defined themselves by their connection to Utah, even before they emigrated, Samuelsen was able to assert his identity as a Danish Mormon in Denmark. While the LDS Church had not yet gained full acceptance as a part of Danish society by the time Samuelsen became a member, the effective and influential combination of his political success and faithful church membership demonstrated the viability of being both Danish and Mormon without having to compromise on either affiliation.

Conclusion

Although most Danish media representations of Mormonism during the late nineteenth and early twentieth centuries emphasize the foreignness of the Mormon religion and its incompatibility with Danishness by underscoring both the doctrinal differences between Lutheranism and Mormonism and the American origins and orientation of the early LDS Church, the earnest, emotionally charged personal narratives of individual Danish Mormons tell a more nuanced story.

Particularly for early converts to the LDS Church, the decision to become a Mormon entailed severing certain ties to Danish culture, including (in many cases) geographical proximity and family connections, but not necessarily, as has often been assumed, the Danish language, traditions, or even social norms, such as the consumption of coffee, tea, and beer. Identification with the group self-conception of Danish Mormons as God's "chosen people" and the decision to immigrate to Utah had an empowering effect on many early converts, particularly those belonging to the lowest social classes in Denmark, who gained social status within their faith community and generally experienced upward social mobility as a result of their emigration.

The construction of a dual cultural identity as a Danish Mormon was a highly individualistic process that involved a vast array of subjective decisions about matters both trivial and profound. While some Danish Mormons became very American in their self-identification—choosing to Anglicize their names, speak primarily English, and concentrate on realizing the dual promises of America that Utah offered, such as economic advancement and spiritual redemption—the majority maintained some degree of connection to their cultural heritage through use of the Danish language, membership in Scandinavian organizations, and participation in Scandinavian worship services and festivities. While such decisions were common aspects of the Danish American immigrant experience, regardless of religious affiliation, other issues requiring cultural adaptation were unique to the Mormon community. Some Danish Mormons adhered strictly to the Word of Wisdom and embraced, enthusiastically even, the controversial doctrine of plural marriage, while others (not only Scandinavian converts) insisted on their culturally determined right to imbibe proscribed beverages and refused to condone the practice of polygamy within their own homes.

As the personal narratives examined in this chapter reveal, the position of Danish Mormons relative to their Danish Lutheran country and countrymen shifted considerably over the course of the late nineteenth and early twentieth centuries, from Hans Jørgensen's mistreatment by his employer after his baptism in 1863 to F. F. Samuelsen's vigorous defense of the Mormons' right to fair treatment by the Danish state in 1915. When the first LDS missionaries arrived in 1850 and began baptizing converts, public persecution was so fierce and the call to gather to Zion so strong that becoming a Mormon meant incurring the enmity of one's neighbors and friends, vastly increasing the convert's likelihood of emigrating within a few short years, as both Hans and Mine Jørgensen did.

In subsequent decades, after nearly every household in Denmark had some form of contact with Mormonism (though the novelty that had inspired such violent opposition to it had worn off), the decision to join the LDS Church no longer brought about such drastic transformations, as Mads Nielsen's prolonged investigation of Mormonism and postponed decision to emigrate reveals. However, the personal cost of leaving loved ones behind and starting a new life under different social and economic conditions remained high. By the end of the century, public disdain for Mormonism had become almost reflexive but no longer malicious, while the establishment of permanent LDS congregations in major Danish cities made it possible—as F. F. Samuelsen's harmonious integration of political activism and evangelical fervor illustrates—for converts to stay in Denmark and continue their ordinary lives while exploring the ramifications of their new religious identity. These developments, along with a fundamental shift in LDS church policy with regard to gathering new converts to Utah, ushered in a new era of Danish Mormon history in the twentieth and twenty-first centuries.

Conclusion

While the Church of Jesus Christ of Latter-day Saints has not yet become a mainstream religion in Denmark in the early twenty-first century, it is no longer perceived as a threat to the fabric of Danish society, as it was for much of the late nineteenth century. During the period of time covered in this study, Danish responses to Mormonism gradually evolved from hostility and alarmism on the part of the majority, coupled with enthusiastic adoption by a minority, to curiosity and prurience regarding emigration and polygamy, and finally to a diminished sense of Mormon "difference" and quiet acceptance of Mormons as neighbors and compatriots. Once the flood of emigration to America began tapering off in the late nineteenth century, Danish Mormons began to establish themselves as productive, respected, long-term members of Danish society who followed the path marked by F. F. Samuelsen's work in the Danish Parliament, rather than transients eager to shake the dust of their homeland from their feet. The first permanent LDS meetinghouse in Copenhagen was built in the late 1920s, on Priorvej in Frederiksberg, which demonstrated the rootedness of the Danish Mormon community in the Danish capital. (Incidentally, this chapel and adjacent missionary housing were converted in 2004 to serve as an LDS temple, the second in Scandinavia after the Stockholm Sweden Temple).

The tumultuous geopolitical events and far-reaching social transformations that Denmark experienced during the twentieth century, particularly in connection with World War II, went a long way toward lessening the stigma associated with Danish Mormonism and facilitating integration efforts. Several members of LDS congregations were active in the Danish resistance during World War II, with at least two losing their lives to Gestapo bullets in the process—a powerful reminder that

Danish Mormons were as dedicated to their country as their Lutheran neighbors. As the Danish LDS newspaper *Skandinaviens Stjerne* reported in May 1945, more than five thousand mourners turned out for the funerals of Mormon resistance fighters Poul Møller Rasmussen (twenty-four years old) and Arly Hess Thomsen (twenty-one years old), whom the mayor of Silkeborg commended for their courage in standing up to Nazi oppression.[1]

The reorientation of the Danish Mormon community toward integration rather than emigration paralleled the improving relationship between the LDS Church and the American government in the years following the conclusion of the Reed Smoot hearings in 1907. Under the leadership of President Joseph F. Smith, nephew to the church's founder Joseph Smith, the Mormons made a concerted effort to demonstrate their loyalty to American political and moral values. That this effort had the intended effect of mainstreaming the church is evident not only in the increasingly viable candidacies of several Mormon politicians over the course of the past century—of which former Massachusetts governor Mitt Romney's presidential run in 2012 was the most highly publicized and came closest to being successful—but also in the increasing attractiveness of Utah as a tourist destination. When Denmark's then-Crown Prince Frederik (later King Frederik IX) and his wife, Princess Ingrid, visited Salt Lake City in April 1939, they were greeted by thousands of Utahns of Danish ancestry, including Provo mail carrier William Knudsen, a former LDS missionary in Denmark and director of a regional Scandinavian choir, who sang a Danish aria at the welcome reception.[2] The Danish royal couple was apparently impressed by the strong Danish heritage of so many of Utah's inhabitants, as well as with the state's prosperity more generally.

The increased secularism and multiculturalism of Denmark in the postwar era caused a sharp decline in both the influence of *Folkekirken*'s clergy on public opinion as well as the perceived need to shelter Danes from foreign ideas, although other cultural differences took the place of Mormonism in demarcating dangerous "otherness." So many new cultural traditions were introduced into Denmark in the second half of the twentieth century that the perceived Americanism of the LDS Church no longer seemed extreme or unusual. If anything, it appeared rather quaint and charmingly wholesome. When the famous Mormon singing group the Osmonds were at the height of their international popularity in the 1970s, quite a few Danes sought out the LDS Church in order to feel closer to the singers, especially Donny and Marie.[3] By the end of the twentieth century, the sight of pairs of clean-cut Mormon missionaries biking through Danish cities in white shirts, suits, and ties (or dresses, blouses, and skirts, in the case of female "sister" missionaries) seemed innocuous, particularly in comparison with media hysteria about a perceived flood of immigrants wearing headscarves and burkas that inspired a host of corporate regulations and national legislation in the late 1990s and early 2000s. When politicians from the far-right Danish People's Party trumpet the need to "protect the country, the people, and the Danish legacy"[4] against immigrants, they are not, as a rule, referring to Mormons.

However, although the turbulent reception of Mormonism has faded from the collective memory of the Danish people and Danish Mormons are regarded as full-fledged members of Danish society, one goal of this book is to show that many of today's struggles over national belonging and cultural identity—both in Denmark and elsewhere—are neither unique nor unprecedented and are thus not necessarily grounds for decrying the degenerate state of modern society. The various examples of high and popular culture portrayals of Mormonism in this book reveal how the generally negative, initially violent reception of Mormonism in Denmark in the late nineteenth and early twentieth centuries changed over time, becoming increasingly self-deprecating and eventually disappearing altogether from public discourse. One consistent aspect of all of these treatments of Mormonism is the way in which its perceived otherness and foreignness was always constructed in opposition to the prevailing norms of Danishness. Since those norms had been based primarily on Denmark's Lutheran religious identity until 1849, that dimension plays a central role in the high culture depictions of the 1850s. Over the next sixty years, however, popular culture depictions engaged more with emigration, sexual morality, and women's emancipation, reflecting the increasing centrality of those concerns for Danish society as the new century progressed.

Meanwhile, for the many hundreds of thousands of Americans whose ancestors were among the seventeen thousand Danish Mormon convert-emigrants, this book has striven to depict not only the social

Conclusion 247

challenges they faced after conversion, but also the ways in which they were required to redefine their cultural identity as a result of their altered relationship to their native culture, their new self-identification as members of the LDS Church, and the conditions of life they faced as immigrants in Utah. While the increasingly international membership of the LDS Church in the twenty-first century poses new challenges to the church as a global institution, Mormon converts all over the world find themselves confronted with similar issues of cultural identity negotiation as early Danish Mormons, despite very different sociopolitical circumstances. What is the relationship between a person's faith and his or her cultural identity? How does converting to the LDS faith complicate their sense of belonging at home, even without the pressure to gather to Zion that nineteenth-century converts faced?

As Denmark struggles to come to terms with the new challenges to its cultural identity posed by the recent influx of immigrants from regions such as the Middle East, Africa, and Southeast Asia, emotionally charged controversies like the Mohammad cartoon crisis of 2005[5] are bound to flare up from time to time as both sides feel their identity is being destabilized or disrespected. Taking the longer view that this book has attempted to provide regarding the reception of Mormonism in Denmark may offer hope that the ultimate outcome of such conflicts—and the cultural tensions that occasion them—will be a positive one, which allows both groups to be enriched rather than threatened by contact with each other.

Seen from this perspective, the legacy of nineteenth-century Danish Mormons is greater than just their impressive number of descendants in America and the modest but well-regarded status of the LDS Church in Denmark today. In addition to both of those important accomplishments, early Danish Mormons' courage to embrace religious difference gave Danish society a valuable opportunity to develop tolerance at a critical juncture on the path to its modern incarnation as an egalitarian social democracy. By interacting with and reacting to Mormons in their midst, Danes learned to reconsider their priorities and define their cultural identity according individuals' self-identification with Danishness rather than on the basis of arbitrary collective attributes.

Notes

Notes to Introduction

1. Using the lengthy official name of the Church of Jesus Christ of Latter-day Saints would render this book twice as long as it already is. I will instead use the terms Latter-day Saint, LDS, Mormon, and Mormonism, the latter two of which derive from the name of the book of scripture, *The Book of Mormon*, that the LDS Church regards as a companion to the Bible.
2. Katty Kay, "Utah Loves Jell-O, Official," BBCNews.com, February 6, 2001.
3. In Danish, the definite article, when used without an adjective, is attached to the end of the noun, as in *Folkekirken*, meaning "the People's Church." Without the definite article, the form of the word is *Folkekirke*, meaning simply "People's Church." 4,430,643 Danes, or nearly 80 percent of the country's population, were registered members of *Folkekirken* at the end of 2013, according to Statistikbanken.dk on February 12, 2014.
4. The Danish government does not collect statistics on religious affiliation. This percentage is based on statistics for first- and second-generation immigrants to Denmark from predominantly Muslim countries, published by the Ministry for Refugees, Immigrants and Integration Affairs, Facts and Figures, July 2009.
5. Jens Rasmussen, *Religionstolerance og Religionsfrihed. Forudsætninger og Grundloven i 1849* (Odense, Denmark: Syddansk Universitetsforlag, 2009), 9. All translations from Danish sources are my own unless otherwise cited.
6. Jørgen Würtz Sørensen, *Rejsen til Amerikas Zion: Den Danske Mormonudvandring før Århundredeskiftet* (Aalborg, Denmark: Forlaget Fenre, 1985), 8–9.
7. Sørensen, *Rejsen til Amerikas Zion*, 9.
8. Sørensen, *Rejsen til Amerikas Zion*, 11.
9. William Mulder, *Homeward to Zion: The Mormon Migration from Scandinavia* (Minneapolis: University of Minnesota Press, 1957), 56. The Nobel Prize-winning Icelandic author, Halldór Laxness, describes this phenomenon in his 1960 novel *Paradísarheimt* (*Paradise Reclaimed*).
10. Margit Egdal, *Mads Nielsen, David og Mette Marie in Guds Eget Land: En Slægtskrønike* (Otterup, Denmark: Landbohistorisk Selskab, 2000), 9.
11. George Santayana, *Reason in Common Sense*, vol. 1 (New York: Scribner, 1905), 284.
12. Stephen Greenblatt, "Cultural Mobility: An Introduction," *Cultural Mobility: A Manifesto* (Cambridge: Cambridge University Press, 2010), 2.

13. Carol Gold, *Danish Cookbooks* (Seattle: University of Washington Press, 2007), 115.

14. Stuart Hall, "Introduction: Who Needs 'Identity'?" *Questions of Cultural Identity*, edited by Stuart Hall and Paul du Gay (London: Sage, 1996), 2.

15. Hall, "Identity," 4.

16. Hall, "Identity," 3.

17. Stuart Hall, "The Spectacle of the 'Other,'" *Discourse Theory and Practice* (London: Sage, 2001), 338.

18. Andrew Jenson, *History of the Scandinavian Mission* (Salt Lake City, Utah: Deseret News Press, 1927), 283.

19. Kathleen Flake, *The Politics of American Religious Identity: The Seating of Senator Reed Smoot, Mormon Apostle* (Chapel Hill: University of North Carolina Press, 2004), 26–27.

20. Alexander Baugh, "Defending Mormonism: The Scandinavian Mission Presidency of Andrew Jenson, 1909–1912," *Go Ye into All the World: The Growth and Development of Mormon Missionary Work*, edited by Reid L. Neilson and Fred E. Woods (Provo, Utah: Brigham Young University Religious Studies Center, in cooperation with Deseret Book, 2012), 524.

Notes to Chapter 1

1. The absolute monarch King Frederik VI granted Danish Jews citizenship after a series of anti-Jewish riots in 1814. Many people feared that the children of Danish Jews would now become fully integrated into Danish society, which is exactly what happened but with positive rather than negative results, as the lives of the famous literary critic Georg Brandes and his brother, the statesman Edvard Brandes, illustrate. The evolving relationship between the Danish Lutheran society and Denmark's Jewish community has been carefully documented by historian Martin Schwarz Lausten in seven volumes; cf. *Frie Jøder? Forholdet Mellem Kristne og Jøder i Danmark fra Frihedsbrevet 1814 til Grundloven 1849* (Copenhagen: Anis, 2005) and *Folkekirken og Jøderne: Forholdet Mellem Kristne og Jøder i Danmark fra 1849 til Begyndelsen af det 20. Århundrede* (Copenhagen: Anis, 2007).

2. Jacob Peter Mynster, *Grundlovens Bestemmelser med Hensyn til de Kirkelige Forhold i Danmark* (Copenhagen: C. A. Reitzel, 1850), 1.

3. Mynster, *Grundloven*, 3, 5.

4. Those Danes who did pay attention to politics, like Peter Andreas Heiberg (1758–1841), often ran afoul of the country's strict censorship laws. As punishment for criticizing the government in his plays, essays, and novels, P. A. Heiberg, father of the celebrated Danish golden age dramatist Johan Ludvig Heiberg, was banished from Denmark on Christmas Eve 1799 and lived the rest of his life in Paris.

5. P. G. Lindhardt, *Vækkelse og Kirkelige Retninger* (Copenhagen: Hans Reitzel, 1959), 9, 46.

6. Bruce Kirmmse, *Kierkegaard in Golden Age Denmark* (Bloomington: Indiana University Press, 1990), 381. Large parts of the Danish peasantry were already literate in this period, but there did not yet exist a public education system outside of parish schools.

7. Thorkild Borup Jensen, ed., *Danskernes Identitetshistorie* (Copenhagen: C. A. Reitzel, 1993), 190.

8. Johan Schioldann Nielsen, *D. G. Monrad: En Patografi* (Odense, Denmark: Odense Universitetsforlag, 1983), 2.

9. P. Stavnstrup, *D. G. Monrad: Politiker og Geistlig* (Copenhagen: Berlingske Forlag, 1948), 11.

10. Stavnstrup, *D. G. Monrad*, 16.

11. In an interesting convergence, Peter Christian Kierkegaard, who is discussed in chapter 2, was instrumental in drafting a conservative, alternative (or "loyalist") petition at the same time. In his diary for December 1839, Kierkegaard notes, "On the 3rd Frederik 6 died, the same evening a meeting at Knirsch's [a café and meeting place] to present a petition by university students, next day our meetings, which ended by the retreat home to me and signing it there, continued on the 5th. Delivered the 7th and printed in the three principal newspapers the same day" (Peter Christian Kierkegaard, *Dagbog*, Danish Royal Library, Copenhagen, NKS 2656, 40, I). The petition received 426 signatures and was read by P. C. Kierkegaard at Amalienborg, the royal residence, on December 8. It also appeared in various Copenhagen newspapers, including *Fædrelandet. Extrablad* 2 (December 8, 1839): 87–88. See also Søren Kierkegaard's journal entry NB18: 62 in *Kierkegaard's Journals and Notebooks*, vol. 7 (2014), 299–300, with accompanying notes. Many thanks to Professor Bruce Kirmmse for the reference.

12. Asger Nyholm. *Religion og Politik: En Monrad Studie* (Copenhagen: Nyt Nordisk Forlag, 1947), 52.

13. Nyholm, *Religion og Politik*, 56; *Fædrelandet* 19: 5, 1840, no. 164.

14. Nyholm, *Religion og Politik*, 53; *Fædrelandet* 13: 3, 1840, no. 99, 691.

15. Nyholm, *Religion og Politik*, 55; *Fædrelandet* 1: 4, 1840, no. 118.

16. Nyholm, *Religion og Politik*, 63.

17. Nyholm, *Religion og Politik*, 53; *Fædrelandet* no. 2, 62.

18. Nyholm, *Religion og Politik*, 57; "Tale ved Læseforeningens Fest, d. 31. Maj 1840."

19. Nyholm, *Religion og Politik*, 58; "Tale ved Læseforeningens Fest, d. 31. Maj 1840."

20. Nyholm, *Religion og Politik*, 103.

21. Nyholm, *Religion og Politik*, 107.

22. Nyholm, *Religion og Politik*, 107.

23. Denmark's primary foreign policy challenge in 1848 was dealing with a civil war being waged in the provinces of Schleswig and Holstein between German-speakers in Holstein who wanted to join the German Confederation and Danish-speakers in Schleswig, an issue that would cause Monrad's downfall

as prime minister sixteen years later. Following the national-liberal party line, the March Ministry supported efforts to give Holstein more freedom while formally incorporating the province of Schleswig into the Danish kingdom, despite the traditional indivisibility of the two provinces. The ministry was unsuccessful in this attempt and was replaced by a more conservative government in November 1848. Monrad was invited to remain in his position, but refused because of his support for the division of Schleswig along linguistic lines, a solution that was unpopular among Danes at the time but which ultimately solved the problem (by plebiscite) in 1920.

24. Jeppe Nevers, *Fra Skældsord til Slagord: Demokratiebegrebet i Dansk Politisk Historie* (Odense: Syddansk Universitetsforlag, 2011), 103.

25. Nyholm, *Religion og Politik*, 95; *Fædrelandet* 26: 2, 1849, no. 48.

26. Robert L. Perkins, "The Authoritarian Symbiosis of Church and Crown in Søren Kierkegaard's 'Attack upon Christendom,'" *Anthropology and Authority: Essays on Søren Kierkegaard*, edited by Poul Houe, Gordon D. Marino, and Sven Hakon Rossel (Amsterdam: Rodopi, 2000), 137.

27. Niels Thulstrup, *Kierkegaard and the Church in Denmark*, translated by R. M. Summers, *Bibliotheca Kierkegaardiana* 13 (Copenhagen: C. A. Reitzel, 1984), 12.

28. For more on the Danish forts in West Africa, see Pernille Ipsen, *Daughters of the Trade: Atlantic Slavers and Interracial Marriage on the Gold Coast* (Philadelphia: University of Pennsylvania Press, 2015).

29. Jens Rasmussen, *Religionstolerance og Religionsfrihed: Forudsætninger og Grundloven i 1849* (Odense: University of Southern Denmark Press, 2009), 56.

30. Rasmussen, *Religionstolerance*, 57.

31. Rasmussen, *Religionstolerance*, 32.

32. Rasmussen, *Religionstolerance*, 170.

33. Rasmussen, *Religionstolerance*, 170–71.

34. Hans Lassen Martensen, *Den Christelige Daab Betragtet med Hensyn paa det Baptistiske Spørgsmaal* (Copenhagen: Reitzel, 1843).

35. Rasmussen, *Religionstolerance*, 189.

36. Martin Schwarz Lausten, *A Church History of Denmark*, translated by Frederick H. Cryer (Aldershot, England: Ashgate, 2002), 229.

37. Rasmussen, *Religionstolerance*, 194.

38. Jes Fabricius Møller, *Grundtvigianisme i det 20. Århundrede* (Copenhagen: Vartov, 2005), 11.

39. Kaj Thaning, *Grundtvig* (Copenhagen: Gyldendal Norsk Forlag, 1983), 9.

40. H. N. Clausen, *Catholicismens og Protestantismens Kirkeforfatning, Lære og Ritus* (Copenhagen: Seidelin, 1825).

41. N. F. S. Grundtvig, *Kirkens Gienmæle imod Professor Theologiae Dr. H. N. Clausen* (Copenhagen: Wahlske Boghandels Forlag, 1825).

42. N. F. S. Grundtvig, *Skolen for Livet og Akademiet i Sorø, Borgerlig Betragtet* (Copenhagen: Wahlske Boghandels Forlag, 1838).

43. Quoted in Thaning, *Grundtvig*, 89.

44. Thaning, *Grundtvig*, 9.

45. Thaning, *Grundtvig*, 86.

46. Claus Bjørn, "Grundtvig-skitse: Grundtvig som Politiker 1848–50," *Grundtvig som politiker*, edited by Thorkild Lyby (Copenhagen: Forlaget ANIS, 2007), 17.

47. Quoted in Andreas Pontoppidan Thyssen, *Den Nygrundtvigske Bevægelse med Særligt Henblik paa den Borupske Kreds, vol. 1, 1870–1887* (Copenhagen: Det Danske Forlag, 1958), 25.

48. Edvard Brandes, "Grundtvigs 100. Fødselsdag," *Morgenbladet* (Copenhagen), September 9, 1883. Also quoted in Jes Fabricius Møller, *Grundtvigianisme*, 10.

49. Quoted in Thaning, *Grundtvig*, 58.

50. Bjørn, "Grundtvig-skitse," 20.

51. Quoted in Bjørn, "Grundtvig-skitse," 33.

52. N. F. S. Grundtvig, "Den Danske Konge og de Tydske Forrædere," *Danskeren*, I, 76.

53. N. F. S. Grundtvig, "Om Constitution og Statsforfatning i Danmark," *Danskeren*, I, 373.

54. *Beretning om Forhandlingerne paa Rigsdagen*, vol. 1 (Copenhagen, 1848), 2513–14, 2548–50.

55. Quoted in Johan Borup, *N. F. S. Grundtvig* (Copenhagen: Reitzels Forlag-Axel Sandal, 1944), 249.

56. *Beretning om Forhandlingerne paa Rigsdagen*, 253.

57. Bjørn, "Grundtvig-skitse," 90; *Beretning om Forhandlingerne paa Rigsdagen*, 2277.

58. *Beretning om Forhandlingerne paa Rigsdagen*, 3050.

59. N. F. S. Grundtvig, "Danmarks Riges Grundlov," *Danskeren* II, 334.

60. Quoted in Thaning, *Grundtvig*, 107.

61. Quoted in Thaning, *Grundtvig*, 108.

62. Quoted in Thaning, *Grundtvig*, 109.

63. The same language appears as paragraph sixty-seven in the current Danish constitution.

64. Lausten, *A Church History of Denmark*, 230; Personal correspondence between the author and Bruce Kirmmse, February 21, 2015.

65. Martensen, *Af mit Levnet*, vol. 2, 132.

66. J. P. Mynster, *Prædikener Holdte i Aarene 1846 til 1852: Sommer-Halvaaret*, 2nd ed. (Copenhagen: Gyldendal, 1854), 17–18.

67. Quoted in Lausten, *A Church History of Denmark*, 230.

68. Rasmussen, *Religionstolerance*, 243.

69. Rasmussen, *Religionstolerance*, 245.

70. Rasmussen, *Religionstolerance*, 246.

71. Rasmussen, *Religionstolerance*, 246. He gives his source as Sekretariat/Direktoratet, the Magistrate's 1. Division, the Secretariat's Archive (–1938), Civil Marriage 1851–1922, vol. 1, 1851–1875.

72. For more about the reception of Mormonism in Norway, see Gerald M. Haslam, *Clash of Cultures: The Norwegian Experience with Mormonism, 1842–1920* (New York: Peter Lang, 1984).

73. For more about the reception of Mormonism in Iceland, see Fred E. Woods, *Fire on Ice: The Story of Icelandic Latter-day Saints at Home and Abroad* (Provo, Utah: Brigham Young University, 2005).

74. John Langeland, "Scandinavia, The Church In," *Encyclopedia of Mormonism*, edited by Daniel H. Ludlow (New York: Macmillan, 1992), 1262–63.

75. Langeland, "Scandinavia," 1263.

76. Haslam, *Clash of Cultures*, 7.

77. Very little is known about Peter Clemensen, aside from some information included in P. O. Hansen's autobiography. Hansen reports that Clemensen lost his wife in childbirth in the summer of 1845, after which he came to Nauvoo from St. Louis. Clemensen's experiences in Nauvoo were disheartening; he was apparently dismayed at the coarse language of some of his fellow Latter-day Saints, distressed at losing his fifteen-year-old daughter to illness, and concerned by the persecution of the saints by their neighbors. As a result, Clemensen "took fright and went away," which prompted Hansen to remark, "This man was the first Danish man in the church, but made shipwreck of his faith. My brother Hans C. Hansen is the next & your humble servant is the 3rd." P. O. Hansen, *Autobiography*, 60–61. P. O. Hansen, *Autobiography*, MS 1437, Peter Olsen Hansen Collection, LDS Church History Library, 45.

78. P. O. Hansen's handwritten autobiography has been published by his great-granddaughter: Leland Hansen Ashby, ed., *An Autobiography of Peter Olsen Hansen, 1818–1895: Mormon Convert and Pioneer Missionary, Translator of Book of Mormon into Danish* (Salt Lake City, Utah: Leland Hansen Ashby, 1988).

79. Hans Christian Hansen was among the first group of Mormons to cross the plains to Utah in July 1847, where he lived out the rest of his life. Although his brother reports in his autobiography that Hans Christian was married in Nauvoo, the entry about him in Andrew Jenson's biographical encyclopedia notes that he "lived a lonely life without the care of a family." P. O. Hansen, *Autobiography*, 61; Andrew Jenson, *Latter-day Saint Biographical Encyclopedia: A Compilation of Biographical Sketches of Prominent Men and Women in the Church of Jesus Christ of Latter-day Saints*, vol. 2 (Salt Lake City, Utah: Andrew Jenson History Company, 1914), 766.

80. P. O. Hansen, *Autobiography*, 52.

81. P. O. Hansen, *Autobiography*, 61.

82. P. O. Hansen, *Autobiography*, 62. Hansen does not specify whether this was a legal or ritual adoption, perhaps as part of a sealing in the Nauvoo LDS Temple. In his description of the journey west, Hansen comments on how fortunate he was to have been adopted by Kimball, particularly because it gave him the means to go west immediately rather than remaining in St. Louis to earn money for the trip. He also expresses gratitude for the opportunity he had to volunteer for the Mormon Battalion, which was organized in July 1846 and marched to San Diego to support the U.S. Army in the Mexican-American

War, but his name does not appear on the roster of any Mormon Battalion company, so he was presumably not accepted for service.

83. P. O. Hansen, *Autobiography*, 77.

84. Erastus Snow, Letter to his family, July 7, 1850, Erastus Snow Collection, LDS Church History Library. Quoted in Haslam, *Clash of Cultures*, 10.

85. Jenson, *History of the Scandinavian Mission*, 5.

86. Haslam, *Clash of Cultures*, 14–15.

87. P. O. Hansen, *Autobiography*, 84.

88. Haslam, *Clash of Cultures*, 15.

89. Erastus Snow, *Journal*, vol. 5, n.d, Erastus Snow Collection, LDS Church History Library. Quoted in Jenson, *History of the Scandinavian Mission*, 6.

90. Jenson, *History of the Scandinavian Mission*, 9.

91. Langeland, "Scandinavia," 1262. Particularly in the 1850s and 1860s, the large number of Danish Mormon converts was paired with a large number of people leaving the church as well, often after a relatively short time—a fact that is often obscured by the apparently steady growth of membership numbers.

92. Snow, *Journal*, vol 6, 21. Quoted in Haslam, *Clash of Cultures*, 182.

93. Kristian Hvidt, *Flugten til Amerika eller Drivkræfter i Masseudvandringen fra Danmark 1868–1914* (Aarhus, Denmark: Aarhus Universitetsforlag, 1971), 293.

94. Jenson, *History of the Scandinavian Mission*, 17.

95. Langeland, "Scandinavia," 1262.

96. Jenson, *History of the Scandinavian Mission*, 11.

97. Snow, *Journal*, vol. 6, 16. Quoted in Haslam, *Clash of Cultures*, 15.

98. Jørgen W. Schmidt, *En Dansk Mormon Bibliografi, 1837–1984* (Aalborg: Forlaget Fenre, 1984), 1.

99. George Parker Dykes, *Diary*, February 24, 1851. Quoted in Haslam, *Clash of Cultures*, 18.

100. Dykes, *Diary*, vol. 2, December 2, 1850. Quoted in Haslam, *Clash of Cultures*, 15.

101. Sørensen, *Rejsen til Amerikas Zion*, 35.

102. Haslam, *Clash of Cultures*, 16. Because the early Mormon missionaries were instructed to travel "without purse or scrip" (according to the Bible), Dykes lived in squalid conditions in Aalborg, traveled everywhere on foot, and was frequently reduced to scrounging weeds, hay, and cabbage leaves to stave off starvation.

103. Quoted in Sørensen, *Rejsen til Amerikas Zion*, 36.

104. J. P. Mynster, *Grundlovens Bestemmelser*.

105. Jesper Stenholm Paulsen, *De Danske Mormoners Historie* (Copenhagen: A. Broberg Forlag, 2012), 35.

106. Knud Banning, *Forsamlinger og Mormoner* (Copenhagen: Gad, 1960), 12.

107. William Mulder, *Homeward to Zion: The Mormon Migration from Scandinavia* (Minneapolis: University of Minnesota Press, 1957), 54.

108. Schmidt, *Bibliografi*, 2–5.

109. Jørgen W. Schmidt, *Oh, Du Zion i Vest: Den Danske Mormon-Emigration 1850–1900* (Copenhagen: Rosenkilde and Bagger, 1965), 36–37.

110. Mulder, *Homeward to Zion*, 55.

111. Mulder, *Homeward to Zion*, 55.

112. Quoted in Sørensen, *Rejsen til Amerikas Zion*, 26.

113. Haslam, *Clash of Cultures*, 17.

114. "Mormonerne i Roeskilde," *Flyveposten* (Copenhagen), February 6, 1851.

115. Paulsen, *De Danske Mormoners Historie*, 43.

116. Jenson, *History of the Scandinavian Mission*, 28.

117. Dykes, *Diary*, June 30, 1851. Quoted in Haslam, *Clash of Cultures*, 21.

118. Ibid.

119. Sørensen, *Rejsen til Amerikas Zion*, 33.

120. Sørensen, *Rejsen til Amerikas Zion*, 28

121. Quoted in Sørensen, *Rejsen til Amerikas Zion*, 33.

122. Sørensen, *Rejsen til Amerikas Zion*, 46.

123. Sørensen, *Rejsen til Amerikas Zion*, 10.

124. Banning, *Forsamlinger*, 195.

125. Hans Lassen Martensen, *Af mit Levnet*, vol. 3 (Copenhagen: Gyldendal, 1882), 108.

126. Claus Bjørn, *Kampen om Grundloven* (Copenhagen: Fremad, 1999), 7.

Notes to Chapter 2

1. The original title in Danish is *Tvende Mormoner ere paa deres Vandring komne ind i et Tømrehus paa Landet, hvor de ved Prædiken og ved Fremvisning af nogle af deres Sekts Skrifter søger at vinde nye Tilhængere.*

2. Haavard Rostrup, "Et Brev fra Christen Dalsgaard," *Kunstmuseets Aarsskrift 1942* (Copenhagen: Nordisk Forlag, 1942), 145.

3. Quoted in Inge Bucka, "Værk og Virkelighed—Realismen i Christen Dalsgaards Billeder," *Christen Dalsgaard 1824–1907*, edited by Charlotte Sabroe, Christine Buhl Andersen, and Inge Bucka (Vestsjællands Kunstmuseum, 2001), 51.

4. This version of the painting, called "A Carpenter's Workshop" (1855), belongs to the Hirschsprung Collection in Copenhagen.

5. Rostrup, "Et Brev," 146.

6. Rostrup, "Et Brev," 147.

7. Matthew 28:19 (King James Version).

8. Reid L. Neilson, "The Nineteenth-Century Euro-American Mormon Missionary Model," *Go Ye into All the World: The Growth and Development of Mormon Missionary Work*, edited by Reid L. Neilson and Fred E. Woods (Provo, Utah: Religious Studies Center at Brigham Young University and Deseret Book, 2012), 67.

9. Jenson, *History of the Scandinavian Mission*, 22.

10. Neilson, "Euro-American," 69, 73.

11. Mynster, *Grundlovens Bestemmelser,* 5.

12. Thorkild C. Lyby, "Peter Christian Kierkegaard: A Man with a Difficult Family Heritage," *Kierkegaard and His Danish Contemporaries, Tome II: Theology,* edited by Jon Stewart (London: Ashgate, 2009), 94.

13. Jørgen Schmidt, *O Du Zion i Vest,* 40.

14. Carl Weltzer, *Peter og Søren Kierkegaard* (Copenhagen: Gad, 1936), 252.

15. Peter Christian Kierkegaard, *Diary 1850–1859,* Manuscript Collection NKS 3013 4 II, Danish Royal Library, Copenhagen.

16. L. D. Hass, "Protest," *Fædrelandet,* February 1, 1851.

17. Otto Holmgaard, *Peter Christian Kierkegaard: Grundtvigs Lærling* (Copenhagen: Rosenkilde & Bagger, 1953), 22.

18. Hans Christian Rørdam, "Om Besættelsen af det Ledige Theologiske Professorat," *Berlingske Tidende,* Number 124, May 31, 1854.

19. Mulder, *Homeward to Zion,* 55.

20. Susan Easton Black, Shauna C. Anderson, Ruth Ellen Maness, eds., *Legacy of Sacrifice: Missionaries to Scandinavia, 1872–1894* (Provo, Utah: Brigham Young University Religious Studies Center, 2007), 111.

21. Black, *Legacy of Sacrifice,* 111.

22. Mulder, *Homeward to Zion,* 54.

23. Rex Thomas Price, *The Mormon Missionary of the Nineteenth Century* (Unpublished dissertation, University of Wisconsin–Madison, 1991), 334–35.

24. Julie K. Allen and David L. Paulsen, "The Reverend Dr. Peter Christian Kierkegaard's 'About and Against Mormonism' (1855)," *BYU Studies* 46: 3 (2007), 115.

25. Allen and Paulsen, "Peter Christian Kierkegaard," 125.

26. Allen and Paulsen, "Peter Christian Kierkegaard," 114.

27. In his entry for June 1855, for example, Peter mentions the conversions of the farmer Niels Nielsen and his hired hand Jens Hansen, whose confirmation Kierkegaard had just performed the previous spring, as well as the farmer/carpenter Nicolai Sørensen, his wife, and his sons Isaac and Frederick. Peter Christian Kierkegaard, *Diary 1850–1859,* Manuscript Collection NKS 3013 4 II, Danish Royal Library, Copenhagen.

28. The membership records of the Haugerup Branch from 1855 to 1859, when it was dissolved again due to the emigration of most of its members, are available on microfilm at the LDS Church Family History Center Archives in Salt Lake City, Utah. The entries for the Hemerdt family are found in the Haugerup Branch Records, 1855–59, 12–13, entries 7–8.

29. Baron von Münchhausen is a fictional character in several collections of stories from the late eighteenth century, which recount his adventures and impossible exploits, such as climbing to the moon on a rope of chaff. The character is based on the historical figure of the German nobleman Karl Friedrich Hieronymous (1720–97), who served in the Russian military and entertained his friends by telling tall tales. See Gottffried August Bürger, et. al., *Die wunderbaren Reisen und Abenteuern des Freiherrn von Münchhausen* (Zurich: Nord-Süd Verlag, 1977).

30. Peter Christian Kierkegaard, *Diary 1850–1859*, Manuscript Collection NKS 3013 4 II, Danish Royal Library, Copenhagen.

31. Peter Christian Kierkegaard, *Om og mod Mormonismen* (Copenhagen: C. G. Iversen, 1855). For the full text in English translation, see Julie K. Allen and David L. Paulsen, "The Reverend Dr. Peter Christian Kierkegaard's 'About and Against Mormonism' (1855)," *BYU Studies* 46: 3 (2007), 100–156.

32. Allen and Paulsen, "Peter Christian Kierkegaard," 118.

33. Reverend Kierkegaard seemed to be wary of "M" alliteration in general. In a letter to C. J. Brandt from early 1855, he described the alliteration between the names Münter, Müller, Mynster, and Martensens as "quite suspicious." Peter Christian Kierkegaard, Letter to C. J. Brandt, 1855, Manuscript Collection, Danish Royal Library, Copenhagen.

34. Allen and Paulsen, "Peter Christian Kierkegaard," 128.

35. Allen and Paulsen, "Peter Christian Kierkegaard," 139.

36. Christian Anker Winther, Letter to P. C. Kierkegaard, October 5, 1854, NKS 3174.4, no. 113, Danish Royal Library, Copenhagen.

37. Christian Anker Winther, Letter to P. C. Kierkegaard, January 18, 1855, NKS 3174.4, no. 114, Danish Royal Library, Copenhagen.

38. Peter Christian Kierkegaard, "Polemik mod Mogens Sommer," *Aalborgposten* (Aalborg), February 21–22, 1866.

39. Holmgaard, *Grundtvigs Lærling*, 49.

40. Flemming Lundgreen-Nielsen, "Grundtvig og Danskhed," *Dansk Identitets-historie*, vol. 3: Folkets Danmark 1848–1940, edited by Ole Feldbæk (Copenhagen: C. A. Reitzel, 1992), 89.

41. Bjørn, "Grundtvig-skitse," 20.

42. Bjørn, "Grundtvig-skitse," 21.

43. Birgitte Stoklund Larsen, "The Tradition of Freedom: N. F. S. Grundtvig and His Influence on the Church," *A Brief Guide to the Evangelical Lutheran Church in Denmark*, edited by Rebekka Højmark Svenningsen (Copenhagen: Aros Forlag and Folkekirkens Mellemkirkelige Råd, 2013), 26.

44. Larsen, "The Tradition of Freedom," 27.

45. Elise Stampe, "Mormonismen," Constantin Hansen Family Collection, NKS 4987 4, Manuscript Department, Royal Danish Library, Copenhagen. The document is filed under the title "Forarbejder til en Bog om Mormonismen" ("Preparations for a Book about Mormonism"), but the title page of the manuscript states simply "Mormonism."

46. The Stampes' patronage of Thorvaldsen reveals an unusual, albeit indirect, family connection to Mormonism. Thorvaldsen's statue of Jesus Christ, commonly referred to as the *Christus*, is widely used throughout the LDS Church. While the original stands in *Vor Frue Kirke* in Copenhagen, which was Søren Kierkegaard's home parish, copies of the statue stand in nearly every LDS temple visitor center. This particular Mormon affinity for Danish Lutheran art is reinforced by the fact that reproductions of paintings depicting the life of Christ created by Carl Bloch for the royal chapel in

Frederiksborg Castle are often featured in LDS meetinghouses and curricular materials. From November 2013 through May 2014, the Mormon-owned Brigham Young University Museum of Art in Provo, Utah (which owns at least two Carl Bloch originals), hosted an extensive exhibition of Lutheran altarpieces by Bloch, fellow Danish painter Frans Schwartz, and the German painter Heinrich Hoffmann.

47. Thora Constantin-Hansen, *Elise Stampe: Et Billede og en Arv* (Copenhagen: H. Hagerups Forlag, 1931), 15.

48. Quoted in Christine Dalgas Stampe, *Baronesse Stampes Erindringer om Thorvaldsen*, edited by Rigmor Stampe (Copenhagen: Gyldendal/Nordisk, 1912), 87.

49. Constantin-Hansen, *Elise Stampe*, 15.

50. Rigmor Stampe, *Baronesse Stampes Erindringer*, 24. Thora Constantin-Hansen's biography refers to a similar incident, but it features a thirteen-year-old Elise arguing with Thorvaldsen about Napoleon and the English attack on Copenhagen in 1807. Constantin-Hansen, *Elise Stampe: Et Billede og en Arv*, 15.

51. Erik Aalbæk Jensen, "Et Kvindehus Gennem 250 År," *Vallø: Historien om et Slot og Dets Ejere....*, edited by Sys Hartmann (Copenhagen: Gyldendal, 1988), 97.

52. Elise Stampe, Letter to N. F. S. Grundtvig, September 14, 1857, Grundtvig Collection, G 466.VI.d.6, Manuscript Department, Royal Danish Library.

53. Constantin-Hansen, *Elise Stampe: Et Billede og en Arv*, 26.

54. Hans Christian Andersen, Letter to Jonna Stampe, June 20, 1864, Reproduced in Rigmor Stampe, *H. C. Andersen og Hans Nærmeste Omgang* (Copenhagen: Aschehoug, 1918), 155.

55. Constantin-Hansen, *Elise Stampe*, 31.

56. Constantin-Hansen, *Elise Stampe*, 32–33.

57. Elise Stampe, Letter to N. F. S. Grundtvig, September 14, 1857, Grundtvig Collection, G 466.VI.d.6, Manuscript Department, Danish Royal Library, Copenhagen.

58. Elise Stampe, Letter to N. F. S. Grundtvig, September 14, 1857, Grundtvig Collection, G 466.VI.d.6, Manuscript Department, Danish Royal Library, Copenhagen.

59. Constantin-Hansen, *Elise Stampe*, 97.

60. N. F. S. Grundtvig, Letter to Elise Stampe, October 11, 1858, Manuscript Department, NKS 3946 kvart, Royal Danish Library, Copenhagen.

61. Elise Stampe, Letter to Bishop P. C. Kierkegaard, December 13, 1858, Danish Royal Library Manuscript Collection.

62. In a letter to Bishop Kierkegaard dated November 5, 1861, Stampe asks, "Do you still remember when, three years ago, an old maid whom you didn't know at all, wrote to you and burdened you with her authorship?" Elise Stampe, Letter to P. C. Bishop Kierkegaard, November 5, 1861, Manuscript Department, Royal Danish Library, Copenhagen.

63. Elise Stampe, Letter to Bishop P. C. Kierkegaard, January 3–4, 1859, Danish Royal Library Manuscript Collection.

64. All citations from this text are taken from: Elise Stampe, "Mormonismen," Constantin Hansen Family Collection, NKS 4987 4, Manuscript Department, Royal Danish Library, Copenhagen.

65. George Pattison, *Kierkegaard and the Theology of the Nineteenth Century* (Cambridge, U.K.: Cambridge University Press, 2012), 202.

66. Bruce H. Kirmmse, "'But I Am Almost Never Understood': Or, Who Killed Søren Kierkegaard," *Kierkegaard: The Self in Society*, edited by George Pattison and Steven Shakespeare (Basingstoke: Macmillan, 1998), 187.

67. Kirmmse, *Kierkegaard in Golden Age Denmark*, 451

68. Søren Kierkegaard, "Var Biskop Mynster et 'Sandhedsvidne,' et af 'de rette Sandhedsvidner'—er dette Sandhed?," *Samlede Værker*, vol. 19 (Copenhagen: Gyldendal, 1964), 9.

69. Bruce H. Kirmmse, ed., *Encounters with Kierkegaard: A Life as Seen by His Contemporaries* (Princeton, New Jersey: Princeton University Press, 1996), 203.

70. Søren Kierkegaard, "Vi er Alle Christne," *Øieblikket*, no. 2, June 4, 1855; *Samlede Værker*, vol. 19 (Copenhagen: Gyldendal, 1964), 117.

71. Søren Kierkegaard, "At Præsterne ere Menneske-Ædere, og paa den Afskyeligste Maade," *Øieblikket*, no. 9, September 24, 1855. English translation from: Søren Kierkegaard, "That the Pastors are Cannibals, and in the Most Abominable Way," *The Moment and Late Writings*, edited and translated by Howard V. Hong and Edna H. Hong (Princeton, New Jersey: Princeton University Press, 1998), 321.

72. Søren Kierkegaard, "Christendom med Kongelig Bestalling og Christendom uden Kongelig Bestalling," *Fædrelandet* 83: April 11, 1855. English translation from: Søren Kierkegaard, "Christianity with a Royal Certificate and Christianity without a Royal Certificate," *The Moment and Late Writings*, edited and translated by Howard V. Hong and Edna H. Hong (Princeton, New Jersey: Princeton University Press, 1998), 54.

73. Søren Kierkegaard, "Er det Forsvarligt af Staten, Christeligt, at Forlokke en Deel af den Studerende Ungdom?" *Øieblikket*, no. 3, June 27, 1855. English translation from: Søren Kierkegaard, "Is it Defensible, Christianly, for the State to Entice Some of the Young Students?" *The Moment and Late Writings*, edited and translated by Howard V. Hong and Edna H. Hong (Princeton, New Jersey: Princeton University Press, 1998), 145.

74. Søren Kierkegaard, "Vil Staten i Sandhed Tjene Christendommen, saa lad den Tage de 1000 Levebrød Bort," *Øieblikket*, no. 3, June 27, 1855. English translation from: Søren Kierkegaard, "If the State Truly Wants to Serve Christianity, Then Let It Eliminate the 1000 Livelihoods," *The Moment and Late Writings*, edited and translated by Howard V. Hong and Edna H. Hong (Princeton, New Jersey: Princeton University Press, 1998), 153.

75. Kirmmse, *Kierkegaard in Golden-Age Denmark*, 365.

76. Søren Kierkegaard, "Hvad man Saadan Kalder en Christen," *Øieblikket*, no. 7, August 30, 1855. English translation from: Søren Kierkegaard, "The Sort of Person Who is Called a Christian," *The Moment and Late Writings*, edited and

translated by Howard V. Hong and Edna H. Hong (Princeton, New Jersey: Princeton University Press, 1998), 229–30.

77. Søren Kierkegaard, "Læge-Skjønnet," Øieblikket, no. 4, July 7, 1855. English translation from: Søren Kierkegaard, "A Medical Opinion," *The Moment and Late Writings*, edited and translated by Howard V. Hong and Edna H. Hong (Princeton, New Jersey: Princeton University Press, 1998), 158.

78. Kierkegaard, "Medical Opinion," 159.

79. Søren Mørch, *Den Sidste Danmarkshistorie* (Copenhagen: Gyldendal, 1996), 50.

80. Kirmmse, *Kierkegaard in Golden-Age Denmark*, 381.

81. Leif Grane, "Sørens Broder: Om Peter Christian Kierkegaard," *Fra Egtvedpigen til Folketinget* (Copenhagen: Munksgaard, 1997), 81.

82. Otto Holmgaard, *Exstaticus: Søren Kierkegaards Sidste Kamp, Derunder hans Forhold til Broderen* (Copenhagen: Nyt Nordisk Forlag Arnold Busck, 1967), 9.

83. Hans Lassen Martensen, Letter dated November 18, 1855, quoted in Kirmmse, *Encounters*, 135.

84. Kirmmse, *Encounters*, 134.

85. Journals NB32:78, *Søren Kierkegaards Skrifter*, edited by Niels Jørgen Kappelørn, vol. 26 (Copenhagen: Gad, 2009), 172.

86. Journals NB32:84, *Søren Kierkegaards Skrifter*, 176.

87. Anonymous article in *Kjøbenhavnsposten*, Number 109, May 12, 1855.

88. Vilhelm Birkedal, "Lidelse for Christi Skyld, dens Nødvendighed for den Christne osv.," *Dansk Kirketidende* 37 (August 26, 1855): Columns 593–604.

89. Søren Kierkegaard, "Guds Uforanderlighed: En Tale," August 1, 1855, *Samlede Værker*, vol. 19 (Copenhagen: Gyldendal, 1964). English translation from: Søren Kierkegaard, "The Changelessness of God," *The Moment and Late Writings*, edited and translated by Howard V. Hong and Edna H. Hong (Princeton, New Jersey: Princeton University Press, 1998), 271–72.

90. Søren Kierkegaard, "Den Religieuse Tilstand," *Fædrelandet* 72: March 26, 1855. English translation from: Søren Kierkegaard, "The Religious Situation," *The Moment and Late Writings*, edited and translated by Howard V. Hong and Edna H. Hong (Princeton, New Jersey: Princeton University Press, 1998), 36.

91. Søren Kierkegaard, "The Religious Situation," 37.

92. Søren Kierkegaard, "Confirmationen og Vielsen; Christeligt Comedie-Spil Eller Det, Som Værre Er," Øieblikket, no. 7, August 30, 1855. English translation from: Søren Kierkegaard, "Confirmation and the Wedding; Christian Comedy or Something Worse," *The Moment and Late Writings*, edited and translated by Howard V. Hong and Edna H. Hong (Princeton, New Jersey: Princeton University Press, 1998), 248.

93. Søren Kierkegaard, "Et Ganske Simpelt Regnestykke," 1854, *Søren Kierkegaards Skrifter*, 469.

94. Søren Kierkegaard, "Præsten Ikke Blot Beviser Christendommens Sandhed, men Han Modbeviser den med det Samme," Øieblikket, no. 9, September 24, 1855. English translation from: Søren Kierkegaard, "The Pastor Not Only Demonstrates the Truth of Christianity, but He Simultaneously Refutes It,"

The Moment and Late Writings, edited and translated by Howard V. Hong and Edna H. Hong (Princeton, New Jersey: Princeton University Press, 1998), 324.

Notes to Chapter 3

1. Claude M. Steele, "The Psychology of Self-Affirmation: Sustaining the Integrity of the Self," *Advances in Experimental Social Psychology*, vol. 21, edited by Leonard Berkowitz (New York: Academic Press, 1988), 261–302.
2. Kim Östman, *The Introduction of Mormonism into Finnish Society, 1840–1900* (Åbo, Finland: Åbo Academy University Press, 2010), 89.
3. Östman, *Introduction of Mormonism into Finnish Society*, 87.
4. Östman, *Introduction of Mormonism into Finnish Society*, 86.
5. Jørgen W. Schmidt and Hans Billeskov Jansen, *Mormonerne (Medlemmer af Jesu Kristi Kirke af Sidste Dages Hellige) i Danske Aviser i Årene 1850–1851* (Lynge, Denmark: Jørgen W. Schmidt, 1980).
6. Jørgen W. Schmidt, *En Dansk Mormon Bibliografi, 1837–1984* (Aalborg: Forlaget Fenre, 1984).
7. Quoted in Sørensen, *Rejsen til Amerikas Zion*, 37.
8. Jørgen W. Schmidt, *Mormonernes Flerkoneri, 1843–1890: Baggrund, Udbredelse, Reaktioner i Litteratur og Presse, Indvirkning på Samfundsstrukturen, Vurdering af Årsag og Virkning* (Lynge, Denmark: Forlaget Moroni, 1983), 31.
9. Jørgen W. Schmidt, *Flerkoneri*, quoted in Sørensen, *Rejsen til Amerikas Zion*, 39.
10. Quoted in Sørensen, *Rejsen til Amerikas Zion*, 39.
11. The number of Brigham Young's wives illuminates the complexity of the Mormon system of plural marriage. While it is true that Young married dozens of women, including sixteen women who bore him a total of fifty-seven children, the vast majority of his plural marriages were nonconjugal relationships, particularly as many of his "wives" were elderly women or widows. Additionally, several of his wives later chose—and were allowed—to terminate their marriages to him. According to Jeffrey Ogden Johnson, "At the time of his death on August 23, 1877, Young had married fifty-six women—nineteen predeceased him, ten divorced him, twenty-three survived him, and four are unaccounted for. Of the twenty-three who survived him, seventeen received a share of his estate while the remaining six apparently had non-conjugal roles." For more information, see Jeffery Ogden Johnson, "Determining and Defining 'Wife': The Brigham Young Households," *Dialogue: A Journal of Mormon Thought*, vol. 20, no. 3, Fall 1987; Leonard J. Arrington, *Brigham Young: American Moses*, (New York: Knopf, 1985).
12. Axel Liljefalk, *Den Hvide Slavehandel* (Copenhagen: E. Jespersens Forlag, 1911), 7.
13. Liljefalk, *Slavehandel*, 7.
14. Jette D. Søllinge and Niels Thomsen, *De Danske Aviser 1634–1989*, vol. 2: 1848–1917 (Odense, Denmark: Odense Universitetsforlag, 1989), 26.

15. During this same period (and, to an extent, as a result of its disastrous alliance with Napoleon), Denmark divested itself of its colonies in India (ceded to the United Kingdom in 1845), Africa (sold to the United Kingdom in 1850), and the West Indies (sold to the United States in 1917). While it still controlled Iceland, Greenland, and the Faroe Islands, they were either independent, small, or far enough away to have little influence on domestic Danish public discourse.

16. Flake, *The Politics of American Religious Identity*, 2.

17. Jan Shipps, *Sojourner in the Promised Land: Forty Years among the Mormons* (Urbana: University of Illinois Press, 2000), 69.

18. "Uddrag af et Brev," *Flyveposten* (Copenhagen), June 28, 1851.

19. "En Advarsel mod de Falske Profeter," *Flyveposten* (Copenhagen), September 29, October 2, October 15, November 6, and November 7, 1851.

20. Schmidt, *Bibliografi*, 1.

21. "Brigham Young," *Ilustreret Magazin*, no. 36 (Copenhagen), September 2, 1854, 281.

22. "Brigham Young," *Illustreret Magazin*, no. 36 (Copenhagen), September 2, 1854, 291.

23. "Brigham Young," *Illustreret Magazin*, no. 36 (Copenhagen), September 2, 1854, 290.

24. "Uddrag af et Brev," *Flyveposten* (Copenhagen), June 28. 1851.

25. "En Advarsel mod Falske Profeter," *Flyveposten* (Copenhagen), October 2, 1851.

26. "En Advarsel mod Falske Profeter," *Flyveposten* (Copenhagen), October 15, 1851.

27. "En Advarsel mod de Falske Profeter," *Flyveposten* (Copenhagen), October 15, 1851.

28. This Danish newsweekly must be distinguished from a satirical Norwegian magazine of the same name that appeared from 1849 to 1855. The Danish *Krydseren* often printed entire series of anti-Mormon articles.

29. "De ti Bud, Saaledes som en Mormon-Huus-Bonde i al Durkdrevenhed Skal Foreholde sit Tyende Dem," *Krydseren* 11, April 4, 1856, 5.

30. Nicolai Edinger Balle, *Lærebog i den Evangelisk Christelige Religion, Indrettet til Brug i de Danske Skoler* (Copenhagen, 1791).

31. Haslam, *Clash of Cultures*, 18.

32. Henrik Cavling, *Fra Amerika*, 2 vols. (Copenhagen: Gyldendal, 1897).

33. Jørgen Würtz Sørensen, *Mellem Mormonerne: En Artikelserie af Henrik Cavling i 'Politiken' Januar 1889* (Aalborg, Denmark: Forlaget Fenre, 1984), 37.

34. Vilhelm Christian Sigurd Topsøe, *Fra Amerika* (Copenhagen: Gyldendal, 1872), 405.

35. Topsøe, *Fra Amerika*, 417.

36. Topsøe, *Fra Amerika*, 413.

37. Robert Watt, *Hinsides Atlanterhavet: Skildringer fra Amerika, vol. 3: Religeuse Sekter* (Copenhagen: P. Bloch, 1874), 2.

38. Watt, *Hinsides Atlanterhavet*, 2.

39. Watt, *Hinsides Atlanterhavet*, 2.

40. Watt, *Religeuse Sekter*, 69.

41. Watt, *Religeuse Sekter*, 97.

42. Henrik Cavling, "Hos Profeten," *Politiken* (Copenhagen), January 13, 1889.

43. Henrik Cavling, "Saltsøstaden," *Politiken* (Copenhagen), January 23, 1889.

44. Henrik Cavling, "Polygami," *Politiken* (Copenhagen), January 14, 1889.

45. Henrik Cavling, "Hos Profeten," *Politiken* (Copenhagen), January 13, 1889.

46. Henrik Cavling, *Journalistliv* (Copenhagen: Gyldendal, 1930), 92.

47. Henrik Cavling, "Edmunds Bill," *Politiken* (Copenhagen), January 20, 1889.

48. Henrik Cavling, "Saltsøstaden," *Politiken* (Copenhagen), January 23, 1889.

49. Henrik Cavling, "Edmunds Bill," *Politiken*, January 20, 1889.

50. Henrik Cavling, *Fra Amerika*, vol. 1 (Copenhagen: Gyldendal, 1897), 442.

51. Rochelle and Robert L. Wright, *Danish Emigrant Ballads and Songs* (Carbon-dale, Illinois: Southern Illinois University Press, 1983), 4.

52. Thomas Thomsen, *Farvel til Danmark: De danske Skillingsvisers syn på Amerika og på Udvandringen Dertil, 1830–1914* (Aarhus, Denmark: Universitetsforlag, 1980), 57.

53. "Langt Bort til Fjerne Strand," Dansk Folkemindesamling 1906/6b: 1, Danish Royal Library, Copenhagen. English translation published in Wright, *Danish Emigrant Ballads and Songs*, 144–46.

54. Wright, *Danish Emigrant Ballads and Songs*, 65.

55. Thomsen, *De Danske Skillingsviser*, 57.

56. Thomsen, *De Danske Skillingsviser*, 58.

57. It is very similar to a somewhat earlier publication, "Lykke og Ulykke Eller: Saltsøens Mysterier. En smuk historie om en ung Pige, der blev forført af Mor-monerne til at rejse til Saltsøen og hvad hun dér oplevede" ("Happiness and Unhappiness; or the Mysteries of the Salt Lake. A lovely story of a young girl who was persuaded by the Mormons to travel to the Salt Lake and what she experienced there"; 1865).

58. "Mormonpigens Klage," Dansk Folkemindesamling Z 190/915, Danish Royal Library, Copenhagen. English translation in Wright, *Danish Emigrant Ballads and Songs*, 142.

59. Wright, *Danish Emigrant Ballads and Songs*, 143.

60. Liljefalk, *Den Hvide Slavehandel*, 31.

61. Wright, *Danish Emigrant Ballads and Songs*, 144.

62. Wright, *Danish Emigrant Ballads and Songs*, 23.

63. Dansk Folkemindesamling 1970/16, XI: 80, Danish Royal Library, Copenhagen.

64. Wright, *Danish Emigrant Ballads and Songs*, 24.

65. Dansk Folkemindesamling 1970/16, IX: 105 Danish Royal Library, Copenha-gen. English translation in Wright, *Danish Emigrant Ballads and Songs*, 144.

66. Alan Lomax, *The Folk Songs of America in the English Language* (Garden City, New York: Doubleday & Co., 1960), 88–89.

67. "In Oleanna, That's Where It's Good to Be," in Wright, *Danish Emigrant Ballads and Songs*, 222.

68. Wright, *Danish Emigrants Ballads and Songs*, 221.

69. Wright, *Danish Emigrant Ballads and Songs*, 146.

70. "Den Sidste nye Vise om de to Kjøbenhavnske Murersvende der Solgte Deres Koner," Dansk Folkemindesamling 1970/16, VIII: 160, Danish Royal Library, Copenhagen. English translation in Wright, *Danish Emigrant Ballads and Songs*, 147.

71. "De to Kjøbenhavnske Murersvende," Dansk Folkemindesamling 1970–71, VIII: 160, Danish Royal Library, Copenhagen. English translation in Wright, *Danish Emigrant Ballads and Songs*, 148.

72. Emil Marott, *Dansk Revy*, vol. 1 (Copenhagen: Borgen, 1991), 17.

73. The contemporaneous terminology used to describe these productions tends to conflate cabaret with revue with variety shows, for which reason I make no distinction between them here.

74. Leif Plenov, *Dansk Revy 1850–2000: Et Uhøjtideligt Tilbageblik* (Gylling, Denmark: L&R Fakta, 2000), 49.

75. Plenov, *Dansk Revy*, 50–51.

76. Plenov, *Dansk Revy*, 62.

77. Georg Prehn, *Sommerrejsen 1911, Københavner-Revy i 2 Akter, af 2x2=5* (Copenhagen: Wilhelm Hansens Musikforlag, 1911).

78. Paul B. Beers, *Pennsylvania Politics Today and Yesterday* (University Park and London: Pennsylvania State University Press, 1980), 51.

79. Jenson, *History of the Scandinavian Mission*, 432.

80. Prehn, *Sommerrejsen*, 12.

81. Prehn, *Sommerrejsen*, 12.

82. Liljefalk, *Den Hvide Slavehandel*, 15–16.

83. Liljefalk, *Den Hvide Slavehandel*, 16.

84. Publicity materials for *Den Hvide Slavehandel* (Copenhagen: Nordisk, 1910).

85. These first Danish anti-Mormon films were quickly followed by a host of French and American productions, including *The Mountain Meadows Massacre* (1912, Pathé Frères, director unknown), *The Danites* (1912, directed by Francis Boggs), and *Riders of the Purple Sage* (1918, directed by Frank Lloyd), based on Zane Grey's 1912 novel of the same name.

86. Clara Wieth Pontoppidan, *Eet Liv–Mange Liv* (Copenhagen: Westermann, 1949), 42.

87. Liljefalk, *Den Hvide Slavehandel*, 16.

88. For more information about the American reception of the film, see Jacob W. Olmstead, "*A Victim of the Mormons* and *The Danites*: Images and Relics from Early Twentieth-Century Anti-Mormon Silent Films," *Mormon Historical Studies*, Spring 2004: 203–21.

89. J.P. Chalmers, ed, *The Moving Picture World*, vol. XI, January–March (New York: The World Photographic Publishing Co., 1912), 315.

90. Olmstead, *A Victim of the Mormons*, 211.

91. Chalmers, *Moving Picture World*, 1170.
92. Marguerite Engberg, *Dansk Stumfilm* (Copenhagen: Rhodos, 1977), 365.
93. Mark B. Sandberg, "Location, 'Location': On the Plausibility of Place Substitution" *Silent Cinema and the Politics of Space*, edited by Jennifer Bean, Anupama Kapse, and Laura Horak (Bloomington: Indiana University Press, 2014), 36.
94. Program notes for *Mormonens Offer: Et Drama om Kærlighed og Sekterisk Fanatisme* (Copenhagen: Nordisk, 1911).
95. Johannes V. Jensen, *Madame D'Ora* (Copenhagen: Gyldendal, 1904), 33, 36.
96. Jensen, *Madame D'Ora*, 121.
97. Program Notes, *Mormonens Offer*, 1911.
98. Program Notes, *Mormonens Offer*, 1911.
99. Program Notes for *Min Svigerinde fra Amerika* (1917), Danish Film Institute, Copenhagen.

Notes to Chapter 4

1. Margit Egdal, *Miraklet på Fyn: De Sidste Dages Hellige på Fyn og Langeland* (Otterup, Denmark: Otterup Lokalhistoriske Arkiv og Forening, 2002), 11.
2. Mulder, *Homeward to Zion*, 107.
3. Richard Jensen, "Mr. Samuelsen Goes to Copenhagen: The First Mormon Member of a National Parliament," *Journal of Mormon History* 36:1 (2013): 10–11.
4. Paulsen, *De Danske Mormoners Historie* (Copenhagen: A. Broberg Forlag, 2012).
5. Virginia Sorensen, *Kingdom Come* (New York: Harcourt, Brace & Co., 1960).
6. Sorensen, *Kingdom Come*, 497.
7. Mary Jo Maynes, Jennifer L. Pierce, and Barbara Laslett, *Telling Stories: The Use of Personal Narratives in the Social Sciences and History* (Ithaca, New York: Cornell University Press, 2008), 6.
8. Jennifer Eastman Attebery, "Claiming Ethnicity: Implicit and Explicit Expressions of Ethnicity among Swedish Americans," In *Not English Only: Redefining "American" in American Studies*, edited by Orm Øverland (Amsterdam: Vu University Press, 2001), 14.
9. Keith W. Perkins, "Andrew Jenson: Zealous Chronologist," *Supporting Saints: Life Stories of Nineteenth-Century Mormons* (Provo, Utah: Brigham Young University, 1985), 95.
10. "Et Gran af Sandhed i et Pund Løgn," *Skandinaviens Stjerne* 1, no. 2 (November 1, 1851), 29.
11. John Taylor, "Kirkens Organisation," *Skandinaviens Stjerne* 1, no. 1 (October 1, 1851), 1.
12. Jenson, *History of the Scandinavian Mission*, 534.
13. Carl Fog, *Nyt Theologisk Tidsskrift*, 1851, 345. Also quoted in Paulsen, *De Danske Mormoners Historie*, 64.

14. Petition to the Danish Parliament, *Skandinaviens Stjerne* 1, no. 7 (April 1, 1852), 102.
15. Doctrine & Covenants 1:30.
16. William Mulder, "Images of Zion: Mormonism As an American Influence in Scandinavia," *The Mississippi Valley Historical Review* 43, no. 1 (June 1956), 22.
17. Egdal, *Miraklet på Fyn*, 148–51.
18. Egdal, *Miraklet på Fyn*, 152.
19. Mulder, "Images of Zion," 19.
20. Sørensen, *Rejsen til Amerikas Zion*, 14.
21. Harald Jensen Kent, *Danske Mormoner* (Udvalget for Utahmissionen, 1913), 3.
22. Mulder, "Images of Zion," 18.
23. Mulder, *Homeward to Zion*, 416.
24. *Skandinaviens Stjerne* 2, no. 110 (January 1, 1853). Quoted in William Mulder, *Homeward to Zion*, 157.
25. Mulder, *Homeward to Zion*, 157.
26. Kent, *Danske Mormoner*, 6.
27. Mulder, *Homeward to Zion*, 164.
28. John S. MacDonald and Leatrice D. MacDonald, ""Chain Migration, Ethnic Neighborhood Formation, and Social Networks," *The Milbank Memorial Fund Quarterly* 42 (1964): 82.
29. Douglas Massey, Jorge Durand, and Nolan J. Malone, *Beyond Smoke and Mirrors: Mexican Immigration in an Era of Economic Integration* (New York: Russell Sage Foundation, 2002), 19.
30. Mulder, *Homeward to Zion*, x.
31. Quoted in Sørensen, *Rejsen til Amerikas Zion*, 37.
32. Mulder, *Homeward to Zion*, 241.
33. Andrew Jenson, *The Autobiography of Andrew Jenson* (Salt Lake City, Utah: Deseret News Press, 1938), 415.
34. Jennifer Eastman Attebery, *Up in the Rocky Mountains: Writing the Swedish Immigrant Experience* (Minneapolis: University of Minnesota Press, 2007).
35. Rachel Gianni Abbott, "The Scandinavian Immigrant Experience in Utah, 1850–1920: Using Material Culture to Interpret Cultural Adaptation" (PhD dissertation, University of Alaska, Fairbanks, 2013).
36. Jennifer L. Lund, "Out of the Swan's Nest: The Ministry of Anthon H. Lund, Scandinavian Apostle," *Journal of Mormon History* 29: 2 (2003), 84.
37. Abbott, "Scandinavian Immigrant Experience," 28.
38. Davis Bitton, "A Reevaluation of the Turner Thesis and Mormon Beginnings," *Utah Historical Quarterly* 34: 4 (October 1966), 331.
39. Conway B. Sonne, *Ships, Saints, and Mariners: A Maritime Encyclopedia of Mormon Migration 1830–1890* (Salt Lake City: University of Utah Press, 1987), 68.
40. 1880 U.S. Census, http://www.censusrecords.com/content/1880_census, accessed September 1, 2016.

41. Beth R. Olsen, "Chronological History of Pleasant Grove, Utah 1850–2000," *Pleasant Grove Sesquicentennial History*, vol. I (Provo, Utah: Stevenson's Supply, 2000), 2.

42. Jenson, *Autobiography of Andrew Jenson*, 128.

43. Olsen, "History of Pleasant Grove," 62.

44. Beth R. Olsen, "Mormon Scandinavian Immigrants' Experiences among English-Speaking Settlers," *Deseret Language and Linguistic Society Symposium* 26 (2000), 60.

45. Olsen, "History of Pleasant Grove," 59.

46. Letter from Hans Jørgensen to Mine Jørgensen, dated May 17, 1881, unpublished letters, copies in the author's possession.

47. Letter from Hans Jørgensen to Mine Jørgensen, dated May 20, 1881.

48. Letter from Hans Jørgensen to Mine Jørgensen, dated June 14, 1881.

49. Attebery, *Up in the Rocky Mountains*, 145.

50. Letter from Hans Jørgensen to Mine Jørgensen, dated June 6, 1881.

51. Letter from Hans Jørgensen to Mine Jørgensen, dated July 19, 1881.

52. Letter from Hans Jørgensen to Mine Jørgensen, dated September 26, 1881.

53. Letter from Hans Jørgensen to Mine Jørgensen, dated June 1, 1881.

54. Letter from Hans Jørgensen to Mine Jørgensen, dated June 14, 1881.

55. Letter from Hans Jørgensen to Mine Jørgensen, dated July 1, 1881.

56. Letter from Hans Jørgensen to Mine Jørgensen, dated July 1, 1881.

57. Letter from Hans Jørgensen to Mine Jørgensen, dated August 20, 1881.

58. Letter from Hans Jørgensen to Mine Jørgensen, dated July 18, 1881.

59. Letter from Mine Jørgensen to Hans Jørgensen, dated June 10, 1881.

60. Ken Cregg Hansen, "'Up the Ditch': The History of Elsinore, Utah, 1874–1977" (master's thesis, Utah State University, 1978), *All Graduate Theses and Dissertations*, Paper 2, 100, http://digitalcommons.usu.edu/etd/2100, 85.

61. Letter from Mine Jørgensen to Hans Jørgensen, dated May 17, 1881.

62. Egdal, *Mads Nielsen, David og Mette Marie i Guds Eget Land: En Slægtskrønike* (Otterup, Denmark: Landbohistorisk Selskab, 2000), 6.

63. Egdal, *Mads Nielsen*, 11.

64. Egdal, *Mads Nielsen*, 16.

65. Egdal, *Mads Nielsen*, 57.

66. Letter from Anders Hansen to Mads Nielsen, dated January 13, 1878, from Ephraim, Utah; Egdal, *Mads Nielsen*, 59.

67. United States, Department of Commerce, Bureau of Census, Manuscript Census for Utah, 1880.

68. Hansen, "Up the Ditch," 86.

69. Hansen, "Up the Ditch," 76. Hansen attributes the name to Brigham Young, president of the LDS Church from 1844–1877, but historian Richard Jensen argues that the anecdote must refer to his son, Joseph Young, instead.

70. Hansen, "Up the Ditch," 11.

71. Egdal, *Mads Nielsen*, 38.

72. Quoted in Egdal, *Mads Nielsen*, 37.

73. Egdal, *Mads Nielsen*, 45.
74. Egdal, *Mads Nielsen*, 33, 71.
75. Egdal, *Mads Nielsen*, 60.
76. Hansen, "Up the Ditch," 3.
77. LDS church president and prophet Brigham Young frequently applied the Bible verse found in Isaiah 35:2 to the pioneers' labors in the Utah desert.
78. Letter from David Madsen to Gjertrud Nielsen, dated March 27, 1887; Egdal, *Mads Nielsen*, 146.
79. Letter from David Madsen to Mads and Gjertrud Nielsen, dated October 11, 1881; Egdal, *Mads Nielsen*, 65.
80. Letter from David Madsen to Mads and Gjertrud Nielsen, dated November 18, 1881; Egdal, *Mads Nielsen*, 68.
81. Egdal, *Mads Nielsen*, 65.
82. Letter from Mads Nielsen to Gjertrud Nielsen, dated July 13, 1884; Egdal, *Mads Nielsen*, 112.
83. Kathryn M. Daynes, *More Wives than One: Transformation of the Mormon Marriage System, 1840–1910* (Urbana, Illinois: University of Illinois Press, 2001), 100.
84. William Mulder reports the percentage of Scandinavian Mormons in polygamous marriages as approximately 12 percent. The most-married Danish Mormon was the patriarch Jens Hansen, who eventually married fourteen wives, but in general most Scandinavian polygamists had only two. Mulder, *Homeward to Zion*, 239–240.
85. Quoted in Egdal, *Mads Nielsen*, 39.
86. Letter from Mads Nielsen to Gjertrud Nielsen, dated July 13, 1884; Egdal, *Mads Nielsen*, 112.
87. Letter from Mads Nielsen to Gjertrud Nielsen, dated August 8, 1887; Egdal, *Mads Nielsen*, 148.
88. Daynes, *More Wives than One*, 160.
89. Quoted in Egdal, *Mads Nielsen*, 40.
90. Marcus Lee Hansen, "The Problem of the Third-Generation Immigrant," *Augustana Historical Society Publications* (Rock Island, Illinois: Augustana Historical Society, 1938), 10.
91. Egdal, *Mads Nielsen*, 22.
92. Steven W. Harris, "Biographical Sketch of Frederik Ferdinand Samuelsen and Mariane Marie Florentine Jensen on the 100th Anniversary of their Baptism into the Church of Jesus Christ of Latter-day Saints on December 21, 1892," unpublished manuscript in the author's possession.
93. Harris, "Biographical Sketch," 13.
94. F. F. Samuelsen diary entry for October 30, 1906, LDS Church History Library, MS 7640.
95. Jensen, "Mr. Samuelsen," 15.
96. By way of example, in a diary entry dated February 9, 1919, Samuelsen reports that he visited his sister and brother-in-law, where he drank coffee with them, LDS Church History Library, MS 7640.

97. Jensen, "Mr. Samuelsen," 15.

98. F. F. Samuelsen diary entry for January 5, 1897, LDS Church History Library, MS 7640, Box 1, Folder 1.

99. Jensen, "Mr. Samuelsen," 12.

100. F. F. Samuelsen diary entry for October 30, 1906, LDS Church History Library, MS 7640, Item 2, 185.

101. F. F. Samuelsen diary entry for December 31, 1906, LDS Church History Library, MS 7640, Item 2, 192.

102. Jørn Holm Bendtsen, "Frederik Ferdinand Samuelsen: Hans liv og Levned 1865–1929," unpublished manuscript, 5.

103. F. F. Samuelsen diary entry for October 30, 1906, LDS Church History Library, MS 7640, Item 2, 185.

104. F. F. Samuelsen diary entry for October 26, 1906, LDS Church History Library, MS 7640, Item 2, 184.

105. Lars Larsen-Ledet, "Det Sidste Torvevalg i Aarhus," *Aarbøger Udgivne af Historisk Samfund for Aarhus Stift* 47 (1954): 232.

106. Paulsen, *De Danske Mormoners Historie*, 101.

107. Paulsen, *De Danske Mormoners Historie*, 102.

108. Quoted in Paulsen, *De Danske Mormoners Historie*, 103.

109. "Mormonerne og den Hvide Slavehandel," *Skandinaviens Stjerne* 63, no. 6 (March 15, 1914), 82.

110. "Mormonerne og den Hvide Slavehandel," 85.

111. "Mormonerne og den Hvide Slavehandel," 92.

112. F. F. Samuelsen diary, June 5, 1915, quoted in Jensen, "Mr. Samuelsen," 30.

113. Quoted in Harris, "Biographical Sketch," 15.

114. F. F. Samuelsen, *Lommekalendar 1919*, LDS Church History Library, MS 7640, Box 2, Folder 1.

115. Quoted in Harris, "Biographical Sketch," 15.

116. Samuelsen's pocket calendar for 1919 is full of notes about his preparations for emigration, including: records of repeated visits to the American consulate, the dimensions of the baggage they would be allowed to bring on board the steamship, addresses for various contacts in Utah (including Andrew Jenson), and the note (on March 14) that he had received a telegram from Reed Smoot confirming they would be given permission to enter the United States. F. F. Samuelsen, *Lommekalendar 1919*, LDS Church History Library, MS 7640, Box 2, Folder 1.

117. F. F. Samuelsen diary entry for November 29, 1919, LDS Church History Library, MS 7640, Box 2, Folder 1.

118. Andrew Jenson, *Autobiography of Andrew Jenson*, 584.

119. Andrew Jenson, *Autobiography of Andrew Jenson*, 604.

120. Andrew Jenson, *Autobiography of Andrew Jenson*, 604.

121. Harris, "Biographical Sketch," 16.

Notes to Conclusion

1. Paulsen, *De Danske Mormoners Historie*, 163.
2. "Royal Pair of Denmark Visits Utah," *The Daily Herald* (Provo, Utah), April 17, 1939, 1.
3. Personal interview with Bent and Charlotte Leit, May 2009, Copenhagen, Denmark.
4. Pia Kjærsgaard, quoted in Ove Korsgaard, *Folk* (Aarhus: Aarhus University, 2013), 7.
5. For more about the cartoon crisis, see Jytte Klausen, *The Cartoons That Shook the World* (New Haven: Yale University Press, 2009).

Bibliography

Abbott, Rachel Gianni. "The Scandinavian Immigrant Experience in Utah, 1850–1920: Using Material Culture to Interpret Cultural Adaptation." PhD dissertation, University of Alaska–Fairbanks, 2013.

Allen, Julie K., and David L. Paulsen. "The Reverend Dr. Peter Christian Kierkegaard's 'About and Against Mormonism' (1855)." *BYU Studies* 46, no. 3 (2007): 100–156.

Arrington, Leonard J. *Brigham Young: American Moses*. New York: Alfred Knopf, 1985.

Ashby, Leland Hansen, ed. *An Autobiography of Peter Olsen Hansen, 1818–1895: Mormon Convert and Pioneer Missionary, Translator of the Book of Mormon into Danish*. Salt Lake City, Utah: Leland Hansen Ashby, 1988.

Attebery, Jennifer Eastman. "Claiming Ethnicity: Implicit and Explicit Expressions of Ethnicity among Swedish Americans." In *Not English Only: Redefining "American" in American Studies*, edited by Orm Øverland, 12–28. Amsterdam: Vu University Press, 2001.

Attebery, Jennifer Eastman. *Up in the Rocky Mountains: Writing the Swedish Immigrant Experience*. Minneapolis: University of Minnesota Press, 2007.

Banning, Knud. *Forsamlinger og Mormoner*. Copenhagen: Gad, 1960.

Baugh, Alexander. "Defending Mormonism: The Scandinavian Mission Presidency of Andrew Jenson, 1909–1912." In *Go Ye into All the World: The Growth and Development of Mormon Missionary Work*, edited by Reid L. Neilson and Fred E. Woods, 503–41. Provo, Utah: Brigham Young University Religious Studies Center in cooperation with Deseret Book, 2012.

Beers, Paul B. *Pennsylvania Politics Today and Yesterday*. University Park and London: Pennsylvania State University Press, 1980.

Bendtsen, Jørn Holm. "Frederik Ferdinand Samuelsen: Hans Liv og Levned, 1865–1929." Unpublished manuscript.

Beretning om Forhandlingerne paa Rigsdagen. Copenhagen, 1848.

Birkedal, Vilhelm. "Lidelse for Christi Skyld, dens Nødvendighed for den Christne, osv." *Dansk Kirketidende* 37 (August 26, 1855): Columns 593–604.

Bitton, Davis. "A Reevaluation of the Turner Thesis and Mormon Beginnings," *Utah Historical Quarterly* 34, no. 4 (October 1966): 326–33.

Bjørn, Claus. "Grundtvig-skitse: Grundtvig som Politiker, 1848–50." In *Grundtvig som Politiker*, edited by Thorkild Lyby, 13–105. Copenhagen: Forlaget ANIS, 2007.

Bjørn, Claus. *Kampen om Grundloven*. Copenhagen: Fremad, 1999.

Black, Susan Easton, Sharon C. Anderson, and Ruth Ellen Maness, eds. *Legacy of Sacrifice. Missionaries to Scandinavia 1872–1894*. Provo, Utah: Brigham Young University Religious Studies Center, 2007.

Borup, Johan. *N. F. S. Grundtvig*. Copenhagen: Reitzels Forlag-Axel Sandal, 1944.

Brandes, Edvard. "Grundtvigs 100. Fødselsdag." *Morgenbladet* (Copenhagen), September 9, 1883.

"Brigham Young," *Ilustreret Magazin,* no. 36 (Copenhagen), September 2, 1854, 281–90.

Bucka, Inge. "Værk og Virkelighed—Realismen i Christen Dalsgaards Billeder." In *Christen Dalsgaard 1824–1907*, edited by Charlotte Sabroe, Christine Buhl Andersen, and Inge Bucka, 48–55. Vestsjællands Kunstmuseum, 2001.

Bürger, Gottffried August, Hieronymous Karl Friedrich von Münchhausen, Rudolf Erich Raspe, Peter Nickl, and Binette Schroeder. *Die Wunderbaren Reisen und Abenteuern des Freiherrn von Münchhausen*. Zurich: Nord-Süd Verlag, 1977.

Cavling, Henrik. "Edmunds Bill." *Politiken* (Copenhagen), January 20, 1889.

Cavling, Henrik. *Fra Amerika*. 2 vols. Copenhagen: Gyldendal, 1897.

Cavling, Henrik. "Hos Profeten." *Politiken* (Copenhagen), January 13, 1889.

Cavling, Henrik. *Journalistliv*. Copenhagen: Gyldendal, 1930.

Cavling, Henrik. "Polygami." *Politiken* (Copenhagen), January 14, 1889.

Cavling, Henrik. "Saltsøstaden," *Politiken* (Copenhagen), January 23, 1889.

Chalmers, J. P., ed. *The Moving Picture World*. Volume XI, January–March. New York: The World Photographic Publishing Co., 1912.

Clausen, H. N. *Catholicismens og og Protestantismens Kirkeforfatning, Lære og Ritus*. Copenhagen: Seidelin, 1825.

Constantin-Hansen, Thora. *Elise Stampe: Et Billede og en Arv*. Copenhagen: H. Hagerups Forlag, 1931.

Daynes, Kathryn M. *More Wives than One: Transformation of the Mormon Marriage System, 1840–1910*. Urbana, Illinois: University of Illinois Press, 2001.

Dykes, George Parker. *Diary*. LDS Church Archives, Salt Lake City, Utah.

Egdal, Margit. *Mads Nielsen, David og Mette Marie in Guds Eget Land: En Slægtskrønike*. Otterup, Denmark: Landbohistorisk Selskab, 2000.

Egdal, Margit. *Miraklet på Fyn: De sidste Dages Hellige på Fyn og Langeland*. Otterup, Denmark: Otterup Lokalhistoriske Arkiv og Forening, 2002.

"En Advarsel mod de Falske Profeter," *Flyveposten*, September 29, October 2, October 15, November 6, and November 7, 1851.

Engberg, Marguerite. *Dansk Stumfilm*. Copenhagen: Rhodos, 1977.

"Et Gran af Sandhed i et Pund Løgn," *Skandinaviens Stjerne* 1, no. 2 (November 1, 1851), 29.

Flake, Kathleen. *The Politics of American Religious Identity. The Seating of Senator Reed Smoot, Mormon Apostle*. Chapel Hill: University of North Carolina, 2004.

Fog, Carl. *Nyt Theologisk Tidsskrift*, 1851, 345.

Gold, Carol. *Danish Cookbooks*. Seattle: University of Washington Press, 2007.

Grane, Leif. "Sørens Broder: Om Peter Christian Kierkegaard." *Fra Egtvedpigen til Folketinget.* Copenhagen: Munksgaard, 1997, 81–108.

Greenblatt, Stephen. "Cultural Mobility: An Introduction." *Cultural Mobility: A Manifesto.* Cambridge: Cambridge University Press, 2010, 1–23.

Grundtvig, N. F. S. "Danmarks Riges Grundlov." *Danskeren* 2, 334.

Grundtvig, N. F. S. "Den Danske Konge og de Tydske Forrædere." *Danskeren* 1, 76.

Grundtvig, N. F. S. *Kirkens Gienmæle imod Professor Theologiae Dr. H. N. Clausen.* Copenhagen: Wahlske Boghandels Forlag, 1825.

Grundtvig, N. F. S. Letter to Elise Stampe, October 11, 1858. Manuscript Department, NKS 3946 kvart, Royal Danish Library, Copenhagen.

Grundtvig, N. F. S. "Om Constitution og Statsforfatning i Danmark." *Danskeren* 1, 373.

Grundtvig, N. F. S. *Skolen for Livet og Akademiet i Sorø, Borgerlig Betragtet.* Copenhagen: Wahlske Boghandels Forlag, 1838.

Hall, Stuart. "Introduction: Who Needs 'Identity'?" In *Questions of Cultural Identity,* edited by Stuart Hall and Paul du Gay, 1–17. London: Sage, 1996.

Hall, Stuart. "The Spectacle of the 'Other.'" *Discourse Theory and Practice.* London: Sage, 2001.

Hansen, Ken Cregg. "'Up the Ditch:' The History of Elsinore, Utah, 1874–1977." Master's Thesis, Utah State University, 1978. *All Graduate Theses and Dissertations,* Paper 2100. http://digitalcommons.usu.edu/etd/2100.

Hansen, Marcus Lee. "The Problem of the Third-Generation Immigrant," *Augustana Historical Society Publications.* Rock Island, Illinois: Augustana Historical Society, 1938, 5–20.

Hansen, Peter Olsen. *Autobiography,* MS 1437, Peter Olsen Hansen Collection, LDS Church History Library, Salt Lake City, Utah.

Harris, Steven W. "Biographical Sketch of Frederik Ferdinand Samuelsen and Mariane Marie Florentine Jensen on the 100th Anniversary of their Baptism into the Church of Jesus Christ of Latter-day Saints on December 21, 1892." Unpublished manuscript in the author's possession.

Haslam, Gerald M. *Clash of Cultures: The Norwegian Experience with Mormonism, 1842–1920.* New York: Peter Lang, 1984.

Hass, L. D. "Protest." *Fædrelandet,* February 1, 1851.

Haugerup Branch Records, 1855–59. LDS Church Family History Center Archives, Salt Lake City, Utah.

Holmgaard, Otto. *Exstaticus: Søren Kierkegaards Sidste Kamp, Derunder hans Forhold til Broderen.* Copenhagen: Nyt Nordisk Forlag Arnold Busck, 1967.

Holmgaard, Otto. *Peter Christian Kierkegaard: Grundtvigs Lærling.* Copenhagen: Rosenkilde & Bagger, 1953.

Holy Bible, King James Version.

Hvidt, Kristian. *Flugten til Amerika eller Drivkræfter i Masseudvandringen fra Danmark, 1868–1914.* Aarhus, Denmark: Aarhus Universitetsforlag, 1971.

Ipsen, Pernille. *Daughters of the Trade: Atlantic Slavers and Interracial Marriage on the Gold Coast.* Philadelphia: University of Pennsylvania Press, 2015.

Jensen, Erik Aalbæk. "Et Kvindehus Gennem 250 År." In *Vallø: Historien om et Slot og dets Ejere, Dets Skæbne og Funktion fra Middelalder til Nutid og Fremtid*, edited by Sys Hartmann, 37–100. Copenhagen: Gyldendal, 1988.

Jensen, Johannes V. *Madame D'Ora*. Copenhagen: Gyldendal, 1904.

Jensen, Richard. "Mr. Samuelsen Goes to Copenhagen: The First Mormon Member of a National Parliament," *Journal of Mormon History* 39, no.2 (2013): 1–34.

Jensen, Thorkild Borup, ed. *Danskernes Identitetshistorie*. Copenhagen: C. A. Reitzel, 1993.

Jenson, Andrew. *Latter-day Saint Biographical Encyclopedia: A Compilation of Biographical Sketches of Prominent Men and Women in the Church of Jesus Christ of Latter-day Saints*. 4 vols. Salt Lake City, Utah: Andrew Jenson History Company, 1914.

Jenson, Andrew. *History of the Scandinavian Mission*. Salt Lake City, Utah: Deseret News Press, 1927.

Jenson, Andrew. *The Autobiography of Andrew Jenson*. Salt Lake City, Utah: Deseret News Press, 1938.

Johnson, Jeffery Ogden. "Determining and Defining 'Wife': The Brigham Young Households." *Dialogue: A Journal of Mormon Thought* 20, no. 3 (Fall 1987): 57–70.

Jordan, C. O. "Mormonpigens Klage." 1872. Dansk Folkemindesamling. Danish Royal Library, Copenhagen.

Jørgensen, Hans and Wilhelmine. Unpublished correspondence, 1879–1883. Copies in the author's possession.

Kappelørn, Niels Jørgen, ed. *Søren Kierkegaards Skrifter*, Vol. 26. Copenhagen: Gad, 2012.

Kay, Katty. "Utah loves Jell-O, Official." *BBC News.com*. February 6, 2001.

Kent, Harald Jensen. *Danske Mormoner*. Udvalget for Utahmissionen, 1913.

Kierkegaard, Peter Christian, *Diary 1850–1859*, Manuscript Collection, NKS 3013 4 II, Danish Royal Library, Copenhagen.

Kierkegaard, Peter Christian. Letter to C. J. Brandt, 1855, Manuscript Collection, Danish Royal Library, Copenhagen.

Kierkegaard, Peter Christian. *Om og mod Mormonismen*. Copenhagen: C. G. Iversen, 1855.

Kierkegaard, Peter Christian. "Polemik mod Mogens Sommer." *Aalborgposten*, February 21–22, 1866.

Kierkegaard, Søren. "Et Ganske Simpelt Regnestykke," 1854. *Søren Kierkegaards Skrifter*, Papir 469.

Kierkegaard, Søren. *A Kierkegaard Anthology*, edited by Robert Bretall. New York: Modern Library, 1959.

Kierkegaard, Søren. *The Moment and Late Writings*, edited and translated by Howard V. Hong and Edna H. Hong. Princeton, New Jersey: Princeton University Press, 1998.

Kierkegaard, Søren. "Var Biskop Mynster et 'Sandhedsvidne,' et af 'de rette Sandhedsvidner'—er dette Sandhed?" *Samlede Værker*, Vol. 19. Copenhagen: Gyldendal, 1964, 9–14.

Kierkegaard, Søren. "Vi er Alle Christne." *Samlede Værker*, Vol. 19. Copenhagen: Gyldendal, 1964, 117–18.

Kirmmse, Bruce H. "'But I Am Almost Never Understood': Or, Who Killed Søren Kierkegaard." In *Kierkegaard: The Self in Society*, edited by George Pattison and Steven Shakespeare, 173–95. Basingstoke: Macmillan, 1998.

Kirmmse, Bruce H., ed. *Encounters with Kierkegaard: A Life as Seen by His Contemporaries*. Princeton, New Jersey: Princeton University Press, 1996.

Kirmmse, Bruce. *Kierkegaard in Golden Age Denmark*. Bloomington: Indiana University Press, 1990.

Kjøbenhavnsposten, no. 109, May 12, 1855.

Klausen, Jytte. *The Cartoons That Shook the World*. New Haven: Yale University Press, 2009.

Korsgaard, Ove. *Folk*. Aarhus: Aarhus University, 2013.

Langeland, John. "Scandinavia, the Church In." *Encyclopedia of Mormonism*, edited by Daniel H. Ludlow. 4 vols. New York: Macmillan, 1992, 1262–65.

Larsen, Birgitte Stoklund. "The Tradition of Freedom: N. F. S. Grundtvig and His Influence on the Church." In *A Brief Guide to the Evangelical Lutheran Church in Denmark*, edited by Rebekka Højmark Svenningsen, 22–33. Copenhagen: Aros Forlag and Folkekirkens Mellemkirkelige Råd, 2013.

Larsen-Ledet, Lars. "Det Sidste Torvevalg i Aarhus." *Aarbøger Udgivne af Historisk Samfund for Aarhus Stift* 47 (1954): 210–38.

Lausten, Martin Schwarz. *A Church History of Denmark*. Translated by Frederick H. Cryer. Aldershot, England: Ashgate, 2002.

Lausten, Martin Schwarz. *Frie Jøder? Forholdet Mellem Kristne og Jøder i Danmark fra Frihedsbrevet 1814 til Grundloven 1849*. Copenhagen: Anis, 2005.

Lausten, Martin Schwarz. *Folkekirken og Jøderne: Forholdet Mellem Kristne og Jøder i Danmark fra 1849 til Begyndelsen af det 20 Århundrede*. Copenhagen: Anis, 2007.

Leit, Bent and Charlotte. Personal interview. May 2009. Copenhagen, Denmark.

Liljefalk, Axel. *Den Hvide Slavehandel*. Copenhagen: E. Jespersens Forlag, 1911.

Lindhardt, P. G. *Vækkelse og Kirkelige Retninger*. Copenhagen: Hans Reitzel, 1959.

Lomax, Alan. *The Folk Songs of America in the English Language*. Garden City, New York: Doubleday & Co., 1960.

Lund, Jennifer L. "Out of the Swan's Nest: The Ministry of Anthon H. Lund, Scandinavian Apostle." *Journal of Mormon History* 29, no. 2 (2003): 77–105.

Lundgreen-Nielsen, Flemming. "Grundtvig og Danskhed." *Dansk Identitetshistorie*, vol. 3. Folkets Danmark 1848–1940, edited by Ole Feldbæk, 9–187. Copenhagen: C. A. Reitzel, 1992.

Lyby, Thorkild C. "Peter Christian Kierkegaard: A Man with a Difficult Family Heritage." In *Kierkegaard and His Danish Contemporaries, Tome II: Theology*, edited by Jon Stewart, 189–209. London: Ashgate, 2009.

MacDonald, John S., and Leatrice D. MacDonald, "Chain Migration, Ethnic Neighborhood Formation, and Social Networks." *The Milbank Memorial Fund Quarterly* 42 (1964): 82–97.

Marott, Emil. *Dansk Revy*, vol. 1. Copenhagen: Borgen, 1991.

Martensen, Hans Lassen. *Af mit Levnet*. 3 vols. Copenhagen: Gyldendal, 1882.

Martensen, Hans Lassen. *Den Christelige Daab Betragtet med Hensyn paa det Baptis-tiske Spørgsmaal*. Copenhagen: Reitzel, 1843.

Massey, Douglas, Jorge Durand, and Nolan J. Malone. *Beyond Smoke and Mirrors: Mexican Immigration in an Era of Economic Integration*. New York: Russell Sage Foundation, 2002.

Maynes, Mary Jo, Jennifer L. Pierce, and Barbara Laslett. *Telling Stories: The Use of Personal Narratives in the Social Sciences and History*. Ithaca, New York: Cornell University Press, 2008.

Ministry for Refugees, Immigrants, and Integration Affairs. *Facts and Figures*. July 2009.

Møller. "Jes Fabricius." *Grundtvigianisme i det 20. Århundrede*. Copenhagen: Vartov, 2005.

Mørch, Søren. *Den Sidste Danmarkshistorie*. Copenhagen: Gyldendal, 1996.

"Mormonerne i Roeskilde," *Flyveposten* (Copenhagen). February 6, 1851.

"Mormonerne og den Hvide Slavehandel," *Skandinaviens Stjerne* 63, no. 6 (March 15, 1914): 82.

Mulder, William. *Homeward to Zion: The Mormon Migration from Scandinavia*. Minneapolis: University of Minnesota Press, 1957.

Mulder, William. "Images of Zion: Mormonism As an American Influence in Scandinavia." *The Mississippi Valley Historical Review* 43, no. 1 (June 1956): 18–38.

Mynster, Jacob Peter. *Grundlovens Bestemmelser med Hensyn til de Kirkelige Forhold i Danmark*. Copenhagen: C. A. Reitzel, 1850.

Mynster, Jacob Peter. *Prædikener Holdte i Aarene 1846 til 1852: Sommer-Halvaaret*, 2nd ed. Copenhagen: Gyldendal, 1854.

Nevers, Jeppe. *Fra Skældsord til Slagord: Demokratiebegrebet i Dansk Politisk Historie*. Odense: Syddansk Universitetsforlag, 2011.

Neilson, Reid L. "The Nineteenth-Century Euro-American Mormon Missionary Model." In *Go Ye into All the World: The Growth and Development of Mormon Missionary Work*, edited by Reid L. Neilson and Fred E. Woods, 65–90. Provo, Utah: Religious Studies Center at Brigham Young University and Deseret Book, 2012.

Nielsen, Johan Schioldann. *D. G. Monrad: En Patografi*. Odense, Denmark: Odense Universitetsforlag, 1983.

Nissen, H. "Langt Bort til Fjerne Strand." 1855–1859. Dansk Folkemindesamling. Danish Royal Library, Copenhagen.

Nyholm, Asger. *Religion og Politik: En Monrad Studie*. Copenhagen: Nyt Nordisk Forlag, 1947.

Olmstead, Jacob W. "*A Victim of the Mormons* and *The Danites*: Images and Relics from Early Twentieth-Century Anti-Mormon Silent Films." *Mormon Historical Studies*, Spring 2004: 203–21.

Olsen, Beth R. "Chronological History of Pleasant Grove, Utah 1850–2000." *Pleasant Grove Sesquicentennial History*, vol. 1: Chronology and Early Topics. Provo, Utah: Stevenson's Supply, 2000, 15–155.

Olsen, Beth R. "Mormon Scandinavian Immigrants' Experiences among English-Speaking Settlers." *Deseret Language and Linguistic Society Symposium* 26 (2000): 59–68.

Östman, Kim. *The Introduction of Mormonism into Finnish Society, 1840–1900.* Åbo, Finland: Åbo Academy University Press, 2010.

Pattison, George. *Kierkegaard and the Theology of the Nineteenth Century.* Cambridge, U.K.: Cambridge University Press, 2012.

Paulsen, Jesper Stenholm. *De Danske Mormoners Historie.* Copenhagen: A. Broberg Forlag, 2012.

Perkins, Keith W. "Andrew Jenson: Zealous Chronologist." In *Supporting Saints: Life Stories of Nineteenth-Century Mormons.* Provo, Utah: Brigham Young University, 1985, 83–99.

Perkins, Robert L. "The Authoritarian Symbiosis of Church and Crown in Søren Kierkegaard's 'Attack upon Christendom.'" In *Anthropology and Authority: Essays on Søren Kierkegaard*, edited by Poul Houe, Gordon D. Marino, and Sven Hakon Rossel, 137–43. Amsterdam: Rodopi, 2000.

Plenov, Leif. *Dansk Revy 1850–2000: Et Uhøjtideligt Tilbageblik.* Gylling, Denmark: L&R Fakta, 2000.

Pontoppidan, Clara Wieth. *Eet Liv-Mange Liv.* Copenhagen: Westermann, 1949.

Prehn, Georg. *Sommerrejsen 1911, Københavner-Revy i 2 Akter, af 2x2=5.* Copenhagen: Wilhelm Hansens Musikforlag, 1911.

Price, Rex Thomas. "The Mormon Missionary of the Nineteenth Century." Unpublished dissertation. University of Wisconsin–Madison, 1991.

Program notes for *Min Svigerinde fra Amerika* (1917). Danish Film Institute, Copenhagen.

Program notes for *Mormonens Offer: Et Drama om Kærlighed og Sekterisk Fanatisme.* Copenhagen: Nordisk, 1911.

Publicity materials for *Den Hvide Slavehandel.* Copenhagen: Nordisk, 1910.

Rasmussen, Jens. *Religionstolerance og Religionsfrihed: Forudsætninger og Grundloven i 1849.* Odense, Denmark: Syddansk Universitetsforlag, 2009.

Rørdam, Hans Christian. "Om Besættelsen af det Ledige Theologiske Professorat." *Berlingske Tidende*, no. 124, May 31, 1854.

Rostrup, Haavard. "Et Brev fra Christen Dalsgaard." *Kunstmuseets Aarsskrift 1942.* Copenhagen: Nordisk Forlag, 1942, 145–47.

"Royal Pair of Denmark Visits Utah." *The Daily Herald* (Provo, Utah), April 17, 1939, 1.

Samuelsen, Frederik Ferdinand. *Diary.* LDS Church History Library, MS 7640, box 2, folder 1.

Samuelsen, Frederik Ferdinand. *Lommekalendar 1919.* LDS Church History Library, MS 7640, box 2, folder 1.

Sandberg, Mark B. "Location, 'Location': On the Plausibility of Place Substitution." In *Silent Cinema and the Politics of Space*, edited by Jennifer Bean, Anupama Kapse, and Laura Horak, 23–46. Bloomington: Indiana University Press, 2014.

Santayana, George. *Reason in Common Sense*, vol. 1. New York: Scribner, 1905.

Schmidt, Jørgen W. *En Dansk Mormon Bibliografi, 1837–1984*. Aalborg: Forlaget Fenre, 1984.

Schmidt, Jørgen W., and Hans Billeskov Jansen. *Mormonerne (Medlemmer af Jesu Kristi Kirke af Sidste Dages Hellige) i Danske Aviser i Årene 1850–1851*. Lynge, Denmark: Jørgen W. Schmidt, 1980.

Schmidt, Jørgen W. *Mormonernes Flerkoneri, 1843–1890: Baggrund, Udbredelse, Reaktioner i Litteratur og Presse, Indvirkning på Samfundsstrukturen, Vurdering af Årsag og Virkning*. Lynge, Denmark: Forlaget Moroni, 1983.

Schmidt, Jørgen W. *Oh, Du Zion i Vest: Den Danske Mormon-Emigration 1850–1900*. Copenhagen: Rosenkilde and Bagger, 1965.

Shipps, Jan. *Sojourner in the Promised Land: Forty Years among the Mormons*. Urbana: University of Illinois Press, 2000.

Snow, Erastus. *Journal*, vol. 5. Erastus Snow Collection, LDS Church History Library, Salt Lake City, Utah.

Søllinge, Jette D., and Niels Thomsen. *De Danske Aviser 1634–1989*, vol. 2, 1848–1917. Odense, Denmark: Odense Universitetsforlag, 1989.

Sonne, Conway B. *Ships, Saints, and Mariners: A Maritime Encyclopedia of Mormon Migration 1830–1890*. Salt Lake City: University of Utah Press, 1987.

Sørensen, Jørgen Würtz. *Mellem Mormonerne: En Artikelserie af Henrik Cavling i 'Politiken' January 1889*. Aalborg, Denmark: Forlaget Fenre, 1984.

Sørensen, Jørgen Würtz. *Rejsen til Amerikas Zion: Den Danske Mormonudvandring før Århundredeskiftet*. Aalborg, Denmark: Forlaget Fenre, 1985.

Sorensen, Virginia. *Kingdom Come*. New York: Harcourt, Brace & Co., 1960.

Stampe, Christine Dalgas. *Baronesse Stampes Erindringer om Thorvaldsen*, edited by Rigmor Stampe. Copenhagen: Gyldendal/Nordisk, 1912.

Stampe, Elise. Letter to Bishop P. C. Kierkegaard, December 13, 1858. Manuscript Department, NKS 4987 kvart, Royal Danish Library, Copenhagen.

Stampe, Elise. Letter to Bishop P. C. Kierkegaard, November 5, 1861. Manuscript Department, NKS 4987 kvart, Royal Danish Library, Copenhagen.

Stampe, Elise. Letter to Bishop P. C. Kierkegaard, January 3-4, 1859. Manuscript Department, NKS 4987 kvart, Royal Danish Library, Copenhagen.

Stampe, Elise. Letter to N. F. S. Grundtvig, September 14, 1857. Grundtvig Collection G 466.VI.d.6, Manuscript Department, Royal Danish Library.

Stampe, Elise. "Mormonismen." Constantin Hansen Family Collection NKS 4987 4, Manuscript Department, Royal Danish Library, Copenhagen.

Stampe, Rigmor. *H. C. Andersen og Hans Nærmeste Omgang*. Copenhagen: Aschehoug, 1918.

Stavnstrup, P. *D. G. Monrad: Politiker og Geistlig*. Copenhagen: Berlingske Forlag, 1948.

Steele, Claude M. "The Psychology of Self-Affirmation: Sustaining the Integrity of the Self." In *Advances in Experimental Social Psychology*, vol. 21, edited by Leonard Berkowitz, 261–302. New York: Academic Press, 1988.

Strandberg, Julius. "Den Sidste nye Vise om de to Kjøbenhavnske Murersvende der Solgte Deres Koner." 1884. Dansk Folkemindesamling. Danish Royal Library, Copenhagen.

Strandberg, Julius. "Jeg er Mormon, som Du nok Ved." 1871. Dansk Folkemindesamling. Danish Royal Library, Copenhagen.

Strandberg, Julius. "Ole Peersen og Hans Kone Dorthes Rejse til Mormonerne." 1874. Dansk Folkemindesamling. Danish Royal Library, Copenhagen.

Taylor, John. "Kirkens Organization." *Skandinaviens Stjerne* 1, no. 1 (October 1851): 1.

Thaning, Kaj. *Grundtvig*. Copenhagen: Gyldendal Norsk Forlag, 1983.

Thomsen, Thomas. *Farvel til Danmark: De Danske Skillingsvisers Syn på Amerika og på Udvandringen Dertil 1830–1914*. Aarhus, Denmark: Universitetsforlag, 1980.

Thulstrup, Niels. "Kierkegaard and the Church in Denmark," translated by R. M. Summers. *Bibliotheca Kierkegaardiana*, vol. 13. Copenhagen: C. A. Reitzel, 1984.

Thyssen, Andreas Pontoppidan. *Den Nygrundtvigske Bevægelse med Særligt Henblik paa den Borupske Kreds*, vol. 1, 1870–1887. Copenhagen: Det Danske Forlag, 1958.

Topsøe, Vilhelm Christian Sigurd. *Fra Amerika*. Copenhagen: Gyldendal, 1872.

"Uddrag af et Brev," *Flyveposten* (Copenhagen), June 28, 1851.

Watt, Robert. *Hinsides Atlanterhavet: Skildringer fra Amerika*. 3 vols. *Vol. 3: Religieuse Sekter*. Copenhagen: P. Bloch, 1874.

Weltzer, Carl. *Peter og Søren Kierkegaard*. Copenhagen: Gad, 1936.

Winther, Christian Anker. Letter to P. C. Kierkegaard, October 5, 1854. NKS 3174.4, no. 113. Danish Royal Library, Copenhagen.

Winther, Christian Anker. Letter to P. C. Kierkegaard, January 18, 1855. NKS 3174.4, no. 114. Danish Royal Library, Copenhagen.

Woods, Fred E. *Fire on Ice: The Story of Icelandic Latter-day Saints at Home and Abroad*. Provo, Utah: Brigham Young University, 2005.

Wright, Rochelle and Robert L. *Danish Emigrant Ballads and Songs*. Carbondale, Illinois: Southern Illinois University Press, 1983.

Films
Den Hvide Slavehandel, directed by Alfred Cohn (1910; Aarhus: Fotorama)

Den Hvide Slavehandel, directed by August Blom (1910; Copenhagen: Nordisk)

Den Hvide Slavehandels Sidste Offer, directed by August Blom (1911; Copenhagen: Nordisk)

Den Hvide Slavinde, directed by Viggo Larsen (1907; Copenhagen: Nordisk)

Han er Mormon / Nalles Forlovelse, directed by Lau Lauritzen (1922; Copenhagen: Nordisk)

Min Svigerinde fra Amerika, directed by Lau Lauritzen (1917; Copenhagen: Nordisk)

Mormonbyens Blomst, director unknown (1911; Aarhus: Fotorama).

Mormonens Offer, directed by August Blom (1911; Copenhagen: Nordisk).

Index

Giants in the Earth (Rølvaag), 187
Glahn, Sophie Henriette, 86
godly awakenings, 25, 49, 59, 85, 90, 185
"Gran af Sandhed i et Pund Løgn, Et."
 See "Grain of Truth in a Pound of
 Lies, A"
"Grain of Truth in a Pound of Lies, A,"
 193. See also *Scandinavia's Star*
Greenblatt, Stephen, 10
Gregory XVI, Pope, 40
*Grundlovens Bestemmelser med Hensyn
 til Religiøse Forhold i Danmark.* See
 *Provisions of the Constitution with
 Regard to Religious Conditions in
 Denmark, The*
Grundtvig, Johan, 46, 102–3
Grundtvig, Meta, 102
Grundtvig, Niels Frederik Severin
 (N. F. S.), 45; and church reforms,
 15, 43–54; criticism of, 49, 53, 104,
 112; and the constitution, 52–54;
 and Danishness, 5, 52, 98; and Elise
 Stampe, 99–108, 111; followers of,
 49, 78–79, 86, 99, 122, 236; and
 freedom of religion, 52, 79, 98, 128;
 separating national and religious
 identity, 53, 97–99; teachings of, 47,
 49, 97–98 works of, 47–48, 50
Grundtvig, Svend, 102–3
Grundtvigianism. *See* Danish Lutheran
 Church, reform in
gudelige Vækkelser. See godly
 awakenings

Hall, C. C., 30
Hall, Stuart, 10-11
Hals, Hans Jensen, 210
Han er Mormon. See *He's a Mormon*
 (film)
Hansen, Abelone, 209
Hansen, Anders C., 209, 222, 225–26
Hansen, Carl Christian Constantin, 29,
 55, 101–2
Hansen, Hans, 52

Hansen, Hans Christian, 62
Hansen, Jørgen, 208–9
Hansen, Ken Cregg, 224–25
Hansen, Peter Olsen (P. O.), 62–63, 63,
 65, 83, 104
Harris, Steven Wilford, 241
Hass, L. D., 70, 88, 134
Haugerup (Haverup), 88–89, 92, 114,
 127
He's a Mormon (film), 176, 180–82. *See
 also* Lauritzen, Lau
Heiberg, Johan Ludvig, 129, 159
Hemerdt, Christine, 92
Hemerdt, Mathias C., 88, 92–93
Herrnhuters, 39
Hill, C., 209
*Hinsides Atlanterhavet: Skildringer fra
 Amerika.* See *Beyond the Atlantic:
 Depictions of America*
History of the Danish Mormons, The
 (Paulsen), 187
History of the Scandinavian Mission
 (Jenson), 84, 194
Hjulet. See *Wheel, The*
Høegh-Guldberg, Ove, 24
Holst, Fritz, 159
Holst, H. P., 100
Holstein, 7, 25, 27-28, 32, 33, 38, 77, 136
Home Mission, 49, 99, 235
Homeward to Zion (Mulder), 200
Høyen, N. L., 79–81
"Hvad Man Saadan Kalder en Chris-
 ten." *See* "The Sort of Person Who
 Is Called a Christian"
Hvide Slavehandel, Den. See *White Slave
 Trade, The* (film)
Hvide Slavinde, Den. See *White Slave
 Girl, The* (film)
Hvidt, L. N., 34

"I Am a Mormon, You Surely Know"
 (street ballad), 154
identity, cultural. *See* cultural identity,
 Danish

Lund, Jutta, 160, *161*
Lund, Sarah Peterson, 205
Lundbye, Johan Thomas, 102–3
Lundgreen-Nielsen, Flemming, 97
Lüpke, Carl Anton, 40
Lütthans, Emilie, 30
"LægeSkjønnet." *See* "Medical Opinion, The"

Madame D'Ora (Jensen), 170
Madsen (Bodtcher), Gerda, 230
Madsen, David, 191, 206, 220, 223, 223, 225–28, 230
Madsen, David, Jr., 226
Madsen, Erastus, 230, *230*, 232
Madsen, Leon Torvel, 224, 228
Madsen, Gjertrud Katrine Davidsdatter, 220, 221, 229
Madsen, Mette Marie, 191, 206, 220, 223–24, 226–27, 232
Madsen, Svend, 187–88
Magdalena, Sophia, 39, 102
Malone, Nolan J., 201
Malling, Lauritz B., 65
March Revolution, 33, 51, 75
marriage, civil, 50, 54, 59–60
Martensen, Hans Lassen (H. L.), 42, 57, 74–75, 85–86, 114–15, 122–23
Massey, Douglas, 201
Maynes, Mary Jo, 188
media: antiMormon, 70–71, 131, 136, 138, 161, 167, 172 (*see also* Mormons in Denmark, reaction to); cinema, 5, 14; Danish, 12, 17, 130; films, antifeminist tendencies of, 175–76, 183; humorous, 132, 141 (*see also* street ballads); newspapers, 65; print, 31, 69, 136; response to Mormons, 12–13
McDonald, John, 201
McDonald, Leatrice, 201
"Medical Opinion, The" (S. Kierkegaard), 119–20
Meidell, Ditmar, 155

Min Svigerinde fra Amerika. See My Sister-in-Law from Amerika
Miracle on Funen, The (Egdal), 185
Miraklet på Fyn. See Miracle on Funen, The
missionaries: accused of white slavery, 135; and American culture, 9; of Danish origin, 9, 62, 190, 207, 210–11, 214–17, 233
mob violence: against Mormons, 71–75, 132, 137; Danish condemnation of, 72–73
Moberg, Vilhelm, 187
Mohammad cartoon crisis, xi-xii, 59, 247
Moltke, Adam Wilhelm, 27, 34
Moment, The, 114
Monrad, Ditlev Gothard (D. G.), 29; appointed as a pastor, 35; and the June Constitution, 15, 27–36; Bishop, 195
Mønster, Peter Christian, 40–41, 66–67
Mønster, Ole Ulrich Christian, 67
Mønster, Marie Christine, 67
Mørch, Søren, 120
Morgenstjernen. See Morning Star, The
"Mormon Girl's Lament, The" (song), 151–53, *152*, 163
Mormon Pioneer Day, 189
Mormonbyens Blomst. See Flower of the Mormon City (film)
Mormonens Offer. See Victim of the Mormons, A (film)
"Mormoner! Mormoner!" *See* "Mormons, Mormons!"
"Mormonism" (Stampe), 99, 103–4
Mormonism. *See* Mormons in Denmark
"Mormonismen." *See* "Mormonism"
"Mormonpigens Klage." *See* "Mormon Girl's Lament, The"
Mormons Bog. See Book of Mormon
Mormons in Denmark: Danish view of, 2–6, 9, 15, 16, 23, 60–61, 69, 130,